CONTENTS

Introduction
Matthew W. Charlton

The biblical account of John the Baptist portrays a rough-edged soul, who stalked the edges of civil society, proclaiming a new message of repentance and forgiveness. His home was the wilderness and his food the insects thereof. Yet, his appearance belied his deep wisdom and vision for God's future for the creation. He possessed the prophet's voice, using it to declare the coming of the kingdom into the world. In the Gospel of Matthew, he dies by execution, beheaded, the victim of the stratagems of power and the folly of youth. The cover of this volume depicts John, an image from a mosaic found in Hagia Sophia mosque in Istanbul, Turkey. At the center is the adored Son of God, Jesus. To his left is the God-bearer, Mary. On the right, is John, the prophet who proclaimed the presence and power of God in Jesus. Perhaps in John, we discern that we never truly see or hear what God is speaking to the people, if only because our common reaction to those who speak against abusive power, oppression, and "the way things are" is to find a way to silence these voices, settling for the worst instead of hoping for the best.

The essays in this book are presented in an effort to speak with the prophet's voice toward making peace among God's people. Specifically, these essays seek to speak with a prophetic voice toward making peace in the context of higher education and collegiate ministry. In essence, this book proposes a formula that, in speaking in a prophetic way to the issues that impact the lives of college students, we aid in the possibilities of peace for God's people. This is the ground of human flourishing after all, that we might live in peace with one another, a peace that gives shape to hope.

Written by campus ministers and college and university chaplains, as well as by staff members of the General Board of Higher Education and Ministry, these essays convey the belief that young people, and especially college students, are given gifts of life when they are presented with the opportunity to be heard, to make a difference, and to bring peace to their world. The essays cover five topics that are of importance today in campus life: ecology and environmental ethics; interreligious understanding and dialogue; systemic and interpersonal racism; sexual ethics; and Christian vocation.

When the coordinating committee developed this list of topics, I was convinced that we would be overwhelmed with proposals on race and sexuality. The original call for papers was posted while we were living in the echoes of Ferguson and ongoing campus protests on race, as well as in anticipation of the 2016 United Methodist General Conference, where the church's positions on human sexuality will again be an important axis of discussion and protest. Yet, this did not happen. In fact, essays that dealt with these topics were difficult to come by, while proposals on the other topic areas were numerous. We experienced some considerable difficulty in generating interest from people of color and, to a lesser degree, from women. I remain concerned that the realities of race, gender, and sex have yet to be adequately addressed by our church. We must take up these concerns with serious, critical inquiry. There is just too much at stake in our world to continue demonizing difference at the expense of peace and human flourishing. The gospel of Jesus unerringly points us toward love of neighbor, yes, even the neighbor that all others would stone to death. As Sheila Bates argues in her chapter, it is incumbent on each of us to open up space for each other, despite and because of difference.

As the general editor of this volume, I commend to you this collection of essays as a collective effort to speak prophetically in our time. They were written with college students in mind, but each has relevance for the broader church. These may be used as resources for you as you prepare for your ministry, as readings for discussion, or as research for your own efforts at making peace in this troubled world.

I would like to extend my gratitude to those who engaged in this project, chiefly to the contributors. Each of them engaged fully in this project, working through ideas with each other, arguing and struggling through concepts, and generally caring for the process and each other. If you know any of these contributors personally, I believe you already know the blessing of their friendship.

Significant and heartfelt thanks go to the coordinating committee of Jane Ellen Nickell (Allegheny University), Ron Robinson (Wofford College), and Tiffany Steinwert (Wellesley College). We consulted via phone call and many e-mails to create a conference that was amenable to collegial conversation around important and difficult topics. The conference was held at Syracuse University in August of 2015, where we were fantastically hosted by Tiffany Steinwert, who was then the Dean of Hendrix Chapel at Syracuse, and her very helpful staff. The weather was nearly perfect and there was not a snowflake in sight!

Sincere thanks goes to Kathy Armistead, who served as the project manager and content editor for this volume. Many of the contributors commented on the excellence of her engagement with their work and the value her expertise added. I am pleased now to call Kathy a valued colleague, as she has recently joined the staff of GBHEM as Publisher.

I am also grateful for the work of Kristi Stephens Walker, who worked on the copyediting and proofing of the manuscript; to Donnie Reed for patiently preparing the cover design; and to Sarah Porter, who did the work of making sure all our participants were able to arrive, work, and depart safe and sound from our conference at Syracuse. Sarah originally contributed an essay on human sexuality that was quite spectacular. However, she was not able to finish the essay due to her matriculation into the PhD program at Harvard. One day, though, I trust that we will benefit from her thoughtful and careful scholarship.

I would like to extend gratitude to Rev. Dr. Kim Cape, the General Secretary of GBHEM, for her support of thinking differently and prophetically about collegiate ministry in the United Methodist context. Dr. Gerald Lord and Dr. Ken Yamada are also to be thanked for their support as the Associate General Secretary for the Division of Higher Education. On their shoulders rested the approval of this project and I am grateful that, through our collective work, GBHEM continues to see the value in this form of theological reflection.

Finally, I am grateful for The United Methodist Church, a church that by doctrine and discipline is committed to nurturing the whole person. We have that commitment even as there remain sharp disagreements about who and how the nurturing of soul and mind should be part of our shared ministry. As a people who believe in sanctification, we know that we have not yet arrived at perfection. We continue always to strive for it, with God's help.

Matthew Charlton
Palm Sunday 2016

ECOLOGY

*A United Methodist Reading of
Francis's* Laudato Si'

*Making Shalom: The Body of
Christ within the Household of God*

*A Theological Response to the
Ecological Crisis*

A UNITED METHODIST READING OF
FRANCIS'S *LAUDATO SI'*
Matthew W. Charlton

The purpose of this chapter is to offer a reading of Pope Francis's recent encyclical on ecology, *Laudato Si'*, in the context of the United Methodist positions on environment and ecology as found in the doctrines and Social Principles of The United Methodist Church (UMC). This brief study is offered in the context of the broad interest and reach of this encyclical as well as in harmony with the UMC's tradition of seeking unity (the Catholic Spirit) in the Body of Christ through understanding and critical inquiry. In the spirit of the common home, a theme prominent in the encyclical, it is hopeful to note that there are many areas of convergence between the United Methodist Social Principles and *Laudato Si'*. In the absence of a comprehensive United Methodist ecological ethic (more on this in the second and third parts of this chapter), this chapter will do three things: first, briefly summarize the major arguments of the encyclical; second, offer some reflections on the encyclical from the perspective of the United Methodist Social Principles; and third, in solidarity with Francis's call, offer a call to action for United Methodists, giving particular attention to the collegiate ministry context.

I. *Laudato Si'*: On Care for Our Common Home

"Laudato Si', mi' Signore"—*"Praise be to you, my Lord."* In the words of the beautiful canticle, Saint Francis of Assisi reminds us that our common home is like a sister with whom we share our life

and a beautiful mother who opens her arms to embrace us. "Praise be to you, my Lord, through our Sister, Mother Earth, who sustains and governs us, and who produces various fruit with colored flowers and herbs."[1]

The release of Pope Francis's encyclical on the environment, *Laudato Si'*, has provided a fresh profile of the significance of the present environmental crisis. Predictably, it raised various sorts of partisan responses, from high praise for the focus on economic injustice to condemnation of the call for greater economic equality.[2] Francis takes a direct approach by staking out a theological position in the midst of a scientific consensus on climate change, focusing his theological energy on the divine gift of responsibility for creation stewardship and the holy command for the humble care of the most vulnerable and impoverished populations.

For Francis, the primary cause of the present crisis is human sin, and especially human sin as it is presented as capitalist market logic. Accordingly, the solution offered is a call to conversion, an adherence to a new spiritual model, one that seeks to recover and renovate for modern times ancient models of communitarian economics rooted in the economy of God as divine creator, sustainer, and redeemer. These practices

---

[1] There are multiple print versions of the encyclical. It is also available online in several languages on the Vatican website: http://w2.vatican.va/content/francesco/en/encyclicals.index.html#encyclicals. The entire document is divided into 246 paragraphs. For reference purposes, and to make it as easy as possible for the reader to locate the source, I will simply offer the paragraph number and, as needed in longer sections, additional information to help locate the source. LS = Laudato Si'. LS, ¶1. All references to Laudato Si', used by permission, © Copyright Libreria Editrice Vaticana.

[2] One starting place would be to conduct a web search on "responses to Laudato Si'. Commonweal has offered a "roundup" of responses: https://www.commonwealmagazine.org/blog/laudato-si-response-roundup. One might also read various responses in *First Things, New York Times, Wall Street Journal*, and other places. I would highly recommend Bill McKibben's review of the encyclical in the New York Review of Books, http://www.nybooks.com/articles/archives/2015/aug/13/pope-and-planet/.

then work as a guide and corrective to the consumptive energy of what Francis sees as destructive economic practices—practices that destroy both the earth (our common home) and terrorize the well-being of our neighbor. It is important to note, however, that Francis does not cast his solutions solely as economic in nature. His call is for an "integral ecology," an ecology that takes care of all parts of the whole, one that understands each part as having intrinsic value: "We are faced not with two separate crises, one environmental and the other social, but rather with one complex crisis which is both social and environmental. Strategies for a solution demand an integrated approach to combating poverty, restoring dignity to the excluded, and at the same time protecting nature."[3]

As such, *Laudato Si'* is not simply a theological statement on the environment. One would err to think that this is all the encyclical addresses. It is rather a call to an "integral ecology" rooted in a holistic Trinitarian spirituality. This is an ecology that takes into consideration the many facets of human practices and experiences as well as recognizing the great gift and value of creation. Francis suggests that an integral ecology is needed, because we are facing a "complex crisis which is both social and environmental."[4] It is environmental in the sense of what is commonly understood in the science of climate change. It is social because climate change and environmental degradation have social effects. The interplay between the social and the environmental can either create opportunity for healing and wholeness (that is, create the likelihood for the working out of an integral ecology) or the interplay may result in political, economic, and cultural decisions that continue to degrade the creation and, with it, human society and culture.

Francis writes that the Christian understanding of the

---

[3] LS ¶139.
[4] LS ¶139.

Trinity undergirds and informs the integral ecology he is calling for: "Everything is interconnected, and this invites us to develop a spirituality of that global solidarity which flows from the mystery of the Trinity."[5] Thus, the integral ecology is an expression of a holistic Trinitarian spirituality, one that honors God as Trinity, God's creation as worthy of human care, and human beings as spiritual beings in need of guidance, hope, and new life through the Spirit of Jesus. Thus, Francis addresses the primary intersections and relationships of creatures, creation, and creator, the present moment of brokenness in these relationships, and how we might go about working toward healing and regeneration.

Essentially, Francis is asking these questions: what is broken, who or what broke it, and how can it be fixed? In response, the answer is that the ecology of our common home is broken. There are the ever-increasing scientific reports that show that human activity is the primary cause for the deterioration of the environment, and that human beings, particularly the poor and most vulnerable people, will be (and in many cases already are) the victims of "the present ecological crisis."[6] Francis is not being apocalyptic here in the sense of crying that "the end is near," but rather stating that the crisis is upon us and not a future prospect. As such, should we not act out of political weakness, ideological prejudice, or simple ignorance of the other—the end is now. For many in the present world, the end has already come, given persistent drought conditions, millions of people fleeing the violence of war and terror, a violence that is part political, part cultural, and part environmental, all of which Francis considers as violations of the required civility to live in a common home.

In chapter 1 of the encyclical, Francis writes about what

---

[5] LS ¶240.
[6] LS ¶15.

is happening now, addressing issues related to pollution; the lack of clean drinking water; the mentality of consumption and its attendant "throwaway culture"; the loss of biodiversity (and its converse, the increase in monoculture and GMOs[7]); the overall breakdown in the quality of human life with a particular focus on inequality; and the weak responses to the present crisis. Private interests obstruct the necessity and health of the common good, "manipulating information so that their own plans will not be affected."[8] In this context, Francis writes, "[T]he most one can expect is superficial rhetoric, sporadic acts of philanthropy, and perfunctory expressions of concern for the environment, whereas any genuine attempt by groups within society to introduce change is viewed as a nuisance based on romantic illusions or an obstacle to be circumvented."[9] And, in the face of "complacency and a cheerful recklessness . . . , [t]his is the way human beings contrive to feed their self-destructive vices: trying not to see them, trying not to acknowledge them, delaying the important decisions and pretending that nothing will happen."[10] The chapter concludes with seeming to ask a question: Is God pleased with what human beings have done? Or are we now, practically speaking, happy atheists, prepared to die in the trash pile of self-created gluttony?[11]

---

[7] "genetically modified organisms"

[8] LS ¶54.

[9] LS ¶54.

[10] LS ¶59.

[11] On this point, I thought of the movie *Wall-E* (Disney/Pixar, 2008), which depicts an earth completely engulfed by the garbage of human consumption. The response to overconsumption and trash is technocratic: create machines to deal with it, compact it, eat it, and then flee into a self-protected sphere of inaction. The irony of Disney producing a movie critical of overconsumption and escapism is a dramatic bit of either practiced corporate naiveté or strategic entertainment marketing that has a deep awareness of its audience's inability or unwillingness to act to change systems of consumption. Interestingly, after watching *Wall-E*, I had a fleeting sense that I had done something good for the environment, even as I tossed my drink cup and popcorn bag in the trash on the way out the door.

Chapter 2, titled "The Gospel of Creation," adds the particular wisdom of the biblical text to the development of an integral ecology. Francis admits that there are those who do not see the inclusion of religion in the landscape of science in general and ecology in particular as rational. In order to develop an "integral ecology," however, "[r]espect must be shown for the various cultural riches of different peoples, their art and poetry, their interior life and spirituality. If we are truly concerned to develop an ecology capable of remedying the damage we have done, no branch of the sciences and no form of wisdom can be left out, and that includes religion and the language particular to it."[12] Thus, there is no rational reason to exclude religion from the interpretation of and interaction with scientific findings. Rather, in the whole scope of an integral ecology, it is as irrational for science and politics to exclude religion as it is for religion to fail to engage them. At the very least, religion offers an account of what creates and maintains culture, which manifestly informs how we receive and act on scientific knowledge.

Francis rejects the notion that the biblical category of "dominion" means an "absolute dominion over other creatures."[13] He writes, "The biblical texts are to be read in their context, with an appropriate hermeneutic, recognizing that they tell us to 'till and keep' the garden of the world (cf. Gen 2:15). "Tilling" refers to cultivating, ploughing, or working, while "keeping" means caring, protecting, overseeing, and preserving. This implies a relationship of mutual responsibility between human beings and nature."[14] In this sense, "absolute ownership" is rejected, and the requirement of the human care and responsibility for "God's earth" is affirmed: "Clearly, the Bible has no

---

[12] LS ¶63.
[13] LS ¶67.
[14] LS ¶67.

place for a tyrannical anthropocentrism unconcerned for other creatures."[15] It is therefore crucial that we avoid and seek to rectify any "disordered use" of created goods; but rather, in an effort to use all things well (or use rightly what is meant to be used), understand that "all of us are linked by unseen bonds and together form a kind of universal family, a sublime communion which fills us with a sacred, affectionate and humble respect."[16]

Chapter 2 concludes with a call to the common good. In a world created for all, there must be an equal dignity afforded to all persons. The present context requires that a special concern must be given for "the fundamental rights of the poor and underprivileged."[17] The common good requires that all have access to what is necessary for life and that none hold more than is required. It is in this context that Francis writes, "The Christian tradition has never recognized the right to private property as absolute or inviolable, and has stressed the social purpose of all forms of private property."[18] As we ponder the fundamental rights of all, Francis reminds us that we do so under the "gaze of Jesus." The Lord of Creation, who is within and without, is watching and judging regarding our care of what is made and our concern for the equal dignity of all.[19]

The third chapter builds on the cultural, scientific, and biblical observations of the previous chapters. Here, Francis traces the genealogy of the ecological crisis through technology, global-

---

[15] LS ¶68.
[16] LS ¶89.
[17] LS ¶93.
[18] LS ¶93. This statement marks the closest connection point with United Methodist doctrine, to which I will return shortly.
[19] LS ¶99–100. We are reminded here that: "One Person of the Trinity entered into the created cosmos, throwing in his lot with it, even to the cross. From the beginning of the world, but particularly through the incarnation, the mystery of Christ is at work in a hidden manner in the natural world as a whole, without thereby impinging on its autonomy."

ization, and what might be called a destructive anthropology rooted in a warped ontology. On this latter point, Francis is the most strident. "An inadequate presentation of Christian anthropology gave rise to a wrong understanding of the relationship between human beings and the world. Often, what was handed on was a Promethean vision of mastery over the world, which gave the impression that the protection of nature was something that only the fainthearted cared about."[20] The result is a "constant schizophrenia," where we consistently fail to see value where we should and, conversely, assign value where there is none. It should be noted that he writes this in the context of affirming that human beings have a special responsibility for the care and stewardship of the creation due to our God-given sentience. As such, Francis draws a straight line from an appropriate anthropology and an integral ecology.[21] Human beings are responsible for the mess we have created, we must take responsibility for it, work to repair it, and seek technical solutions that are ethically balanced (i.e., tech held in check by ethics—not all things are allowable that are possible), and honor the human person in each one's integrity, vocation, and culture.[22]

In order to arrive at the beginning of an integral ecology, Francis gives attention to local order and economy. Whereas the local perspective is a first order for individuals, the root of an integral ecology must begin with what the people know and how the people live. In this way, Francis gives special attention to local thinking and indigenous communities. Two lengthy quotations serve to illuminate this point.

---

[20] LS ¶116.

[21] LS ¶118.

[22] "We forget that the inalienable worth of a human being transcends his or her degree of development. In the same way, when technology disregards the great ethical principles, it ends up considering any practice whatsoever as licit. As we have seen in this chapter, a technology severed from ethics will not easily be able to limit its own power." LS ¶136.

There is a need to respect the rights of peoples and cultures, and to appreciate that the development of a social group pre-supposes a historical process which takes place within a cultur-al context and demands the constant and active involvement of local people *from within their proper culture*. Nor can the notion of the quality of life be imposed from without, for qual-ity of life must be understood within the world of symbols and customs proper to each human group.[23]

The imposition of a dominant lifestyle linked to a sin-gle form of production can be just as harmful as the alter-ing of ecosystems . . . In this sense, it is essential to show special care for indigenous communities and their cultural traditions. They are not merely one minority among oth-ers, but should be the principal dialogue partners, especially when large projects affecting their land are proposed. For them, land is not a commodity but rather a gift from God and from their ancestors who rest there, a sacred space with which they need to interact if they are to maintain their identity and values.[24]

The chapter addresses several other themes that are related to the development of a local integral ecology: poverty, design (aesthetics matter—they are reflection of God's goodness), landscapes, housing, human dignity, and staking out a position on gender roles.[25] While we may disagree with some of Pope Francis's thinking, his conclusion offers a brief defense of the principle of the common good, which he defines from *Gadium et Spes*: "the sum of those conditions of social

---

[23] LS ¶144.

[24] LS ¶145–146.

[25] On the point of gender roles, United Methodists will not have much resonance as the UMC seeks to avoid making distinctions in gender from a doctrinal perspective. However, the UMC has several resolutions that provide positions against domestic violence, sexual violence, prostitution, and pornography—all issues that disproportionately affect women's lives.

life which allow social groups and their individual members relatively thorough and ready access to their fulfillment."[26] Francis then deploys both the notion of integral ecology and common good to lift up the "preferential option for the poor," raising from theological dustbins the operative maxim of Latin American liberation theology.

In the final two chapters the encyclical concludes with a call to action, education, and conversion, which includes dialogue in the context of recognizing that we are one people on one planet. Francis helpfully suggests that while contemplation may provide the intellectual basis one needs for action, action itself is another thing altogether. Thus, he seeks to "outline the major paths of dialogue, which can help us escape the spiral of self-destruction which currently engulfs us."[27] Briefly, these "major paths" include: dialogue in the international community; dialogue aimed at new national and local policies; dialogue and transparency in decision-making; dialogue between politicians and economists for the sake of human fulfillment; and dialogue between the religious and scientific communities. All of these dialogues have as their purpose the creation of holistic, integral solutions of the serious concerns of climate change, public health and welfare, relationships between people and governments, and relationships among the world governments and powers. Thus, "[a]ny technical solution which science claims to offer will be powerless to solve the serious

---

[26] LS ¶156. I am appreciative of this appeal to the common good. Yet, I feel that the notion of the commons should play a stronger and more central role in this integral ecology, if only because technocracy and neoliberalism do not know what to do with something that is not claimed by the principle of private ownership. For that matter, it is questionable whether United Methodists doctrinally possess a strong enough sense of the commons to make a difference economically or ecologically. But, at the very least, Pope Francis's appeal does point to a need for United Methodists to develop a clearer notion of the commons and the common good.

[27] LS ¶163.

problems of our world if humanity loses its compass, if we lose sight of the great motivations which make it possible for us to live in harmony, to make sacrifices and to treat others well."[28]

The final chapter suggests the question: What is the present status of human freedom? Francis allows that human freedom is constrained by a passive ignorance of the needs of the earth and of neighbor brought about largely as a result of the "techno-economic paradigm" of compulsive consumerism: "This paradigm leads people to believe that they are free as long as they have the supposed freedom to consume. But those really free are the minority who wield economic and financial power."[29] Accordingly, we must be converted to a new way of life, one that honors the earth and neighbors for their own and for God's sake. "Disinterested concern for others, and the rejection of every form of self-centeredness and self-absorption, are essential if we truly wish to care for our brothers and sisters and for the natural environment. . . . If we overcome individualism, we will truly be able to develop a different lifestyle and bring about significant changes in society."[30] Thus, education toward an ecological conversion, a call to a spirituality of joy, peace, and love, and the sacramental celebration and recognition that God is with us all become markers of hope toward the new creation in the midst of the despair of the present age.

---

[28] LS ¶200.

[29] LS ¶203. Note that the latter sentence is suggesting contextually that those who are "really free" are only such in the context of the techno-economic paradigm, not so in the context of the freedom of God.

[30] LS ¶208. Note that "disinterested concern" regards the status of one's engagement with another. For instance, if your "concern" for another is because you stand to make money off of them, then you are not "disinterested." A biblical example of this is the petition against Job indicating that Job's righteousness and faithfulness are only the result of Job's desire to maintain his position, his wealth, and his family. Thus, God allows Job to be tested by the accuser.

United Methodist Environmental Ethics

A colleague sent me a text recently observing the absence from Capitol Hill in Washington, DC, of United Methodist bishops, while judicatory and episcopal leaders from other denominations and faiths were petitioning the US government on environmental issues. The question I posed to her was, "Does The United Methodist Church have an effective social witness anymore?" Her reply was no. Now, the absence of United Methodist bishops may have been that they did not know about this day of petitioning, or some other compelling reason kept them away. Regardless, as a church, the UMC has strong teachings on environmental ethics, poverty, culture, technology, and living with wisdom in a modern world—the topics that Francis addresses in the encyclical. These teachings represent a powerful social witness that United Methodists should be proud to testify to and act upon. The United Methodist social principles and related resolutions express an attempt by the church to give some direction to how one might live a faithful life in the peculiar service to which all Christians are called through baptism, a renewed life of service to God's Kingdom (inclusive of all of God's creation), resulting in a "new ethical orientation under the guidance of the Holy Spirit."[31]

There is no "apples-to-apples" type of comparison between the encyclical, which has the weight of the pontifical office and magisterium, and the social teachings of The United Methodist Church. The UMC's teachings primarily take the form of principles and resolutions that do not carry with them the weight of church doctrine. The statements that come from the

---

[31] World Council of Churches, *Baptism, Eucharist, and Ministry* II.B.4. (Geneva: World Council of Church, 1982).

General Conference represent the official teachings and position of the UMC. As such, they have a claim on the conscience and faith-life of United Methodist Christians. Accordingly, what do United Methodists teach about ecology?

To begin, we turn to the Articles of Religion and Confession of Faith, which, by virtue of their stature as the principle teachings of the church, make a claim of belief upon all those who are joined in membership to the UMC. (It is a chargeable offense to teach contrary to the established doctrines of the church.) Article XV of the Confession of Faith reads:

> We believe God is the owner of all things and that the individual holding of property is lawful and is a sacred trust under God. Private property is to be used for the manifestation of Christian love and liberality, and to support the church's mission in the world. All forms of property, whether private, corporate or public, are to be held in solemn trust and used responsibly for human good under the sovereignty of God.

The UMC affirms that God holds the rightful title to all that is and that human beings have been granted a sacred trust of care. The church affirms private ownership of property, while at the same time not regarding that private ownership as absolute—there is a duty of care both for the land and for the neighbor for no other reason than that the sovereignty of God requires it.[32]

The language of ownership is quite interesting in that it evokes the notion of the *oikonomia*—the law of the home.

---

[32] A corollary may be found in Article XXIV in the Articles of Religion, having to do with the holding of goods in common: "The riches and goods of Christians are not common as touching the right, title, and possession of the same, as some do falsely boast. Notwithstanding, every man ought, of such things as he possesseth, liberally to give alms to the poor, according to his ability."

Timothy Eberhart, writing about the work of M. Douglas Meeks, says that the concept of *oikonomia* means having access to the means to life, which raises a central question: "Will everyone in the household get everything they need to live?"[33] If the answer to the question at any point is no, then the people of God (the church) are called into action by the householder (the Creator and Sustainer) to correct the injustice. "The church, for Meeks, is God's attempt to build a household that will join God in making the world into home."[34] To create a home is to create the possibility of life for all and to practice fruitfully the gift of hospitality, which is expressed as care of and for the other. In the context of an integral ecology (and I see no reason why United Methodists should not adopt both the language and the concept) and Article XV, this care necessarily extends to the created order and to the created other.

In addition to this sacred trust, we must also take account of the notion of responsible use. Doctrinally, responsible use is for the human good, which must of necessity encompass care for the creation. As Meeks suggests, the absence of home puts the possibility of life into question. This would include the home of "otherkind": the flora, fauna, and land that are also alive and deserving of the care of a home.[35] This is a home with its own natural rhythms, an ability to nourish life without the technological interference of human beings. Think of the forest bed, covered, in the autumn of the year, with fallen leaves. These leaves decompose and nourish the ground, become a home for all manner of critters, and through decay support new life in the spring. Rake

---

[33] Jürgen Moltmann, Timothy R. Eberhart, and Matthew W. Charlton, eds., *The Economy of Salvation* (Eugene:OR: Cascade, 2015), 5.

[34] Ibid., 6.

[35] Mark Wallace, *Finding God in the Singing River: Christianity, Spirit, Nature* (Minneapolis: Fortress, 2005).

up all those leaves, and the process of nourishment and home is interrupted. Imagine this on a larger scale: poorly planned clear-cutting and burning of forests to make way for crop and pastureland; removing the tops of mountains to get at the coal underneath; the manifold environmental devastations that continue to emerge as a result of climate change. This notion of "responsible use" calls into question practices that disrupt, diminish, and destroy the good rhythms of creation. Rather, responsible use would suggest that we (re)discover ways in which human beings might live within these natural good rhythms.

While doctrine has a claim on United Methodist belief, the practice of a United Methodist environmental ethics must begin with an individual conscious motivation to engage faithfully and fruitfully in local and global contexts, particularly holding in mind the Wesleyan understanding of Christian perfection. Wesley expressed the operative sense of Christian perfection through the General Rules of the United Societies, which were formed to aid those "having the *form* and seeking the *power* of godliness, united in order to pray together, to receive the word of exhortation, and to watch over one another in love, that they may help each other to work out their salvation."[36] Those who "desired to flee the wrath to come and to be saved from their sins" joined these societies in order to nurture in each other the fruit of salvation, in essence, to encourage their progress in the grace of God. Accordingly, society members were expected to live by a three basic rules:

First: By doing no harm, by avoiding evil of every kind, especially that which is most generally practiced, such as . . .

Doing to others as we would not they should do unto us.

Doing what we know is not for the glory of God, as:

---

[36] *The Book of Discipline of The United Methodist Church—2012*, para. 104 (p. 76).

... Softness and needless self-indulgence.

Laying up treasure upon earth.

Secondly: By doing good; by being in every kind merciful after their power; as they have opportunity, doing good of every possible sort, and, as far as possible, to all men . . .

Thirdly: By attending upon all the ordinances of God . . . [37]

In sum, the baseline of a United Methodist ecological ethic begins with a duty of care for the creation and a corresponding responsible use of God's creation for the good of all, while avoiding that which may cause harm, for the glory of God.

United Methodists expand on this baseline ethic in the Social Principles and in Book of Resolutions, the latter being resolutions affirmed by the General Conference as official positions of the church on a variety of social, political, economic, and ecological issues. The Social Principles constitute a body of teachings that extend from "a prayerful and thoughtful effort of the General Conference to speak to the issues in the contemporary world from a sound biblical and theological foundation as historically demonstrated in United Methodist traditions. They are a call to faithfulness and are intended to be instructive and persuasive in the best of the prophetic spirit."[38]

Ideally, these statements and resolutions are structured to express the best spirit of the United Methodist and Wesleyan understanding of grace and Christian perfection—the pursuit of holiness of heart and life. Accordingly, many of the resolutions call for societal, economic, and political change that seems, in the gathered wisdom of General Conference delegates, to express the expected progress of grace-filled human beings interacting in a world infused with sinful expression. This may

---

[37] Ibid., para. 104.2 (pp. 76–78). I have emphasized several specific instances of the rules as seem appropriate to the topic of environment and integral ecology.

[38] *The Book of Resolutions of the United Methodist Church—2012*, preface (p. 43).

be seen in the forceful principles and resolutions related to the environment: "Therefore, let us recognize the responsibility of the church and its members to place a high priority on changes in economic, political, social, and technological lifestyles to support a more ecologically equitable and sustainable world leading to a higher quality of life for all of God's creation."[39] The resolutions that speak to this social principle are as follows: energy policy (1001); energy policy in the US (1002); nuclear safety in the US (1003); mountaintop removal coal mining (1021); ending the use of dioxins (1022); environmental justice (1023); affirmation of the precautionary principle: "lack of full scientific certainty shall not be used as a reason for postponing cost-effective measures to prevent ecological degradation" (1024); environmental racism (1025); environmental stewardship (1026); God's creation and the church (1026); law of the sea (1028); protection of water (1029); recycling (1030); and, global warming (1031).

Within these resolutions there are brief statements of theological reflection that fall along three primary lines. First, there is the repetition of the psalm (in various themes) that the earth is the Lord's and all that is in it. Second, there is concern over human abuse of the good creation, cast provisionally as a result of human brokenness and misunderstanding of the principle of dominion. Third, there are actions we can and must take to heal the brokenness in creation and in human communities. We see here similarity not only with the structure but also with the overall intention of *Laudato Si'*: a recognition that acts upon God's expectation of us as caretakers of God's good creation.

Because of the nature of the statements as individual resolutions, there is a lack of internal cohesion; and, perhaps as

---

[39] Ibid., Social Principle: The Natural World (p. 45).

a result of that which makes the statements problematic as specifically UM statements on the environment, there is no in-depth, coherent theological rationale offered.

There are a number of other social principles/resolutions that take up themes from the encyclical: social community (rights of the racial and ethnic groups, population, medical experimentation and genetic technology, rural life, suburban and urban life, health care); economic community (property, consumption, poverty, family farms, corporate responsibility); and the world community (national power and war). Below is a list of the associated resolutions organized around these Social Principles:

3124:	The church's response to ethnic and religious conflict
3161:	Education
3162:	Right to a quality education
3181:	Genetics
3182:	Human cloning
3183:	Stem cell research
3201:	Health care for all in the United States
3202:	Health and wholeness

There are several resolutions between 3202 and 3361 that take up in some fashion racial/ethnic concerns and cultural and religious practices, which are related to the sense of the encyclical in expressing the value of culture and religious practice for the fulfillment of proper human ends.

3361:	Population
3371ff.:	Racism
3391ff.:	Rural issues
3411ff.:	Urban issues
4001:	Appalachia
4051:	Justice and world hunger

4052: Economic justice
4054: Pathways to economic justice
4056: Greed
4058: Privatization
4059: Global economy and the environment
4091: Poverty, welfare reform
4092: Poverty
4132: Environmental health and safety in work and community
4133: Rights of African American farmers
6025: Globalization
6081: Development in Africa
6127: Justice, peace, and the integrity of creation
6129: United Methodism and Peace
8006: Embryonic stem cell research
8017: Cultural competency training

The UMC has much to say that echoes and reinforces Pope Francis's call for an integral ecology. United Methodists believe that all people have a right to life, health, and culture; that the earth must be protected and preserved; that greedy wealth leads to a breakdown in the hope of interpersonal and culture reconciliation; and that we are not so far gone yet as to have no hope for a better future, with God's help and our hands.

Call for Action

I struggle with what I can do personally and what institutions are able to accomplish corporately to nurture the care of our common home. For instance, how should I respond to news that 2015 was the "hottest year on record?" Some would say nothing, because these are natural cycles upon which human beings have no impact. This is rubbish—the preponderance of evidence is that the present climate change is "extremely likely" to be caused by human activity.[40] No doubt, there are both radical solutions and lifestyle changes that one could apply that would have an aggregate impact on the health of the planet and its peoples and ecosystems. Somebody should do those. But, is it me? Is it you? Can you or I tolerate making changes to our lifestyle and culture in order to support the life and health of communities now and into the future? For me, doing so is not a question of willingness. I am willing to want to live in such a way on this common planet that is not detrimental to others living across oceans and across time. But, how should I? If you and I are the only two, then we make a minimal impact and very likely appear ridiculous to others. Perhaps that is all right, but it is certainly not sufficient. Several weeks ago, I saw a news report about a young woman who collected all of her trash from the last two years in a single small jar. It was not much trash at all, especially compared to the huge cart of garbage I haul up to the street once a week.

Here are the things I have been told are the right things to do: buy less stuff, drive less and in smaller, fuel efficient cars or take public transit, turn down the heat and turn up the air conditioner, recycle, compost, buy carbon offsets for flying (I fly quite a bit and am suspicious when the airline asks if I want to buy a carbon offset—what would that money do, who gets it, would that make any kind of difference?), eat organic, don't

---

[40] See the most recent summary report of the Intergovernmental Panel on Climate Change. "Anthropogenic greenhouse gas emissions have increased since the pre-industrial era, driven largely by economic and population growth, and are now higher than ever. This has led to atmospheric concentrations of carbon dioxide, methane and nitrous oxide that are unprecedented in at least the last 800,000 years. Their effects, together with those of other anthropogenic drivers, have been detected throughout the climate system and are *extremely likely* to have been the dominant cause of the observed warming since the mid-20th century." http://ar5-syr.ipcc.ch/topic_summary. php. Also, see the IPCC full website: ipcc.ch. For a more "popular" approach, see Bill McKibben's book, *The End of Nature* (1989), and the follow-up to that book published more recently, *Earth: Making a Life on a Tough New Planet* (2011).

eat stuff that has to fly to get to you, eat local and seasonally, eat less meat (or go full-veggie), lose weight so I eat less meat or less veggies, don't drink bottled water instead use a refillable container. This is all very confusing. Perhaps this is why Francis is calling for a conversion.

What can we do? Contemplation and action are the two sides of the holistic spiritual life. Action in the absence of wonder may too easily become another form of selfishness, while contemplation that does not lead to difference is time ill-spent. Accordingly, a call to action must be thoughtful, giving consideration to the theological and anthropological concerns that shape our understanding.

United Methodist churches and campus ministries have much to consider in plotting their collective way forward. There are churches, campus ministries, and other institutions in the United Methodist connection that are using their green space to grow community gardens, recycle and compost food-waste, as well as taking other measures to approach greater sustainability. Methodists plant trees, install solar panels, use green energy sources, advocate for climate action on local and global scales, and develop networks of faithful people who commit to a covenanted ecological spirituality. As always, there is more that can be done, and more people who can choose to live and act differently in the world in order to protect and preserve our planet for God's sake and for the sake of the future.

Briefly, I propose a call to action with three parts. These are reasonable and valuable in support of our common home. Taken together, this call can help United Methodists make a greater impact.

First, read and contemplate Francis's encyclical letter and the resolutions of the UMC. Consider how these texts might be calling you and the institutions with which you affiliate to a way of life which points toward a holistic, integral ecology. In the context of college ministry, these can be offered as small group studies or as a retreat, with appropriate action to balance the work of contemplation.

Second, act on what you can do and call your organization to action. Do something that makes a difference. Choose to live differently. Contact those in power, encouraging them to act for the sake of all people, creatures, and places. Political movements can make a big difference, slowly paying dividends on all the time and passion invested.

The more that young adults are invested in the protection and flourishing of our common home, the greater the likelihood that we will be able to make a difference in the quality of that home for all. This is already happening in many places. One movement that I became aware of recently is led by students at the Methodist Theological School in Ohio. It is called "The Wesleyan Order of St. Francis." It is described as,a dispersed monastic Order whose members are disciples of Jesus Christ committed to its rule of life to live simply in solidarity with the marginalized, voiceless, and undervalued members of God's creation. Members live this way as witnesses to the church's care for all of God's creation and as leaders in the movement for change in their communities. Members of this Order affirm the legacies and ministries of Saint Francis of Assisi and John Wesley and see their work as a continuation of it.[41]

The call is to live simply and to live "in solidarity with the creation." Note that this represents both contemplation and action. Discernment is met with vocation, an engagement of the spirit with the body at work in the world.

Finally, I sense that it would be extraordinarily powerful for college students in United Methodist-related ministries to petition General Conference to establish a study committee to

---

[41] See the website: www.wesleyanosf.com.

develop a holistic ecological theology for United Methodists. The goal would be to produce a coherent document that fully reflects our church's understanding of ecology with appropriate courses of action that the church as a body and that each of us as individuals may take.

If we would do these things in order to help guide each other into the hope of God's future, we can stand with Pope Francis and advocate for a world that is not threatened by death, but rather a home that flourishes with the creativity of the Spirit and fully respects the life that God has made.

Making Shalom:
The Body of Christ
within the Household of God
Jane Ellen Nickell

We live in an increasingly fractured world. Technology enables us to connect with people across the globe, but we are so glued to our smart phones that we do not notice those we pass on the sidewalk. Machines allow us to do more work in less time, carving our lives into ever-smaller segments, while modern society is overall compartmentalized by function, profession, and class. Technological connections allow us to stay busy socially without necessarily forming deep, meaningful relationships. Our students are prime examples of this segmentation, as they juggle multiple demands, interests, and identities.

This fragmenting of our lives also contributes to ecological problems. While individualism is central to American identity, consumerism amplifies that ideal by urging us to fulfill our every desire, without considering the effect on others. Our disposable economy gobbles up resources and creates mountains of waste. For example, we spend more than fifty billion dollars per year on bottled water, leaving behind 1.5 million pounds of plastic bottles, only 13 percent of which get recycled.[1] We act on what is convenient for us, not recognizing how that habit impacts other people or the natural world.[2] Our blindness to how our

---

[1] Christina Peppard, "Message in a Bottle," *Reflections* 101, no. 2 (2014): 31–33.
[2] At Allegheny College, only 21 percent of students use bottled water, but half of those students say they use it because of convenience, as revealed by a survey that an

lifestyle affects the natural world creates distance from it. We live in a bubble of our own making, with light and darkness at the flip of a switch, climate-controlled buildings, and layers of concrete between our feet and the earth itself. Because we have less physical contact with the natural world and its cycles, we remain unaware of the environmental costs of our lifestyle. Modern life is powered by fossil fuels, whose greenhouse gas emissions contribute to climate change. Climate change is a factor in other environmental issues such as rising sea levels, severe storms, drought, and extinction of species through loss of habitat. The persistence of climate change deniers in the face of overwhelming scientific agreement is evidence of how carefully most developed societies conceal the effect of their lifestyle on the world around us.

Collegiate ministry can address our isolation from each other and the rest of creation by encouraging ties of community and a sense of interconnection that does not sever our life choices from their consequences. Indeed, many students long for such connections, more so than they realize. Student membership in civic, service, and social clubs, including fraternities and sororities, remains strong on most campuses. Recent research about the spiritual lives of young adults[3] tells us that while some students walk away from organized religion, many still seek engagement with the world through community service and meaningful, shared spiritual experiences.

While community can become a buzzword with shallow commitment, religion is steeped in concepts, symbols, and

---

Environmental Science class conducted (Fall 2014). The college addressed that by giving each incoming student in Fall 2015 a stainless steel water bottle and installing fifteen refill stations around campus.

[3] See the work of Christian Smith, the Barna Group, and the "Spirituality in Higher Education" research at the Higher Education Research Institute at UCLA.

practices that foster deep connection. The Hebrew term *shalom*, often translated as peace, is a rich concept referring to a sense of wholeness, harmony, and completeness, especially as it relates to society. The phrase *tikkun olam* means repairing the world and is a key concept in Jewish environmentalism, where it is extended to both the natural and social worlds. As Paul describes in his Epistles, the image of the body of Christ encourages a sense of unity that embraces diverse gifts under the common purpose of serving Jesus Christ. Theologian Sallie McFague extends that metaphor to the entire created universe in describing the body of God. This essay explores these concepts and suggests ways that collegiate ministry can overcome the fragmentation of modern life in developed, differentiated societies. As United Methodists, we can look to our own tradition, with its connectional structure and long tradition of social holiness.

Christian Environmentalism

Almost fifty years ago, Lynn White Jr. laid the blame for the ecological crisis at the feet of Western Christianity,[4] claiming that Christians have taken our God-given dominion over other creatures (Gen 1:26) as license to exploit the rest of creation. Technological changes, combined with scientific exploration as early as eleven centuries after Christ, radically altered our relationship with the earth. A religious worldview interpreted the biblical creation story in ways that allowed not just dominance but exploitation of nature.

Lynn White's solution was to look to St. Francis of Assisi, who cared for all creatures and anthropomorphized the

---

[4] Lynn White Jr., "The Historical Roots of Our Ecologic Crisis," *Science* 155 (1967): 1203-07. This now-famous article prompted in large part the religious environmental movement that addresses White's critique and offers new theological constructions, as well as practical environmental actions for people of faith.

elements of nature—sun, moon, wind, water, earth, and fire—not just as neighbors but also as kin.[5] White focused on ecological harm to nature, yet humans also suffer from loss of ties to the world around us. More recently, an editorial in *Perspectives on Science and Christian Faith* makes that link explicit: "Christian thinking—and environmental thought, in general—needs a deeper understanding of humanity's relationship with nature as it is lived out in society and in communities."[6] Seeking connection can address both the social isolation created by fragmented lives and the degradation of the natural world.

Ecological issues matter to many young adults, who carry a sense of responsibility to repair what previous generations have broken. When polled about global warming, 70 percent of eighteen- to twenty-nine-year-olds worry a great deal or a fair amount, 10 percent more than thirty- to forty-nine-year-olds, with even less concern among older generations. Young Christians, including evangelicals, share this concern, as illustrated by such groups as Renewal: Students Caring for Creation and Young Evangelicals for Climate Action (YECA). Ben Lowe has been a leader in both groups, working as well with A Rocha and the Evangelical Environmental Network. Deeply involved in the environmental movement, Lowe published his first book, *Green Revolution* (2009), when he was twenty-five, and followed that up with *Doing Good without Giving Up* (2014). These books are part of Lowe's ongoing advocacy to inspire more young adult Christians to join him.

---

[5] See St. Francis of Assisi's "Canticle of the Sun," which inspired the hymn "All Creatures of our God and King." The pope who bears Francis' name continues the saint's work in his deep compassion for all people and his environmental awareness, expressed most thoroughly in *Laudato Si'*, the 2015 encyclical about climate change (see essay by Matthew Charlton in this volume).

[6] John R. Wood et al., "Christian Environmentalism: Cosmos, Community, and Place," *Perspectives on Science and Christian Faith* 57, no. 1 (2005): 1–5.

These young evangelical Christians represent a convergence of conservative theology and progressive politics that sets them apart from older generations of evangelicals. Such students illustrate a segment of this generation that Naomi Schaefer Riley names the Missionary Generation.[7] For these students, religion remains central to their identity, and they stay connected to faith communities through involvement in congregations and/or religious clubs on campus, whereas an increasing number in that age group claim to be unaffiliated.[8]

Motivation for Lowe and other Christian environmentalists is twofold. First is a sense of stewardship for God's creation, based on scriptures that extoll the natural world (Job 38–39, Psalm 104) and that recognize God as sovereign over creation (Psalms 8 and 24), with humans serving as caretakers, or stewards. Submitting our aims and desires to God runs counter to a culture that urges us to indulge ourselves with the acquisition of material wealth and power. A commitment to creation care requires reading the dominion language of Genesis 1:26, cited by White as problematic, in light of Genesis 2:15, which charges humans with tending and keeping their garden home. Human use of the earth and its resources should be tempered by God's sovereignty.

Second, Christians are motivated by environmental justice, recognizing that those who bear the consequences of

---

[7] Naomi Schaefer Riley identified and named this segment of young adults in her book *God on the Quad: How Religious Colleges and the Missionary Generation Are Changing America* (New York: St. Martin's, 2005), documenting increased enrollment at faith-based schools.

[8] "Unaffiliated" is the fastest growing religious category in the country, with almost one-fourth (23 percent) of the US population claiming that status, up from 16 percent in 2008. Among eighteen- to twenty-five-year-olds, that number is 35 percent (http://www.pewforum.org/religious-landscape-study).

environmental problems had little to do with causing them. In 2014, the people of the Carteret Islands became the first climate change refugees, abandoning their island home for life in the mountains before the islands become entirely submerged by the rising sea. Yet, this low-tech society did little to generate the carbon emissions that contribute to climate change.[9] Young adults who grew up in a globalized era are concerned for neighbors around the world, as well as those in their local communities.

Addressing these concerns requires expanding the idea of community beyond any one campus or hometown to include humanity on a global scale, since climate change is a global problem. Confronting the related problem of species extinction and loss of biodiversity requires broadening our sites beyond the human community to consider all creation. The idea of an interconnected web resonates with quantum physics[10] and Eastern religions such as Buddhism. Biblical resources begin with Genesis 1, in which God declares every aspect of creation "good," and include Ecclesiastes 3:19, both of which connect the fate of humans to all other creatures.

Adopting a global and interspecies concept of community offers a different set of values than consumer culture—as some say, a good life rather than a "goods" life. Following the example of Jesus, St. Francis, and John Wesley, among others, leads us to build intentional communities while reducing our acquisition of wealth and material goods. Students longing for authentic community can enjoy the wealth of deep relationships with God, each other, and the natural world.

---

[9] The Carteret people's transition is documented in the film *Sun Come Up* (2011).
[10] See Barbara Brown Taylor's "Physics and Faith: The Luminous Web" in *The Christian Century* 116, no. 17 (1999): 612-61), and her subsequent volume *The Luminous Web: Essays on Science and Religion* (Cambridge, U.K.: Cowley, 2000).

Communal Theology: Reclaiming the Body

The theological image of the body of Christ offers layers of meaning while addressing the issues that students and the larger Christian community face, although it has suffered some misperceptions over time. The image is, first of all, incarnational, asserting a central doctrine of Christianity—that God took human form to live and die as an embodied being. The incarnated Christ affirms our own embodiment, as well as the material world in which we live. Incarnation gives intrinsic value to the world and everything in it, rather than being valued only for how it can resource human lifestyles and habits.[11] Furthermore, just as Christ's resurrected body promises life and regeneration, our own self-giving can reveal new ways of being in the world, when we step out of our role as "takers" and embrace the identity of "givers."

A primary strength of this image is its ability to unify diverse entities into an organic whole dedicated to God's purposes, providing the sense of community that many young adults seek. Paul uses this image throughout 1 Corinthians to urge that fractured community to find a sense of unity that uses its variety of gifts for the common good (1 Cor 12). By drinking of the one Spirit (1 Cor 12:13), the various members of the community recognize their interdependence and come to a sense of oneness that parallels the unity of the body. Using such passages[12] for worship and Bible study can help focus students on the benefits of community and the gifts they each bring to it.

The image of the body of Christ is distinctly sacramental, recalling that baptism unifies Christians into one body that cares for all its members. The concept takes on two different meanings in the Eucharist: first, as Christ's presence in the ele-

---

[11] See essay in this volume by Domenic Nigrelli.
[12] See also Romans 12:3-8, 1 Corinthians 12, and Ephesians 4:1-6.

ments and second, as the body—the church—that is nourished by the sacrament. Sacraments also provide connection to the natural world by using the element of water in baptism, and grain and grapes transformed into the bread and wine of Communion (to use the name that conveys the corporate nature of this sacrament).

As the body of Christ in the world, Christians are called to continue Christ's work of proclamation and service. The servant aspect of the image makes a strong case for social action, a long-standing part of the Christian (and distinctly Methodist) tradition. In his book *Shalom Church* (2010), Craig Nessan writes that the work of the church, as the body of Christ, is repairing the world in all its brokenness. Nessan's use of the Hebrew terms *tikkun olam* and *shalom* connects Christians to our Jewish roots. *Tikkun olam*, he writes, addresses the mending of society as well as the natural world[13] with the goal being shalom, in its fullest sense as a deeply integrated, harmonious, and life-giving community.[14] The body of Christ achieves this through both evangelism and social ministry. While these impulses are often associated respectively with the Christian right and the Christian left, both are needed or the body is incomplete.[15]

This view of the church is an ideal that, unfortunately, the institutional body often fails to live out. If the institutional body of Christ were deeply committed to this work, the resulting sense of shalom would offer the authentic community that many Christians are longing for, especially college-age adults. There are obstacles within the metaphor, beginning with our

---

[13] Craig L. Nessan, *Shalom Church: The Body of Christ as a Ministering Community* (Minneapolis: Fortress, 2010), 19.
[14] Ibid., 4.
[15] Ibid., 9.

culture's complicated relationship to our own embodiment and sexuality. Voices from feminism and race studies offer the critique that the hegemonic Christian has traditionally been portrayed as a white, heterosexual male who practices a rationalized form of spirituality, and for whom sexual and emotional experiences are a distraction.[16]

Other barriers to the effective use of body imagery are the relationship of the members of the body to each other and the body's relationship to the rest of the world. Robert Bellah and others[17] have noted that American individualism has disrupted a sense of social cohesion. Reflecting a religious take on this idea, Nessan writes that individualized spirituality serves a therapeutic function for the person and views religion as oppressive institutionalization.[18] The power in this theological "body image" is its fundamental unity, albeit with a variety of gifts, working toward the common good.[19] This concept also addresses the human tendency to view ourselves as distinct from the rest of creation and therefore exempt from living within its limits.

The Case of Our Food

The food we eat offers a case study of the interconnection between our bodies, other people, the natural world, and spirituality. The shiny fruits and vegetables, colorful boxes of food, and plastic encased meat products we see in the grocery store conceal some unsavory practices in food production. Farming on an industrial scale[20] relies on heavy machinery,

---

[16] Sallie McFague, *The Body of God: An Ecological Theology* (Minneapolis: Fortress, 1993), 33–35.

[17] Robert Bellah et al., *Habits of the Heart: Individualism and Commitment in American Life* (Berkeley: University of California Press, 1985).

[18] Nessan, *Shalom Church*, 1.

[19] Ibid., 37.

[20] Michael Pollan details the unsustainable practices involved in industrial agriculture

genetically engineered seeds, and chemicals in the form of fertilizers, pesticides, and herbicides that contaminate ground water and flow into rivers, creating "dead zones" where marine life cannot be sustained.[21] In some places, mono-cropping has replaced crop rotation, so chemical fertilizer is used to restore nutrients in the depleted soil.

Most of our meat, eggs, and dairy come from a livestock industry that uses Concentrated Animal Feeding Operations (CAFOs). The animals live in horrific conditions and receive antibiotics to prevent the spread of disease. With a thousand or more cows or pigs, or hundreds of thousands of chickens in a single facility, the concentration of waste pollutes the air and groundwater. The living bodies of these animals are carefully hidden from us, along with the bodies of farm workers, who receive low wages and are exposed to the chemicals used in industrial farming. Small farms and farming communities often cannot compete with farming on this scale. Such farming practices are unhealthy for the land, the animals, the workers, and we, the consumers. They are destructive to community.

The government subsidizes these practices, making food that is factory farmed and heavily processed cheaper than fresh food grown in more sustainable ways. Cost is also determined by the location of grocery stores, so that fresh food is not sufficiently cost effective for inner city stores with high rent and small square footage, leading to "food deserts." In addition, food cost reflects the 40 percent of food that is wasted in the

---

in his book *The Omnivore's Dilemma: A Natural History of Four Meals* (New York: Penguin Books, 2007). In addition, the Fall 2014 issue of Yale Divinity School's *Reflections* magazine featured articles on the theme "At Risk: Our Food, Our Water, Ourselves." Copies can be ordered at http://reflections.yale.edu.

[21] Pollan, *Omnivore's Dilemma*, 47. Pollan describes a "dead zone" at the mouth of the Mississippi River the size of the state of New Jersey.

United States. This includes produce deemed too gnarly or misshapen for the grocery store, food discarded after its "best by" date, and the large portions served in many restaurants, such as supersized fast food meals.

The cumulative effect is that the food that should nourish our bodies is harming us, and the cost of food produced in healthy, sustainable ways is out of reach for many lower income families. This has contributed to the ironic reality that many poor folks in the United States, including many children, suffer from obesity and diabetes, rather than hunger.

Fortunately, there are ways that communities can address food inequities and inadequacies by providing a market for locally grown food. In Consumer Supported Agriculture (CSA), community members subscribe to a farm in their area, and each week they receive locally grown, fresh produce, a practice that is healthy for the farm, the consumer, and the community. Another alternative is community gardening, in which community members share the work and the harvested produce. Urban gardens may occupy spaces once marked by urban blight. In some areas, churches, campuses, and other religious communities sponsor gardens,[22] as do campuses. Even students who are away during the summer can provide needed labor in preparing and planting a community or campus garden in the spring and harvesting in the fall.

All such efforts contribute to healthy bodies and healthy communities, while giving us an up-close view of nature in all its complexity. We feed our own bodies, while discerning the needs of others and not exploiting farm animals or workers, as the body of Christ requires us to do. This is the essence of

---

[22] A booklet on "Why Every Church Should Plant a Garden . . . and How" is available as a free download from A Rocha USA at http://arocha.us/wp-content/uploads/2012/05/GardenManual.pdf.

Communion, in which we envision a banquet where all are fed the bread of life, and no one goes away hungry.

Body of God

In expanding the concept of the body of Christ and its Eucharistic implications, Sallie McFague looks to the Greek word *oikos* or "household" to envision the household of God[23] that embraces all members of creation and erases human exception. The word is the basis for the terms ecology, economy, and ecumenical, all of which suggest ways to live with each other on this planet and within the religious community. Whereas the word *environment* looks at what is around us, *ecology* includes the human subject, and, as it does in science, describes an organic, interconnected system. Likewise, it resembles the image of the body of Christ in noting the value that all parts contribute to the health of the entire system.

Drawing on this common root of the words ecology and economy, McFague offers an economic ecological model that is communal and egalitarian, seeking the well-being of all members of the planetary household. This proposal counters the current Western ambition to achieve personal happiness through the accumulation of material wealth that spurs economic growth. Even though unlimited economic growth within a limited planetary system is unsustainable on a global scale, the free market economy, with its goal of unchecked growth, is rapidly becoming a worldwide market. With increasingly more wealth concentrated in increasingly fewer individuals, the consumer culture nevertheless dangles before us the goal of material abundance that could land us in the "1 percent" at the top.

---

[23] Sallie McFague, *Life Abundant: Rethinking Theology and Economy for a Planet in Peril* (Minneapolis: Fortress, 2001), 36.

In contrast, McFague describes an economic system in which communal life seeks the good of all, balancing individual freedom with the integrity of the community.[24] Rather than depicting society as a linear structure, like a ladder one climbs or a race to the finish line, she offers a circle that includes and supports every member.[25] Love of neighbor is a critical aspect of this ecological economics, and distributive justice should ensure that all have enough, without extreme wealth or poverty on either end of the economic scale.[26]

Being a theologian rather than an economist, McFague offers a theological construct that undergirds a sustainable society and, in place of material wealth, promises abundant relationships. McFague imagines the entire physical universe as the body of God,[27] or the God in whom "we live and move and have our being" (Acts 17:28). God is both body and spirit, as are humans. God's love is incarnated not just in Jesus, but throughout the created universe. McFague contrasts this model to the radical transcendence she sees in some traditional theologies. Instead she offers radical immanence in the form of panentheism, in which God contains the totality of the physical universe, and yet surpasses or transcends it. God is everywhere, like the Islamic concept of *ayat*, which sees signs of God throughout the world.[28]

For McFague, this concept escapes some of the difficulties she sees with traditional theology and its coherence with

---

[24] Ibid., 103.

[25] Ibid., 106.

[26] Ibid., 109.

[27] McFague articulates this theological model in her 1993 book *The Body of God: An Ecological Theology* and in *Life Abundant: Rethinking Theology and Economy for a Planet in Peril* (2001).

[28] See Ibrahim Abdul-Matin's book *Green Deen: What Islam Teaches about Protecting the Planet* (San Francisco: Berrett-Koehler Publishers, 2010) for a discussion of this and more on Islamic environmentalism. Concepts that cut across religious traditions offer rich potential for interfaith discussion, such as the process of scriptural reasoning described in Christopher Donald's essay in this volume.

the Western economic paradigm she critiques. Additionally, Protestant Christianity emphasizes the individual nature of salvation, accomplished through Jesus's redemptive death and resurrection, with faith as our only effort. Confronting her own "trouble with Jesus," McFague articulates three problems with the prevailing Christology: "it is a form of 'Jesusolatry'; it is individualistic and anthropocentric; and it understands salvation in purely spiritual terms."[29] McFague writes that these aspects of Christian theology support consumer patterns that elevate and fulfill individual desire.

McFague claims that orthodox doctrine of a preexistent and ascending Christ, who is both fully human and fully divine, creates tensions with postmodern scientific understanding in a way that serves as a barrier to belief.[30] Many young adults experience this tension during college, finding a limited understanding of God's work inconsistent with the diversity of ideas, cultures, and spiritual expressions they are encountering. By focusing on the Incarnation, McFague expands a primary element of Christology beyond Jesus of Nazareth. She summarizes her ecological economic Christology in the phrase "God with us,"[31] and describes it as a Christology that "looks Godward through Jesus," and Jesus as "the lens through whom we see God."[32]

This offers a more approachable view of God to students who may feel alienated from a radically transcendent deity. Technology plops them in the midst of a diverse, teeming, complex world, and McFague's model places God in the middle of that same complexity, rather than being firmly ensconced in heaven. McFague describes a God who literally embraces

---

[29] McFague, *Life Abundant*, 159.
[30] Ibid., 158.
[31] Ibid., 158.
[32] Ibid., 170.

us with wind, water, trees, cats and dogs, each other, and every aspect of the material universe. God is more vast than the universe, yet as near as our next breath. As does the body of Christ, the idea of God's embodiment affirms our own, encouraging a healthy body image in the face of highly sexualized commercial culture. Also like the body of Christ, we are unified in our diversity and find the holy in our midst.

Young Evangelicals for Climate Action (YECA) leader Ben Lowe echoes McFague when he describes incarnational living as a way to overcome our separation from nature and the effects of environmental problems. He writes that the incarnation does not mean God reached down from heaven, but reached out from within humanity, as we must do for each other.[33] One aspect of living incarnationally is building intentional community—using the lessons of the parable of the Good Samaritan to develop relationships with those near and dear, as well as the diverse "others" we encounter. Another element is to live humbly in order to overcome our isolation from nature and the effects of our lifestyle.[34] Lowe speaks for others in his generation who have become actively engaged in addressing environmental problems through intentional, broad-based community, and he embraces this fully, living communally with other young adults.[35]

The United Methodist Connection

Theologies of the body resonate with the thought of John Wesley, as do United Methodist structures and practice. While Wesley does not use language of embodiment,

---

[33] Ben Lowe, *Green Revolution: Coming Together to Care for Creation* (Downers Grove, IL: InterVarsity, 2009), 60–61.
[34] Ibid., 64–65.
[35] See essay by Rimes McElveen in this book.

he envisions God as being present throughout creation, and containing it within Godself. As he writes:

God is in all things and . . . we are to see the Creator in the glass of every creature . . . we should use and look upon nothing as separate from God, which indeed is a kind of practical Atheism; but, with a true magnificence of thought, survey heaven and earth, and all that is therein, as contained by God in the hollow of his hand, who by his intimate presence holds them all in being, who pervades and actuates the whole created frame, and is, in a true sense, the soul of the universe.[36]

Wesley portrays God as loving and relational, and, according to the Great Commandment, we are to do the same: love God and love neighbor. In one of his thirteen sermons on Jesus' Sermon on the Mount, Wesley writes that Christianity is "essentially a social religion; and that to turn it into a solitary religion, is indeed to destroy it."[37] Society—"living and conversing with other [people]"[38] —is critical to faith, and the internal change of heart that signals salvation must be lived out in community.

Like McFague, Wesley has harsh words for the wealthy who disregard the poor and laments growing economic disparity. Both approach the problem theologically, with McFague claiming that accumulating wealth at the expense of others is a form of sin,[39] and Wesley writing that it endangers one's soul.[40] Rather than

---

[36] John Wesley, "Sermon on the Mount" *Sermons of John Wesley*, http://www. umcmission.org/Find-Resources/John-Wesley-Sermons/Sermon-23-Upon-Our-Lords-Sermon-on-the-Mount-3.

[37] JohnWesley, *The Sermons of John Wesley*, "Sermon on the Mount," Sermon 24, Discourse 4. http://wesley.nnu.edu/john-wesley/the-sermons-of-john-wesley-1872-edition/sermon-24-upon-our-lords-sermon-on-the-mount-discourse-four.

[38] Ibid., I.2,

[39] McFague, *Life Abundant*, 116–17.

[40] Wesley, *The Sermons of John Wesley* "Sermon on Mount," Sermon 28, Discourse 8. http://wesley.nnu.edu/john-wesley/the-sermons-of-john-wesley-1872-edition/sermon-28-upon-our-lords-sermon-on-the-mount-discourse-eight/.

exploiting those who have the least, Wesley maintains that the community must defend and care for its poorest and weakest members. No one should have more than they need until all have the essentials of life.

Wesley's ideas are lived out in United Methodist practice, which in theory offers the kind of connection and accountability that young adults seek. A renewal movement in the Church of England, Methodism itself began at a university (Oxford), when John Wesley and his brother Charles, with a small group of friends, devoted themselves to disciplined, holy living, which included outreach to those on the margins. As the movement grew, members gathered in societies, groupings of religious laypersons that were common at the time. The Methodists, however, took these societies to a new level by creating small accountability groups within their societies: geographically formed demographic groups called bands and classes. Like the Wesleys and their friends at Oxford, these groups provided encouragement and spiritual discipline for those striving to live holy lives.

Connection forms the heart of Methodism. Local congregations and campus ministries still provide small groups such as Bible studies, Sunday school classes, and Covenant Disciple Groups that serve a similar purpose as the earlier bands and classes. The United Methodist Church comprises a chain of different levels of conferences—delegated bodies that decide polity—with the General Conference as the only official voice of the denomination. Methodism encourages the ties of community that can connect the pieces of our fractured lives, and United Methodist collegiate ministry can draw on Wesley and on the resources of the Methodist connection to offer the meaningful community that many students desire.

By encouraging this sense of community on campus, in the larger culture, and within the whole created order, United

Methodist collegiate ministers can provide the deep connections that give our lives meaning and resilience. All manner of new religious and communal expressions are attempting to fill this need for those who feel alienated from the institutional church. Methodism offers community and connection with deep roots, along with beliefs and social values that resonate with contemporary theological movements, such as McFague's that address barriers to belief.

In addition, Methodism's long tradition of social justice offers engagement with the global community. The United Methodist Church's "Rethink Church" campaign puts belief into action, drawing on the web of local congregations throughout the world, and demonstrating that United Methodists seek to open hearts, open minds, and open doors as they reach out in service. The program offers volunteer opportunities with a range of social issues, including environmentalism, along with global health, restorative justice, worker rights, immigration, and others. Such efforts balance individualistic impulses with opportunities to serve others, engage with diverse populations, and address pressing problems like climate change.

United Methodist environmentalism can draw on the denomination's Social Principles, which affirm our action on behalf of the natural world (para. 160), the social community (para. 162), and justice within the economic community (para. 163). Each section addresses specific issues, and the United Methodist *Book of Resolutions* includes explicit statements around such issues as energy policy (1001 and 1002), environmental justice (1023), global warming (1031), and Communities of Shalom (3016). The General Board of Church and Society website[41] provides the text of the Social Principles

---

[41] http://www.umc-gbcs.org. As of this writing, the General Secretary of the Global

and some Resolutions, along with suggested actions to address specific issues. These actions range from changing individual habits to advocacy efforts aimed at systemic change, both of which are necessary to address global environmental problems and the entrenched lifestyle patterns that contribute to them. United Methodist colleges and universities that put these principles into practice are leaders in sustainability, with four schools listed among the top fifteen in the Princeton Review's 2015 Guide to Green Colleges—Green Mountain College, Dickinson College, American University, and Willamette University.

These are the issues that concern young adults and that can call them into communities where they can connect more deeply with God, through engagements with other people and the natural world. United Methodist local congregations might partner with student environmental groups for conversation, programs, and projects, especially at schools that have a commitment to sustainability. Through their involvement in environmentalism, college students demonstrate that they are not just leaders of tomorrow, but also leaders of today making significant contributions to the church and the world with energy, fresh thinking, and deep commitment to the issues and concerns that speak to them. In seeking new ways to form meaningful community, young adults find ways to overcome the fragmented lives that are all too common in our society.

Board of Church and Society (GBCS) is Rev. Dr. Susan Henry-Crowe, a former collegiate minister (Emory University).

A Theological Response
to the Ecological Crisis
Domenico Nigrelli
for Filippa Nigrelli

Introduction

Ecological Crisis as a Theological Problem

To think about the current ecological crisis from a theological perspective is an almost intractable task. For one thing, the task is inherently multidisciplinary. Ecological science, ecological philosophy, ecological ethics, and ecological theology, are each specific fields of inquiry with distinct methods, standards of research, and goals. The sheer scope of subject matter and diversity of methods and inquiries are overwhelming. Further, no one can be an expert in all of them. I am rightly intimidated by the volume of knowledge that one would need to have in order to say something meaningful. To say something coherent to all these disparate fields fills me with a debilitating nausea—I have to admit. The responsible thing might be to remain silent, acknowledging the sheer complexity and abstaining from adding another opinion, which would only contribute to the cacophony of voices. And yet, because of the urgency and importance of an informed theological response to the ecological crisis, to remain silent is equally impossible, even if remaining so is piecemeal, partial, and in need of revision.

This essay is primarily theological in nature, meaning that I am offering a view of why and in what way our relationship with nature ought to be grounded and our conduct ought to be governed by a Christian understanding of God's nature, or being. I shall propose that faith's apprehension of the realities of self, world, and God lead, with a certain necessity, to a deep-ecological framework concerning how we, as Christians, ought to relate to the world. I argue that anthropocentrism and biocentrism are not radical or encompassing enough to face the pernicious state of the health of our planet. Positively stated, I shall offer a holistic theocentric framework that is amenable to a deep ecological ethic. In addition, I will present a specific method to address the question of the reality of God, which is illuminative for a deep ecological ethics and understanding of world as God's creation.[1]

---

[1] The way, or method, to the question of the reality of God is threefold. I shall offer a phenomenological description of the facticity of redemption. Second, the phenomenological insights are mined for the ontological import. Third, the ontology is then transposed into proper theological reflection. Privileging the concept of the *primacy of redemption,* a term of art coined by Edward Farley, I shall give an account of how God comes forth as God in the faith community. Traditional theology would name this theme the "revelation of God" or the "knowledge" of God. But since I am convinced that the traditional understanding of revelation is overburdened with too many ambiguities, I shall retain Farley's term—God's coming forth as God in the facticity of redemption—when I want to distance myself from the classical Christian tradition. Next, the actual occurrence of redemption is experienced as a transformation from evil and corruptions to theological freedoms and theonomous existence. Because the primordial event of redemption is a lived-out experience touching the very depths of the being of the human being, it is ontological, and not merely psychological, emotional, or socially induced. The interpretation of the lived experience of redemption gives rise to relevant symbolic content which origin is itself pre-linguistic and pre-theological. In the facticity of redemption God comes forth into meaning content in the primary symbol God the Redeemer. Once this primary symbol is theologically established, it is fertile ground for further theological insights. I shall argue that from the primacy of the experience of redemption certain discernments of faith come to the fore in which the reality of God is correlated to the meaning of redemption. Although the primary symbolics of God the redeemer is already present in the authoritative texts (scripture, doctrines, and confessions), I shall not make use of that taken-for-granted authority but shall offer a phenomenological-

I offer this chapter to chaplains and campus ministers, who, by nature of their vocation, understand what it means to be multidimensional and multifunctional. This is because their role is to be pastor, counselor, program coordinator, leadership coach, Bible study leader, spiritual director, administrator, theologian, or whatever their community needs. This paper highlights their role as theologian and how they

---

ontological-theological approach to the reality-bearing status of this primary symbol: God the Redeemer or Spirit. The reasons for this move into theological prolegomena will become clearer as I develop the essay. Suffice now to say it that in scripture and tradition, the primary symbol is too ambiguous for our concerns, because it is burdened with anthropocentric, geocentric, patriarchal, and other distortions. But there is a way, I hope to show, to retain the primary symbol of God the Redeemer without these distortions. The symbolics of God in itself is a necessary but not sufficient source for an ecological theology. A third moment of argument is needed. How is it that God as redeemer relates to the totality of the world? The symbol of God as Redeemer contains in itself another semantic field that yields another basic symbol: God as Creator and Sustainer of the totality of creation. Both primary symbols, God the Redeemer and God the Creator thematize the God–world relationship, but they do not give an account of this relationship adequate to our epistemic context and in view of the contemporary ecological crisis. To that end, the symbolics of God have to be worked over and deepened by a framework of the God world relation. The articulation of a new "contemporary" framework can be accomplished by specifying (a) an empirical-scientific, and (b) a generic ontological understanding of how the world is and works, in our case the biosphere and the many ecological systems in it. Furthermore, the empirical-scientific and ontological understanding of nature must be related to the symbolic content of the Christian faith, an account of that relation that is rather difficult. This is where proper theological thinking has to do its main work. I shall propose that the facticity of redemption will give us a linguistic unit, the "ecclesial universal" — again, a term of art coined by Edward Farley — that is the hinge point between science, ontology (philosophy), and theology. We have already mentioned that the symbols of redemption give rise to the divine name of God as Holy Redeemer or Spirit. In the next move, I will try to show that a further inquiry in the symbolics of God, grounded in the redemptive activity of God, gives rise to the primary Name or Designation of God as Creativity. This primary designation of Creativity is further explicated by the ciphers or attributes of Eternality, Empowerment, and Aim, and a paradigm of God's relation to the world can be constructed from the way God comes forth as God in redemption, from the symbolics grounded in that redemption, and from a metaphysical ontological interpretation of how the world works and is.

Lastly, if all of these theses to be elaborated and explicated are acceptable, I shall finally argue that the Christian faith suggests a deep ecological framework of how we live in, with, and as nature.

can respond thoughtfully and guide their students to think about how God fits into the big picture when confronting the ecological crisis.[2]

A Prolegomenon to a Practical/Political/Liberation Theology

This paper is not biblical theology or systematic theology. It is a prolegomenon to a practical/political/liberation theology. As a prolegomenon it is not yet liberation/political theology proper. It belongs to a philosophical theology that attempts to investigate the question of the reality of God and the best way to approach this question of God and the God–world relation. Hence this investigation proceeds at a general and abstract level. But it is useful, I suggest, because it provides an overview of the pervasive issues and their interrelations, which is necessary before we can articulate and live out in more concrete systematic, political, ethical, social, and spiritual approaches.

But my proposal is not neutral, rather it seeks to advocate for a certain approach; therefore, I privilege the so-called revisionist theological camp. The works of Schleiermacher, Tillich, Tracy, McFague, Soelle, Farley, Cobb, Chopp, and Anderson are in the background of my thinking.[3] Fundamentalist, neo-orthodox, dialectical, ultra-orthodox approaches, and denominational theologies, though they have a lot to contribute, get no mention here. Needless to say, they deserve a hearing. But they cannot be the focus, given the limited scope of this chapter.

---

[2] One proviso: I shall not offer any pedagogical material. There is no course of study proffered, no suggestions for implementation or action, no spiritual formation.
[3] Premodern theology in the "House of Authority" is deemed relatively inadequate to address the issue under contemporary epistemic contexts. Neo-orthodox theology is also relatively inadequate because of its fideistic elements (Barth, Moltmann, etc.). Post-liberal theologies are also relatively inadequate because they provide a more current content; they turn out to be a more sophisticated fideism (Lindbeck, John Milbank, Jean-Luc Marion).

Ideally, a proposal should not be a monologue. It ought to be situated as an interlocutor in dialogue with other interlocutors, so in addition to theologians there are other conversation partners. For example, ecological/environmental scientists, empirical-nomological researchers, and natural-scientific theorists can help us articulate how nature works and is. Philosophers of science and social science can help us describe the world as nature in its perduring structures, systems, elements, relations, dynamism, temporality, spatiality, and being.[4] Ethicists can help us describe the "good and virtuous life" and our obligations to others (including the nonhuman other) as we all strive to live with dignity, respect, and authenticity.

This proposal is also not neutral in that it is polemical; that is, it comes from a Christian perspective and is contrary to a pervasive cultural attitude, which is often philosophically and ethically articulated by the academy and the cultural elite. Simply put, this prolegomenon is a bio-sociological framework for a normative value theory (axiology), and it expresses a contrary view to what was succinctly expressed by Protagoras: "Man (sic) is the measure of all things." This phrase, played out in the stance of much contemporary philosophy and ethics, argues that: (1) all values are epiphenomenal; (2) all values are subjective or culturally relative; (3) only human beings have intrinsic value; and (4) everything else has only extrinsic value. I shall argue that the experience of Christian faith can give us a radically different framework: a theocentric holism in which values are both objective and subjective and that God is the primordial source of value.

Relating the Ecological Crisis to Theological Thinking

The following theological argument is connected with some considered judgments that need to be aired at the beginning

---

[4] See Hartshorne's metaphysics of any and all possible worlds and Whitehead's/Cobb's metaphysics of the present cosmic epoch.

and substantiated in the course of this chapter. Again in summary fashion, here are the preliminary beliefs and convictions that guide my reflections on the ecological crisis.

First, humanity is facing what is very likely an irreversible ecological catastrophe; the current ecological distress, which is leading to global catastrophic changes, has been brought about by human activity and funded by the rise of modernity in which scientific knowledge of the natural world has changed our way of understanding nature. By this I mean the predominant Enlightenment view and the classical Newtonian-Cartesian mechanistic belief that nature has no value in itself. Therefore it has no intrinsic but only extrinsic value. (This philosophical view also has roots in a certain strand of Christian theology.) Alongside this view, which is still prevalent, there is also the development of ever-new technologies that continually use the earth's resources solely as means for human ends. However, there is also the growing awareness that our impending catastrophe cannot be reversed merely by technological means.

Second, a greater source of the ecological crises is the confluence of a philosophical and religious idea that nature is intrinsically valueless with an economic theory that does not even consider nature as part of the economic output. I argue that what we need is a conversion of mind and heart, a deliberately constructed theological imagination that has a different understanding of the interrelation of cosmos, nature (life), history, society, individuals, and God.

Prelude to a Theological Interpretation: Ecological Science, Economics, Ecological Philosophy, and Ethics

In this section, I shall mention briefly the wide-ranging debates over why humans should value nature. Three overarching themes come to the fore. First, we value nature as a space of aesthetic experience, even a mysterious source of religious feelings. Who has not been moved by the sheer, gracious beauty, and religious feelings lavished by mountains, streams, forests, oceans, sunsets, and other marvelous natural phenomena? In this rather romantic notion, nature is seen as originally pure, uncorrupted by humans, and a source of moral and spiritual contact. Nature has value for us as moral, aesthetic, and religious human beings. I note that this relation to nature leaves the question open whether nature has intrinsic value in itself or whether it is valuable to human being as sources of the "moral self," as Charles Taylor has remarked.

The second way is to value nature only for its own sake: its value is intrinsic regardless of whatever derived value it might have for human beings. Many people, religious and nonreligious alike, are drawn to this evaluating stance. Although I am sympathetic to this view and believe it is the best way to acknowledge and respond to ecological crisis, it is insufficient and lacking, even though the spiritual and intuitive pull is undeniable.

Third, and arguably the most current attitude toward nature, is that nature can be valued simply as a source of economics. Its value is strictly extrinsic. We extract our food, water, air, clothing, building materials, and so on from nature. We mine its ores, cut its trees, harvest its fish, and develop its land. We value it for the material products it provides us.

Contrary to this last view in particular, I argue that, based on reasons essential to the Christian faith, nature's value resides not in itself nor in our evaluation of it. Rather, I propose that the Christian symbol of the world as creation means that nature has theonomous value, which specifies that nature has intrinsic value beyond its usefulness for humanity.

There are green Christians and their numbers are growing. The view that nature is valuable beyond what it can do for us has become a strong force, pulling our hearts and minds to reconsider our inherited traditional beliefs and practices concerning our relationship with nature before God. But this understanding can also lead us to ask: Is there a faithful living in, with, and as natural beings that is based on a theological understanding of nature as God's creation, and therefore as the bearer of theonomous value?

An Economic Account of the Root of the Ecological Crisis

Before we can answer this ethical-theological question, I want to go deeper into the causes of the ecological crisis itself and offer a summary argument put forth by the environmental philosopher Kenneth Sayre.[5] This may seem like a detour, but Sayre's argument will shed light on the ecological crisis and is important to the argument of this essay. We are learning from the ecological sciences the intricacies of the biosphere and the complex interrelations of the many ecological systems, which are complex systems that are comprised of subsystems, which are comprised of subsystems, etc. There are feed-back loops with, between, and among the various ecological systems. Thus the biosphere is not one thing nor is it static; rather the biosphere is a self-regulating, complex whole in which ecological systems are regulated, which, in turn, make up, comprise, and influence the whole of the dynamic, ever-changing, ever-adjusting biosphere. The biosphere is the global whole of all ecosystems, the zone of life on this vessel called earth in the seemingly infinite ocean of our universe. The atmosphere, the oceans, the landmasses, with their forests, mountains, valleys, plains, fertile lands, seemingly dead deserts, river systems, and all human habitation, whether in small villages or great metropolises, are vast ecosystems with their own subsystems, and together they all comprise the biosphere.

From a theoretical standpoint, which postulates a well-functioning and healthy biosphere, each individual ecosystem

---

[5] For more, see Kenneth Sayre's book *Unearthed: The Economic Roots of Our Ecological Crisis* (Notre Dame, IN: University of Notre Dame Press, 2010).

has an internal regulating mechanism that serves the sustainability of that particular system. An ecosystem is itself made out of many subsystems, which reach to the more subordinate relationships of that system. Furthermore, the self-regulating processes of each ecosystem are conducive for sustainability, preservation, and well-being because the internal processes interact with their environments. These environments are, of course, other ecosystems, which, in their internal self-regulation for self-preservation, sustainable growth, and well-being, are dependent on their part on their context, which turn out to be other ecosystems. We also learn from ecological or environmental science that this interplay of mutually supporting and mutually benefitting coexistence is made up of delicate, dynamic, and, when healthy, resilient sets of relationships. This is also the matrix of evolutionary development.

However, in the last three hundred years, more or less, this resilient, delicate, creative biosphere has been systematically broken down by human activity, purposeful and accidental, and continues to drain the biosphere as part of economic activity. That is, because of internal systematic failures, when one ecosystem breaks down, the whole is negatively affected. For example, let's look at the pollution of land through pesticides, herbicides, and many other chemical discharges. The internal mechanisms that regulate input from the environment affect the preservation and health of that ecosystem, changing the output into its environment, affecting the whole. The land becomes degraded and sick. This, in turn, contributes to the degradation of other complimentary environments; i.e., the river systems, the seas in which the rivers flow into, the oceans, the atmosphere, and so on. The point should be clear. The systematic degradation of one ecosystem has deleterious effects not only on itself but on the other systems that it needs to survive and flourish. The current crisis is systematic, and perhaps, irreversible, because all the major ecosystems have reached a point of critical degradation, which makes for an ever-increasing dysfunction when these degraded systems interact with each other. Thus air pollution contributes to land pollution, contributes to water pollution in the rivers, lakes, seas, and oceans, which leads to extinctions of living species and degrade chemical structures, which in turn weaken land health, air health, and so on.

Humanity has systematically broken down this resilient, delicate, creative biosphere. What are the causes? I shall simply offer an overview of Sayre's analysis. His main thesis is that the current ecological crisis is driven by global economic activity fueled by irresponsible economic theories and suspect morality.

The critique unfolds along three lines. First, using ecological science he shows that negentropic energy is changed into entropic[6] energy with every economic activity that necessarily uses energy for the production of goods and services. This statement is ethically neutral. When the many eco-systems are intact, they have the capacity to absorb entropic energy and stabilize the many ecosystems and the biosphere as a whole. The biosphere either disposes entropy as low grade radiation into space or recycles entropic energy into negentropic or useful energy. In other words, human activity in itself, if it remains within certain limits, does not disrupt the energy cycles of the ecological systems and so does no irreversible harm to the biosphere. Or said more precisely, the harm done by humans can be "absorbed" by the system, yielding no substantial effect. Furthermore, providing empirical data, Sayre argues that eco-

---

[6] Entropy is the degradation of the matter and energy in the universe to an ultimate state of inert uniformity. It is also a process of degradation or running down or a trend to disorder. http://www.merriam-webster.com/dictionary/entropy. Negentropy is the opposite; it is the entropy that a living system exports to keep its own entropy low.

nomic activity produces too much entropy, at a pace in which the biosphere cannot either get rid of it in space or renew it as negentropy. The cycle of degradation is not only widening but also deepening and accelerating.

The second part of Sayre's argument is that economic activity is not morally neutral. It is couched in theoretical or scientific language that actually obscures the causes of the degradation of the biosphere. He says that there is something fundamentally skewed with the classical economic theories in play today, which were birthed by Adam Smith and further developed in most respectable universities and think tanks. These are their operative axioms. (1) In order for an economy to remain healthy it has to grow. (2) A nongrowth, sustainable economy is not a stable economy but one that will die. (3) Economic growth automatically contributes to social and natural well-being. (4) The biosphere and its myriad of ecosystems and subsystems is a limitless resource for material and energy for economic activity. Please note that natural resources, including all forms of energy, are not included in the equations that measure the health or sickness of economic activity. And although some recent economic theories include natural resources in the economic input-output equation, they do so by assigning them a monetary value.

In rebuttal to these assumptions, Sayre says, first, the recognition that natural resources must be part of economic theory is a step forward, but assigning monetary value to natural resources is at best an arbitrary activity. Who decides what a forest, a river, a glacier is worth when it is disrupted or even destroyed in order for economic growth to be maintained?

Second, and this brings us to the more fundamental flaw in this economic theory, which is the assumed but not proven axiom that the biosphere is a limitless and indestructible resource for material and energy for fueling economic activity. Ecological science has shown that far from being limitless and indestructible, the biosphere is limited (bounded), fragile, and vulnerable to negative and irreversible damage. The resources of the biosphere are limited, most of them nonrenewable, once they are taken out of the ecological functional circle, and transformed into non-recyclable or non-recoverable entropic energy—think of the greenhouse effect of gases that trap heat in the atmosphere, rather than letting it escape into space, and the depletion of the ozone layer, which lets in ultraviolet rays increasing global warming.

Third, there is no empirical evidence that economic growth automatically brings social well-being and the protection of nature. In fact, what we are experiencing is that only a relatively few people are enjoying the benefits of wealth, but the negative side effects of ecological distress—draught, pollution, migration, and so on—are felt mostly by the lower classes of developed countries and emerging markets. Furthermore, economic wealth in the hands of the few in the developed nations has come by way of the exploitation of natural resources of the so-called developing countries.

Fourth, classical economic theory has always asserted, but never tested, the axiom that economic health depends on an ever-growing economic output, usually measured in goods and services produced and consumed by citizens of a particular nation.

Fifth, Sayre's argument then turns into ethical questioning. Economic theory, on its face, designates "happiness" of individuals as its highest value. But it turns out, that happiness is equated with the fulfilment of individuals' pleasures, interests, and needs. Furthermore, fulfillment can only be accomplished by producing, buying and selling, and consuming goods and services. That in turn is possible when the accumulation of wealth is the highest good. The pursuit of happiness, which here means the consumption of things that bring pleasure and comfort, can only be realized by the accumulation of private wealth, in the form of disposable income. Disposable income is a value in itself, the capacity to consume as many goods or services that are deemed to bring comfort and pleasure. They are following Adam Smith's dictum that the accumulated wealth of the individual, who pursues his or her own private interest, will result through the working of the "invisible hand" in the accumulation of wealth for everyone else.

However, there is no real basis for the assertion that the accumulation of private wealth leads, by the efficacy of the "invisible hand," the mechanism of free-market capitalism, to the well-being of all; this is a morally dubious premise. Is the capacity for consumption of goods and services that lead to pleasure and comfort the same thing as happiness or a fulfilled life? Also, is it philosophically and morally tenable that only human desires and needs have intrinsic value? Are there nonhuman realities that have intrinsic value and therefore limit economic activity? As one can imagine, for Sayre this is a rhetorical question. In contrast, Sayre proposes a theory of economics that expounds a "sustainable" nongrowth-driven economic activity, which replaces consumption as the highest intrinsic value.

Does Nature Have Any Intrinsic Value?

We are moving now to a crucial juncture of our argument. If Kenneth Sayre is correct in his analysis, the ecological crisis demands a conversion of the heart and mind. We need to see that what fuels the ecological crisis is human desire for consumption gone awry, itself stoked by an anthropocentric ideology, which considers humans as the only beings who have intrinsic worth. It follows then that the natural world only has extrinsic worth or is only a means to desired human ends. So here is the question: In what sense can we articulate the intuitive sense that nature has intrinsic worth in the face of the overwhelming popular sentiment and economic theory that only human beings have intrinsic worth? The theologian and ecologist Holmes Ralston III puts the problem succinctly:

> In an age of naturalism, philosophers seem as yet unable to naturalize values. They are naturalizing ethics, epistemology, and metaphysics. They have connected human ethical behavior to Darwinian reciprocity, kin selection, genetic fitness, and so on. They analyze human capacities for epistemology with care to notice how our human perceptions, our sense organs, have an evolutionary history. Our mind and its cognitive capacities are pragmatic ways of functioning in the world. They interpret ideologies and metaphysical views as means of coping, worldviews that enable humans in their societies to cohere and to outcompete other societies. Ethics, epistemology, and metaphysics are survival tools, whatever else they may also become.[7]

We can rephrase Ralston this way: people, as individuals and as a species, are biologically motivated. And all of our mental, physical, and social constructs are meant to help us survive. This means that our morality, beliefs, and all knowledge are self-serving, even if they become more than that. Therefore it is "natural" for human beings to value and evaluate other natural entities in terms of our own survival, as means to our ends. Even if we believe that nature, for example, can be viewed as intrinsically valuable, it's just an illusion or understood that

---

[7] Louis Pojman et al., *Environmental Ethics: Readings in Theory and Application*, 7th ed. (N.p.: Wadsworth Publishing/Cengage Learning, 2016), 130.

extrinsic value always trumps intrinsic value. For example, we might think we value the forest for its own sake, until we are cold, then it becomes a source to provide for our warmth. But is there a deeper, non-extrinsic way that nonhuman nature possesses value?

The question is theologically important. If God is the Creativity that disposes the world, divine Creativity "lets be" creation as nature. Is this divine "letting-be," this empowering of creation to be itself as nature, also a source of bestowing value to the natural reality that God lets be? Is not the divine act of letting-be of creaturely being in its own autonomy-dependence-self-transcendence also not a creation of beauty, of value? The questions are important but it is premature to answer. So, let's follow Ralston a bit further.

There is an aporia in the logic of this anthropocentric, socio-biological way of naturalizing values. On one hand, humans are considered as natural in nature as nature. On the other hand, there seem to be features that distinguish us from nature: capacities for meaning-making, language, morality, aesthetics, faith, and valuing. And yet, these distinguishing features are also emergent capacities rooted in the very way nature works. So here we have a type of natural reality. The human species that emerged from nature and is capable of valuing itself intrinsically values everything else extrinsically or at least relative to the species' own intrinsic worth. In this socio-biological interpretive framework, philosophers and ethicists deny that everything natural, other than the human species, has intrinsic value; that is, that all value is either subjective or culturally relative. Either way, human subjectivity and culture are contingent upon natural processes, but the act of assigning value is an exclusive human activity, which designates humans as intrinsically valuable, basically because we say so.

But why not take the argument on a different route? If we

all are entities whose origin can be traced back to evolutionary processes that gave rise to our type of being with the capacity to value, then it seems that the source of our capacity to value has come to us from a nature that has the potential to contingently produce a natural species with the capacity to value. Given the bio-evolutionary-social framework of the origin of values, another plausible pathway is open to the subjectivists, given their own assumptions.

If subjectivity is a result of natural processes and if valuing is a capacity of subjectivity, then it seems that nature is the objective, nonhuman matrix for the condition with which human beings come into being to begin with. This means that nature could be conceived, without contradiction, to be the objective nonhuman context from which the emergence for the capacity to value becomes viable. Could it be that some of the valuing capacity that human beings have is shared by nonhuman entities, at least in more rudimentary form? To get out of this conceptual gap—that humans are of nature, and abide in nature and as nature, and yet we are the only natural entities capable of bearing intrinsic worth—is to ferret out a category mistake in their argument. The epistemological and the ontological explanatory frameworks are fused and thereby confused.

How We Know Whether Nonhuman Reality Has Intrinsic Value

The following section is rather technical, but necessary to dislodge the argument for exclusively anthropocentric values. I shall begin with the epistemological question: How do we know whether nonhuman reality and the biosphere, in particular, have intrinsic value? To explore this question I shall invite you into a thought-experiment. Consider first the relative epistemological question: as long as human beings exist, it is possible to ask whether or not nature has intrinsic value? This assertion can be modified in order to make the vexing epistemological problem even more acute. As long as human beings exist, we can entertain the question of whether nature has intrinsic value even if human beings did not exist. This presupposes the existence of human beings in their endeavor of thinking about the intrinsic value of nature. One can think for example about the value of nature before human beings existed and the value of nature long after human beings have gone extinct. But the condition for thinking about nature without human beings rests on the fact that human beings exist that "do" the thinking. That is why I have called this the "relative epistemological question." The questioning is relative to or contingent upon the existence of thinking human beings.

Here is a related question: If human beings did not exist as a matter of fact would nature have intrinsic value? As far as I can tell, the only logically possible answer to the factual nonexistence of human beings in relation to the question of the value of nature is the following conclusion. If human beings did not exist as a matter of fact, then we can say neither that nature has value nor that nature does not have value. The conditions for answering the question are simply such that they make the raising of the question impossible. The radical absolute epistemological stance "if human beings never existed, then we can say neither that nature in itself is intrinsically valuable nor that it is not intrinsically valuable" seems to me to be correct—as an epistemological question.

There is an error when the epistemological impossibility to answer the question either way is used to found a reality claim that all values must be emerging with the existence of human beings. Since, epistemologically investigated, we can say neither that nature has value nor that it does not, if human beings did in fact not exist—the absolute epistemological question—that seems to give grounds to the anthropocentrists to argue that valuing depends on the de facto existence of human beings.

Only on the relative epistemological basis can the issue of whether nature is intrinsically valuable even be raised. Here, there is a subtle switch from epistemological considerations— apart from actual human beings, we can say neither that nature has value nor that it does not—to an ontological assertion: that the question of the value of nature depends on the de facto existence of human beings.

Toward a Theological Interpretation

The approach in this section is theological. We want to inquire where discernments of objective values occur, values that come with criteria independent of the human beings who perform the act of perceiving value. From within the Christian faith, does the biosphere have intrinsic value; and if so, what are our ethical responsibilities toward it? Do ecological systems have intrinsic value? Do species have intrinsic value? Do animals have intrinsic value? And so forth.

Ironically, we begin with a theological anthropology to overcome the anthropocentric stance of our relationship to nature. Consider the following model of a theological anthropology. Three mutually interpenetrating spheres comprise human reality. The first consists of the personal sphere or human subjectivity. The second sphere is the interhuman, and the third sphere is the social. Informing this anthropological analytic is a theological question: How does God come forth as God in each of these spheres in such a way that, in this coming forth, meanings and symbols arise, which, in turn, are endowed with conviction that what thus comes into meaning is, at the same time, real?

The adjectival phrase "as God" in the slogan "God coming forth as God," is intentionally employed to highlight the issue that what we are after are neither psychological explanations of the origin of belief in God nor sociological accounts. The question asks about the reality or actuality of God as God, who comes forth with God's own criteria of intelligibility and with fields of evidences that ground the conviction of God's actuality. This basic conviction of faith is what is at stake in the disagreements about socio-biological theories about human reality that propose an anthropocentric understanding of values. For much of socio-biological theory, religious feeling and the power to create values are epiphenomena of subjectivity. They believe that the more fundamental reality is made up of biological-evolutionary processes, which themselves are "blind" or value-neutral.

In Christian anthropology, the personal sphere is itself multidimensional. It is biological; it has phylogenetically rooted desires for well-being and self-preservation. But as personal or as an agent-self, the personal sphere is not merely reducible to natural-biological processes. The self is fundamentally self-interpreting, self-evaluating. It is that kind of entity for which its being, or existence is an issue, to paraphrase a key point of existentialist philosophers and theologians (Pascal, Heidegger, Sartre, Augustine, Rahner, Tillich). To be a self, a person is more a task to be tackled than an unchanging substance already completed. In other words, the person, the agent-self, has elemental passions for the self on behalf of itself. It has a deep an indelible need to be itself. Another elemental unremitting desire is to be in communion with others, to acknowledge the beautiful, but fragile, vulnerable face of the other, and for the other to acknowledge one's own dignity. And perhaps, we can list another fundamental desire: the desire for what is real or actual.

Furthermore, the Judaic-Christian ethos, which embodies various theological anthropologies, shows that a structural feature of human reality is its tragic existence. The elemental passions for self, other, and reality are never satisfied. With each momentary satisfaction, the self moves beyond its fulfilled desire into an infinite horizon of more and other desired goods and conditions for its well-being. This unfillable hole between the desiring heart and what the world can offer, as Augustine well understood, is experienced as a kind of suffering, a permanent lack, an uncrossable void. The quality of the experience of the restlessness of the heart is an unavoidable ontological feature of being a self. Self-transcendence and self-initiation have this concomitant aspect of tragic existence in the sense the humans exist in a world of finite goods that can never unambiguously or permanently satisfy the elementary passions. In other words, the self senses its groundlessness and existential insecurity amidst the worldly goods, an ontological insecurity arising out of its own finitude, the finitude of the worldly goods, and the undeniable breech between what is desired and what is received.

At this juncture, the Christian ethos reveals another anthropological layer constitutive of theological anthropology. Unable to dwell in this ontologically tragic situation, the self has two options. The first option leads to idolatry. The second is faithful existence before God. In the first option, the self insists that ontological insecurity and tragic existence be eliminated, and this elimination is expected from a good or reality in the world. So arises the idol, a worldly good that will secure the human being in its ontological, structural tragic groundlessness. Under the dynamics of idolatry, the ontologically insecurity is not actually removed. Rather, what happens is that the being of the human self is corrupted by self-deception, sin, and evil. The Christian faith insists that once the self is corrupted by sin and enslaved by the idol, nothing in the world can undo this corruption. This conviction that once the human being is corrupted by sin and evil, it has no resources either in itself or in the world to escape the deadening power of the false god, is a cornerstone of the Christian faith. It is also a fundamental insight that can help overcome the anthropocentrism of the socio-biological evolutionary philosophy and ethics that posits human subjectivity to be the sole source of intrinsic value and valuing. If no good in the world or the totality of world-system is capable of removing corruption, sin, and evil, and yet, redemption can occur, then that which brings about redemption must be a world-transcendent reality capable of redeeming. Faith calls this reality God.[8]

This brings us to another major theological insight of the Christian faith: the facticity of redemption.[9] In the Christian faith, redemption is a facticity; it occurs. It is a fact. It is a lived experience that yields meanings and values to be interpreted, assessed, and judged. By redemption, following Tillich, I mean, generally speaking, a transition from the corrupted, idolatrous existence to a theological freedom, theological virtues, or theonomy. If God comes forth as God in redemption, as the interpretations of the facticity of redemption would have it, another momentous insight is opened up. In the redemptive divine coming forth, the believer discerns that which is brought about by redemption cannot be a worldly reality. If it is true, as Christian faith attests, that once in the claws of the idol, we cannot save ourselves or nothing in the world can save us; and yet

---

[8] The term *world-transcendent reality* is ambiguous. In a mythological imaginary, God is envisioned as being outside, beside, above the world; or "existing" prior to the world. Such notions reduce God to an entitized, mundane reality. No such stories are told here. What God transcends in relation to the world is not a spatial or temporal category but a logical one concerning the fact that God is the "One and only One" reality capable to transform corrupted being into a new theonomous being. As the One and only One able to redeem, God is absolutely different than intra-worldly realities or the totality of the world (being) as such. The word *transcendence* refers to this absolute difference.

[9] *Facticity* is a technical term in existentialist theology not to be confused with factuality. Factualities are correlated with the natural aspect of ontic existence, the way an individual goes about living his or her life concretely in the world. Factuality is correlated to the onto-logical-structural features of the human being, in our case the "desiring heart," the elementary passions, the self-transcending, self-interpreting capacities of human subjectivity.

redemption happens, then the redemptive transformation comes from the One and Only One, non-worldly reality that can redeem. God discloses God's self as the world-transcendent Redeemer. It is this lived-experience of redemption by the causal efficacy of divine power that grounds the conviction that God is God apart from our human desires and needs. God comes forth as God with criteria and norms adequate to God and not human needs and desires.[10] This insight into the reality of the Godness of God is the place for faith that de-centers anthropocentrism. God, as the source of redemption and the source for the emergence of new being, has the effect of relativizing human existence with regard to God, replacing the anthropocentric framework with a theo-centric framework for thinking about the God-world-self holism.

But how do the dynamics of idolatry and the dynamics of redemption affect the other spheres of human reality and how do they give rise to meanings and symbolics of God?[11] In the interhuman sphere idolatry engenders the corruption of the community of face-to-face relations. Here violation, resentment, and guilt are the effects of sin and evil. Once this corruption happens, nothing in the world can redeem it. And yet, the Christian faith does experience redemption in relationships. Enemies become friends; violated relations become reconciled. Martin Buber reminds us that faith sees these transitions (from idolatrous corruptions to theological freedoms) as integral to our relationship with an Infinite

---

[10] The facticity of redemption engenders discernments about ontological transformations that rise into meanings of redemption, symbolic language that renders these ontological transformation intelligible and able to be conceptualized, narrated, thought about, and appropriated for judgment. In the ontological transition from corruption to redemption, the meaning of God the Redeemer that arises in the facticity of redemption and comes also with the conviction (judgment) that what is so meant is at the same time real. This is a reformulated ontological proof of God's existence from the framework of redemption.

[11] This discussion merits a more thorough analysis, but that is beyond the scope of this chapter.

Thou. The Infinite Thou, as a deep symbol of faith for God's relationship in the sphere of community, is the One and Only One that empowers reconciliation and relationships characterized by agape. If reconciliation is a facticity of faith, then God is co-present in that reconciliation as the One and only One who could bring about redemption, and the symbol accordingly of God as Reconciler, the Infinite Loving Thou arises. In the sphere of the social, with its institutions, powers, economies, traditions, culture, and so forth, the dynamic of idolatry and evil distorts the social into subjugating unjust societies. If societal redemption is experienced in the faith, then the One and only One who could bring about this transformation is nothing of the world but God as the Norm of Justice. The facticity of societal redemption gives rise to the primary symbol, God of Justice.

Let me summarize. For faith, it is inconceivable that the release from idolatry could be brought about by a worldly reality or power. Since redemption does occur and is a reality that transcends the totality of world-system and being, it is God who comes forth as related to the totality of world and also as the efficient cause of a reborn world. In this coming forth, God cannot be reduced to human acts of experiencing and valuations. God provides God's own criteria independent of human beings. The primacy of God in redemption discloses itself as the source of a valuing, a bestowal of goodness, beauty and autonomy to everything God redeems. Anthropocentrism is deposed as an interpretive scheme. Theo-centrism takes its place and we experience God the Redeemer in the personal sphere as the Meaning of Existence; the Infinite Thou, authentic selfless Love, the search for community; and the Norm of Justice in a corrupt society.

The symbolic field of God the Redeemer uncovers another, hidden field of meanings and primary symbols that have to do with divine creativity. Redemption is Creativity writ large over all reality, including nonhuman reality. How so? The transitions from idolatrous bondage to theological freedom indicate a peculiar kind of creativity. The redemptive power of God creates a new good that was not here before. Thus, redemption is a moment of divine creativity. The primary symbol of God the Redeemer gives rise to another primary symbol, God as the Creativity that disposes human reality towards redemption.

The theological concept of creativity is polysemic in this context. It can mean two different things, although they are intimately related. In one meaning, Creativity bespeaks who God is; it is a designation, a naming of God's actuality, the Name of God as God. In systematic theology, this designation belongs to the doctrine of God. In a second sense, creativity is an activity of God; it is what God does. And so it belongs in the doctrine of God as the creator of creation. The divine activity as creativity is grounded in God's own being as Creativity. Creativity with capital "C" refers to the Name of God, who God is. Creativity with lower "c" refers to God's activity. This distinction is important for our task of showing that nature as creation has intrinsic value, independent of whether or not human beings give value to it. Moreover, if God is the Creativity that lets things be by redeeming them, things have value based on God's gracious act of redeeming/giving new being, regardless of whether or not human beings are the only entities capable of valuing. The intrinsic value of nature comes from the creative activity that God performs, that is the relationship of God and world.[12]

---

[12] This last statement should not be confused with the following statement that, as far as we know, only human beings are aware and have the capacity to value.

The Creativity that God Is:
A Source of Intrinsic Value for Everything Created

If God is Creativity, inherent in that creativity are the attributes of eternality, empowering, and aim. To empower, in an ontological sense, is God's act of letting-be of realities that are dependent-independent of God. The relationship of dependence-independence is understood as dialectical; with dependence there is recognition of the need for the other, with independence this relationship forms a functional whole. The pole of dependence signifies that creaturely reality could not come about without God's creative act. The pole of independence signifies that what is so created, let-be, has the fundamental character of self-initiation, self-determination, and self-creativity. What God empowers is precisely the realities' autonomy-in-relation to its environment. God's creativity is not a heteronomy over created being but a letting-be of creaturely autonomy. Idolatry as a feature of the corruption of an originally good creation is transformed by God into theononomy of a "new being"; but theonomy does not erase creaturely autonomy, but frees it from idolatrously induced heternomy.

Redemption is a sort of empowering. The divine creativity empowers beings to be. God lets being be in its finite goodness. Since the empowering/redemptive activity of God moves human beings into meaningful existence, mutual relations infused by agape and societal justice, the creative empowering also discloses a divine Aim. The creativity of God is not amorphous, chaotic, nor sheer unleashed power. Rather it is a power that works toward harmony, depth, width, and intensity; a matrix for emergent new strata and qualities of being. It moves beings toward complexification, relationality, mutually interdependent symbiosis, and at the same time, individual freedom. Thus, as the outcome of God's creativity, the facticity of redemption bespeaks a divine Aim in God's activity toward the world.

A closer interpretation of the divine Empowering with Aim shows also that the divine creativity is not selective, piecemeal, or limited in scope, time, or place. From the facticity of redemption, it is inconceivable to imagine that there was a time or a space or a region of being in which God was not always already the empowering, purposeful creativity. Thus, another primary cipher or attribute conjoins Empowering and Aim, that is to say., Eternality.

If God is the Creativity that disposes the world with empowering aim and eternality, and these activities in modes of inclusivity, self-sufficiency, and unconditionality, then whatever God creates is also infused with intrinsic value. Or as said in Genesis, God pronounces them "good."

What is the relation between the conviction of the reality of God to the cognitive or epistemological question of how one knows that God is actual and that God's actuality is the source of value for everything that God creates and sustains and redeems? The crux of the argument is whether a socio-biological anthropocentrism of values can sustain the "impossibility stance" of the radically absolute axiom: if there are no human beings, then there would be no intrinsic value in the world. The reformulation of the epistemological and ontological question runs as follows: if there are no human beings at all then there can be neither redeemed human beings nor idolatrously corrupted human beings. In the absolute epistemological sense: if there are no redeemed human beings, then we can say neither that God is, nor that God is not. This is the epistemological agnostic stance or the impossibility thesis.

This impossibility thesis has only epistemological import; it cannot be meant as a theological statement—theological in the strongest sense of positing the question of the reality of God. It is merely an epistemological impasse or non-capacity of knowing. To turn the question of "how we know" about the actuality of God and the conditions necessary to that knowledge into an anti-theological metaphysical claim about the nonexistence of God puts the socio-biological anthropocentric position in a precarious cognitive situation. It has to turn an epistemological agnosticism (if human beings did not exist, then we can say neither that God is nor that God is not) into a most comprehensive metaphysical positive statement: the assertion that God in any and all possible conditions of reality is not real or actual. Such a conflation of the epistemological non-capability of saying whether or not God is actual if human beings do not in fact exist, with the metaphysical atheism that God is in any and all senses non-actual, is possible only on the basis of an anthropocentrism built into their ideology from the very beginning. Socio-biological human-centrism presupposes but does not proffer reasons concerning the facticity of redemption and the discernment of the world-transcendent "One and Only One." It merely treats religious experiences as epiphenomena.

In the faith community, redemption is not merely an epiphenomenon. On the contrary faith has access to realities that come with evidence and reason to ground convictions. The faith community functions as the matrix of its discernments of realities. Faith acknowledges the epistemological paradox: if there are no human beings and if there are no redeemed human beings, then we can say neither that God exists, nor that God does not exist. In the absolute epistemological sense, if there are no redeemed human beings, then epistemologically but innocuously, we can say neither that God is nor that God is not. However, this is an epistemological question about the conditions for the possibility of knowledge. But this epistemological agnosticism cannot be the ground of a metaphysical positive about the non-reality of God. The ontological issues, the question about the reality of God as God, have a different structure and framework. The facticity of redemption leads to a different ontological-theological conclusion about the reality status of God. If the contingency of human being is a dependence-independence dialectic, if redemption gives rise to the conviction that what faith means by God is at the same time real, then we have an insight into the primoridiality of the reality of God as the ground of redemption *independent* of the human being. The independence of God (within the independence-dependence dialectic) simply signifies that nothing in the world nor the totality of the world can bring about redemption of a corrupted world. In positive terms, since redemption happens, God is the One and only One world-transcendent Reality that is experienced as the cause of redemptive activity. As world-transcending Redemptive/Creativity God is intendent of the world and as that Which Redeems/Creatively disposes the world, God is dependent on the world.

The facticity of redemption then gives rise to an insight of the otherworldliness of God, a primordiality expressed in the Creativity that redeems, and therefore establishes a theocentric God-world-self holism. Theocentrism displaces anthropocentrism. Value is bestowed on anything and everything that God makes new through redemption. And since there is no limitation to God's scope of redemptive creativity, no entity or reality in the world is without intrinsic value. This theologically articulated vision of the God who, in creating/redeeming is the source of all value refutes the anthropocentric conviction that only humans have intrinsic value, while everything else has only extrinsic value.

Conclusion

This essay is a theological prolegomenon meant to help us begin to think theologically about the ecological crisis we are facing. The intended reader is the chaplain and the campus minister in his or her role as theologian. My assumption is that the primary professional activities of ministry ought to be complemented by attention to speaking in a prophetic (theological) voice. In addition, practical and even political theology and ministry is impoverished without an understanding of such deep and persistent questions. Thus, I have identified in predominant ethical, philosophical, and economic theories the crucial question: Does nonhuman nature, in our case the biosphere, have intrinsic value; and, if so, does it deserve moral consideration?

I have argued that if the primordial experience of redemption that occurs in the community of faith is taken as the starting point of theological reflection, faith discerns that God comes forth as Redeemer; as Redeemer God discloses a Creativity that bestows new being, a non-idolatrous, theonomous being for human beings. And as Creativity, God has no limitations in scope, aim, space and time. Thus whatever God creates God redeems; concomitantly, whatever God redeems God re-creates. The divine activity of redemption-creation is a bestowal of intrinsic value to the totality of created being, which includes the nonhuman nature.

When redemption happens, anthropocentrism that makes humanity the measure of all things, is replaced by a theocentric holism of the God-world-self relationship. In short, God gives nonhuman nature intrinsic value as God also gives humanity, which deserves our moral consideration and gives witness to our redemption. It is my hope that this thinking will help campus ministers and chaplains develop curricula, Bible studies, or whatever their context needs to help students see how conversation about the relationship of God, world, and self is vital in discussion about ecological crises.

PLURALISM

Transformative Knowing: Scriptural Reasoning and Wesleyan Epistemology

All Faith Chapel or No Faith Chapel? Contours of Diversity and Pluriformity in Collegiate Ministry

Sunesis: Understanding via Interplay

A Particular Ministry in a Pluralistic Context

Practical Divinity: Pluralism in a Liberal Arts Community

Transformative Knowing:
Scriptural Reasoning and Wesleyan Epistemology
Christopher Donald

The Christian faith asserts that humanity lives in a broken, suffering world. Advances in technology bring news of disaster and violence from across the world into our homes, classrooms, and churches. When the terrorist attacks occurred on September 11, 2001, news observers noted that the world had changed. Until that day, many Americans had naively believed the end of the Cold War offered security, prosperity, and freedom from fear. Many people were certain that the world would have no more war or conflict, and so The Millennium Summit, which met in September 2000, had set goals for eliminating poverty, promoting sustainability, and creating meaningful global institutions and democratic civil societies. Instead, September 11, 2001 established a generation shaped by the normality of fear and suspicion and the banality of intrusive security and militarized society.

Children who were unknowing toddlers on September 11 are now college students. They have known nothing of American engagement with the world besides war, besides American soldiers deployed and dying in Iraq and Afghanistan. They have lived in a society shaped by polarizing fundamentalist figures— in the United States and in the Islamic world—seeking to exploit faith and religious identity for political expediency or military advantage. The world did change on September 11. Faith has become a means by which unscrupulous leaders create division and suspicion; consequently, violence, whether between individuals or states, is so often framed in terms of faith. United Methodist college chaplains and campus ministers have a responsibility as both Christian ministers and as campus leaders to discover ways to educate students about issues of faith and to help build community across lines of religious difference.

United Methodist campus leaders are called to the work of peacemaking and peace-building by nurturing a community that offers an alternative narrative to the divisive faith perspectives of fundamentalists. One natural place for United Methodist campus ministers to gain guidance about this community-building across faiths is in the works of John Wesley. Wesley is the founder of the Methodist Movement (of which United Methodism is a part), and his writings provide the formative Methodist theological perspective. In addition, Wesley was a community-builder, bringing together people across lines of difference (most often social class in Great Britain and including race in North America) in the name of the Christian faith. However, depending on the occasion of his writing, Wesley could be either conciliatory or polemical toward other faith traditions. That is to say, Wesley's writing on interfaith concerns is inconsistent at best and offensive at worst. But ultimately, Wesley was a man of his time. His aggressive words toward Catholics were as much the result of jingoistic fervor as they were a theological dispute. His dismissive attitude toward Muslims was grounded in contemporaneous belief in European racial supremacy as much as it was in Christian triumphalism. For present-day chaplains and ministers working on increasingly diverse and religiously plural campuses, Wesley's works on interfaith concerns, when taken at face value, can obscure any meaningful basis for mutual cooperation and relationships across lines of religious difference.

The Wesleyan basis for interfaith cooperation may not be found in his writing about the other faiths of his time, but rather in his more basic way of perceiving, understanding, and interpreting the world. When Kingswood School, the first Methodist institution of learning, was opened in Bristol in 1748, Charles Wesley penned a hymn that proclaimed the school would "unite the pair so long disjoined: knowledge and vital piety, learning and holiness combined." This poetic expression reflects John Wesley's theory of knowing, which asserts that both the intellect and the spirit, and the mind and the heart have roles in the way human beings perceive, understand, interpret, and know the world, relationships with others, and God. Wesley believed that this relationship between experience and reason produces the kind of knowledge that is transformative for individuals and society. The natural knowing of science and the spiritual knowing of faith can combine to motivate and to enact transformation in the world. This Wesleyan epistemological perspective remains relevant today as United Methodist chaplains and campus ministers address a variety of social issues, including interfaith engagement and community, on campus and beyond.

Scriptural Reasoning (SR) is a practice of intellectual and spiritual engagement across faiths that has as its objective nothing less than healing a broken world. People of Abrahamic faiths (Judaism, Christianity, and Islam) share the conviction that divine intent is revealed in their community's sacred texts, and believe that these texts are normative for ordering individual and communal life. In addition, believers within these communities find that critical study of these sacred texts, employing philological, historical, literary, and other methods, enriches and deepens the meanings of sacred texts. Practitioners of SR from these three faiths bring together the life of the spirit and the life of the mind by reading their sacred texts together, which facilitates both personal and social transformation. Reading together creates a community across faith convictions and also helps people of faith read their own sacred text in a new way. This perspective and process have resonance with Wesleyan epistemology: a basis in sacred text, the joining of the spirit, and the intellect and creation of community for personal edification and social transformation. The practice, principles, and outcomes of SR are consistent with transformative knowing, which is the process and objective of John Wesley's epistemological framework. Accordingly, the practice of SR provides a method for United Methodist chaplains and campus ministers to engage in interfaith dialogue with authenticity and conviction.

Scriptural Reasoning Principles, Practices, and Outcomes

Early one Monday evening, a group of six students and two facilitators at a liberal arts college in the Gulf South gather in an unused classroom to read together. They are Jews, Christians, and Muslims, and they bring with them their holy books, the words and stories that give shape and meaning to their lives. One by one they share these sacred words, offering them to the group, and the group receives them with respect and gentleness, certain that meaning can be found in them. Throughout their time together there is laughter, there is joy, there is confession, and there is reflection. New ideas are dawning. As their time draws to a close, a sense arises that something special has happened. In a region dominated by a particular kind of evangelical Christianity, these students have courageously reached across the line of religious difference. Amid a politics that is quick to slander and stereotype, these students have opened their minds and hearts. In an academic culture that often dismisses religious conviction as myth and superstition, these students have found faith a resource and strength to make the world a better place. Something special has happened, as these students from different faiths leave that classroom and make their way to the cafeteria to eat dinner together and to continue their conversation.

Scriptural Reasoning originated from Textual Reasoning, a practice of Jewish scholars, philosophers, and theologians who began meeting during the American Academy of Religion in the early 1990s. Textual Reasoning developed from the conviction that Jewish philosophy and theology could speak to the broken, suffering world, but also that Jewish philosophy and theology had become divorced from the Torah, the source of Jewish identity.[1] Textual Reasoning assumed that the Torah as sacred text, which had been interpreted in different ways by different Jewish communities, spoke to all Jews about Jewish identity in a particular way. Using the model of talmudic discussion, which prized thinking together as much as any conclusive outcome, these Jewish scholars found that the sacred text became a place of meeting, where they brought their human experiences into conversation with the sacred text and Jewish tradition and, through that process, discovered a community of joy, imagination, and healing.[2]

Since the participants in Textual Reasoning met during the American Academy of Religion, scholars from Christianity and Islam (the other Abrahamic, textual traditions) sat in on Textual Reasoning sessions as observers.[3] Soon, scholars from the three Abrahamic faiths, convinced that their traditions

---

[1] David F. Ford, "An Interfaith Wisdom: Scriptural Reasoning between Jews, Muslims, and Christians," in *The Promise of Scriptural Reasoning*, ed. David F. Ford and C. C. Pecknold (Malden, MA: Blackwell Publishing, 2006), 3.

[2] Peter Ochs, "The Society of Scriptural Reasoning: The Rules of Scriptural Reasoning," *The Journal of Scriptural Reasoning* 2, no. 1 (2002): n.p., http://jsr.shanti. virginia.edu/back-issues/volume-2-no-1-may-2002-the-rules-of-scriptural-reasoning/ the-society-of-scriptural-reasoning-the-rules-of-scriptural-reasoning7/.

[3] Ford, "An Interfaith Wisdom," 3.

speak to the broken, suffering world, were seeking a way to read their respective sacred texts together. Scriptural Reasoning (SR) was the fruit of that effort to join intellectual rigor with faith conviction, all for the healing of a broken, suffering world.

Scriptural Reasoning is, first and foremost, a practice that is shared by people of different faiths.[4] Participants in SR speak of "houses," or the Abrahamic faith traditions where participants "live" every day, and the "tent," or the SR session where they gather temporarily. This differentiation means that one central virtue of SR is hospitality, which shapes preparation for the SR session. Sessions normally have a host and convener, who may or may not be the same person, who is responsible for the mutual hospitality that supports SR work. The host arranges a space and chooses a time, sensitive to the religious calendars of the various faiths, and invites participants. Experience has shown that a group from six to ten participants is optimal, any smaller or larger and the discussion may not be as fruitful. The composition of the group should evenly reflect the participating faith traditions, as well as take into account factors such as gender and levels of religious training. The host might also provide light refreshments, again being mindful of any religious restrictions.

Practice in the SR session itself is an engagement of vulnerability and hospitality. The convener facilitates the session, ensuring that boundaries are observed, including

---

[4] Scriptural Reasoning sessions are different from place to place and group to group. This general description is based on: William Taylor, *How to Pitch a Tent: A Beginner's Guide to Scriptural Reasoning* (London: St. Ethelburga's Centre for Reconciliation and Peace, 2008); Steven Kepnes, "A Handbook for Scriptural Reasoning," in *The Promise of Scriptural Reasoning*, ed. David F. Ford and C. C. Pecknold (Malden, MA: Blackwell Publishing, 2006), 23–39; Peter Ochs, "Scripture," in *Fields of Faith: Theology and Religious Studies for the Twenty-First Century*, ed. David F. Ford, Ben Quash, and Janet Martin Soskice (New York: Cambridge University Press, 2012), 117; and the author's own experience with a Scriptural Reasoning group in Charlottesville, Virginia.

maintaining an attitude toward the text of curiosity rather than exposition, ensuring a concrete focus on the text, and seeing that time limits are respected. The scriptural texts are quite short, a few verses at the most, printed in original languages and translation, and typically selected around a particular theme. "House conveners" can assist in selecting the texts and also can advise the group on appropriate behaviors towards sacred text in their tradition. The convener and the group determine the order of reading the texts. Presenters from each of the three traditions introduce their respective text to the group, which may be read in its original language and then read in English. The presenter then takes a few moments to set the passage in its scriptural context or explain its historical context or note textual issues. The presentation aims at being personal and conversational, authentic to the presenter and his or her tradition. If the presenter does not know everything about the text, others from the group may assist. Next, the text becomes the focus for group conversation and discussion, centered on the "plain sense" of the text—the meaning of the words freed from interpretive frames—and what the plain sense of the text communicates about the Divine, people of faith, the world, and the relationships between them. When conversation moves away from the concrete, plain sense of the text, the convener redirects conversation to the plain sense. After the other texts are presented and discussed and before the group adjourns, they might take some time to choose a theme for the next session so house conveners can select texts. In this manner, the SR session is based in hospitality and the engagement is characterized by vulnerability and hospitality, all for authentic mutual relationships.

Since SR is a community practice first, no firm rules or principles guide groups in a directive way. Rather, like Wesley's epistemology, the principles of SR's way of knowing are implicit. However, a variety of SR participants and observers have discerned several principles that guide SR practice and work.[5] First is the value of sacred text for communities. Scriptural Reasoning founders point to the suspicion, conflict, violence, and suffering in the world today and maintain that addressing these problems comes from seeking wisdom in sacred text.[6] Scriptural Reasoning takes scripture seriously as the transmitter of God's wisdom and the experiences of previous generations and as the normative ground upon which communities of faith are built. And SR understands that sacred texts of other faith traditions do the same for the communities of those traditions.

In an SR session, the text is at the center of the group and the foundation of the discussion; when conversation strays, the convener redirects it to the text. Because the text is sacred to one of the traditions, it is treated respectfully by the others, always with the attitude that value and wisdom are inherent in what that text has to say.

Another principle that emerges is the role of tradition in SR, which is present at multiple levels. The houses are the three faith traditions, and within each house are interpretive traditions and practices that shape the reading of sacred texts. Scriptural Reasoning acknowledges readings and welcomes them in the tent of an SR session, but that tradition does not

---

[5] Again, variation among practicing groups creates a variety of perspectives. Helpful here are Kepnes, "A Handbook for Scriptural Reasoning"; Rebekah Ann Eklund, "The Goods of Reading: Theological Interpretation and Scriptural Reasoning," *The Journal of Scriptural Reasoning* 9, no. 1 (2010): n.p., http://jsr.shanti.virginia.edu/back-issues/vol-9-no-1-december-2010-the-fruits-of-scriptural-reasoning/the-goods-of-reading-theological-interpretation-and-scriptural-reasoning/; and David F. Ford, "Seeking Muslim, Christian and Jewish Wisdom in the Fifteenth, Twenty-first and Fifty-eighth Centuries: A Muscat Manifesto" (lecture, Sultan Qaboos Grand Mosque, Muscat, Oman, April 20, 2009), accessed July 31, 2015, http://www.interfaith.cam.ac.uk/resources/journalarticlesandbookchapters/muscatmanifesto.

[6] Ford, "A Muscat Manifesto," lecture.

carry the normative weight that it carries within its house. In fact, innovative and imaginative interpretations by members of other houses in an SR session might initiate deeper reflection on tradition by the presenting house.[7] At the same time, other traditions may emerge within SR, including a foundational story, reports of successful and transformative groups, and over-arching commitments to hospitality, openness, and imagination. At this point, projecting how emerging tradition will continue to unfold in particular SR groups and the movement in general is difficult.[8]

Individual experience and reason are also critical parts of the conversation in SR. By leaving the house and gathering in the tent, the power and possibility of interpretation are in the hands of individuals. Experiences of individuals that are connected to knowledge of scripture, faith traditions, academic disciplines, and other life events shape the hermeneutic lens through which they understand sacred texts.[9] Human reason connects, evaluates, and articulates these experiences and interpretations. This openness to individual experience in SR establishes an environment where a special type of reason (imagination) can make hermeneutic leaps to view new possibilities within the sacred text of how God speaks to a broken and suffering world. Often, these insights of SR lead

---

[7] Ochs, "Scripture," 116.

[8] One interesting development was expansion of the practice beyond Abrahamic faiths, as reported in Samuel Wells, "The Possibilities of a Faith Council," *The Journal of Scriptural Reasoning* 9, no. 1 (2010): n.p., accessed August 12, 2015, http://jsr.shanti. virginia.edu/back-issues/vol-9-no-1-december-2010-the-fruits-of-scriptural-reasoning/ the-possibilities-of-a-faith-council/. Another development is the use of SR framework by the Prison Service in the United Kingdom to develop a Quranic Reasoning program called "Al Furqan" as a way of challenging interpretations of the text by prisoners influenced by radical terrorist groups, as reported in Richard Pickering, "Terrorism, Extremism, Radicalisation, and the Offender Management System," *Prison Service Journal*, no. 203 (September 2012): 12.

[9] Ochs, "Scripture," 116.

individuals to view their own sacred text and interpretive traditions in new ways. Also, the individual's experience of an SR session and the virtues that guide SR help cultivate those virtues in that person's life beyond SR. The SR session can be transformative, not just in the knowledge and insights gained but also in the virtues that are cultivated in the process.

Community experience is also an important element of SR and, like tradition, is observable at multiple levels. Individual experiences within SR and new interpretations of sacred text arise in the midst of that special, temporary community and are carried back to the individual's permanent faith community, where they can be investigated and evaluated based on that community's hermeneutical principles, tradition, and shared experience. But more immediately, the community gathered in the SR tent has a shared experience, which takes the form of the shared understanding that guides the work of SR. A temptation to stray into abstract ideas and an attempt to synthesize the content of the three texts may arise. However, the SR session must stay focused on the plain sense of the text as a way of maintaining attention to the concrete and preserving the particular perspectives of the faith traditions. Speculation that begins to stray from the concrete and particular is typically redirected by the convener or community members to focus on the text. Individual experiences and interpretations of sacred text are also evaluated in light of community virtues demonstrated and cultivated in the practice of SR.

Two of the most significant shared experiences are vulnerability and hospitality. A great deal of vulnerability exists in opening one's sacred text, which contains the principles and narratives that shape one's faith and life, to a community of others and then allowing them to interpret that text. A great deal of hospitality is needed in receiving others and their sacred text with gentleness, respect, and authentic engagement.

A number of other virtues, such as patience, faithfulness, joy, community, and imagination, guide the practice of SR in the moment and also become, in practice, a part of the outcomes of SR. These community experiences become a means of evaluating individual experiences and interpretations that arise by engaging sacred text through SR.

As stated, the founders of SR have maintained that there were no "guiding principles"; however, participants have identified several virtues that guide SR sessions and guide the individual participants beyond a particular session. These virtues have been suggested by New Testament scholar and SR participant Rebekah Eklund, particularly from the perspective of reading Christian scripture in her own study and SR contexts.[10] It is notable that the virtues Eklund identifies in SR also correlate to scriptural virtues of Christian life: the fruit of the Spirit described in Galatians 5:22-23, community as demonstrated in Acts 2:42-47, and imagination as described in Hebrews 11:1. One dimension of the fruit of the Spirit that Eklund names as a virtue in SR is patience. Scriptural Reasoning involves slow, close reading of a small piece of sacred text, often in the original language.

This savoring of sacred text creates a new, deeper appreciation and impression beyond simple meaning and application. The virtue of faithfulness, again part of the fruit of the Spirit, is also part of and nurtured by SR. Faithfulness as a part of engagement with sacred text is, in many ways, contrary to the prevailing view within academic communities. Yet reading sacred text with the assumption that it shares the wisdom of God means reading that text expecting to be transformed in the process. As Eklund observes, "not that one masters it, but that one

---

[10] Eklund, "The Goods of Reading."

is mastered by it." Another aspect of the fruit of the Spirit that guides and is the product of SR is the virtue of joy. Delight in a sacred text for its own sake creates a new perspective on why and how to read that text. Community is a virtue demonstrated in the early church (Acts 2:42-47) which is required to read scripture, whether reading as an individual who is part of a community or as the community together in worship or teaching. A mutual relationship exists between sacred text and community, as the text shapes the life and imagination of the community and the community shapes the way the text is interpreted. Finally, and perhaps most important, SR requires and cultivates the virtue of imagination, as framed by Hebrews 11:1. Imagination is the most important virtue that SR offers to the academy and the church. Eklund writes,

Scriptural reasoning resists the standard academic mode of textual study by emphasizing intuition and even a certain kind of playfulness with the text. It also demands a certain charity: the belief that one might be surprised by even a familiar text, and that a Christian might be taught something new about the Christian scripture by a Jew or a Muslim.[11]

Engaging imagination in SR opens up possibilities—a virtue desperately needed in a hurting and broken world—and helps individuals view the world, and the way the world is addressed by sacred texts, in new ways. These virtues guide the practice of SR, but, through the practice, these virtues are cultivated in the individuals who participate, transforming the way they think about sacred text, their community of faith, and their relationship to the world.

Engagement with sacred texts, in one's house of faith or in the tent of SR, always leaves a person changed. The virtue of imagi-

---

[11] Ibid.

nation, nurtured in SR, opens participants to the surprise that is characteristic of the practice, which is itself a kind of humility. Eklund notes that participants in SR begin to see their own old text in new ways, that they are changed by encounters with the texts of other faiths, and that this willingness to be surprised encourages approaching and reaching across lines of difference with humility. At the same time, hope emerges in the practice of SR. Imagination opens the heart and mind to discovering a better way that is free from pain and conflict. The practice of SR itself opens the possibility that the three Abrahamic faiths can witness together to the healing and peaceful intentions of God for the world. Finally, and most important, SR results in friendship.

SR cofounder David Ford noted, in a speech to Muslim scholars, "It is possible for us to face and discuss our differences without resolving them, while at the same time deepening our mutual respect and friendship."[12] Friendship created through vulnerability and hospitality in the SR tent of meeting is sustained even after an SR session is over. That friendship, across lines of difference, witnesses to the love of God and proclaims the way of peace in a world that desperately needs both love and peace. Scriptural Reasoning, in its practice, its principles, and its outcomes correlate to John Wesley's epistemological framework and thinking, which is a transformative knowing for the end of reconciliation and friendship.

John Wesley's Epistemology or Transformative Knowing

Early in his career, John Wesley was intrigued by the idea of spiritual knowledge as transformative knowledge, in that it changed the way a person perceived and understood the world. This spiritual knowledge was imparted by a personal experience

---

[12] Ford, "A Muscat Manifesto," lecture.

of the "witness of the Spirit" referenced in scripture.[13] In particular, Wesley was exposed to the unswerving faith of Moravian Christians during his journey from his Georgia posting back home to England, and he wondered how they lived and proclaimed their faith with such certainty. Back in London, Wesley engaged the Moravian leader Peter Bohler about the reliability of spiritual knowledge through the witness of the Spirit. When Wesley expressed skepticism about the witness of the Spirit and the reality of spiritual, transformative knowledge, Bohler brought several other members of the Moravian group to Wesley to provide their own affirmation of both the reality of the witness and its content.[14] Not long after, Wesley had his own experience of the witness of the Spirit in Aldersgate, where he received assurance of his saving relationship with God in Christ.[15] This direct revelation of spiritual knowledge required a new epistemological framework that could accommodate knowledge that was spiritual, and was most evident in healing and transforming the broken, suffering lives of believers in Jesus Christ.

Wesley needed to develop a new epistemological perspective, accounting for the intellectual and spiritual knowing he observed first in the Moravians, then in himself, and then, later, in the Methodist Movement more broadly. He was most directly influenced by two dominant schools of thought in eighteenth-century England. The first thinkers, to whom Wesley was reacting, were the theologians and leaders of the seventeenth- and eighteenth-century Church of England,

---

[13] Romans 8:16
[14] Yoshio Noro, "Wesley's Theological Epistemology," *The Iliff Review* 26, no. 1 (December 1971): 62.
[15] John Wesley, "The Witness of the Spirit," in *The Works of John Wesley*: Sermons, vol. 2, ed. Albert C. Outler (Nashville: Abingdon, 1984), 290.

known as the "Anglican Divines."[16] These men stated that the only appropriate sources for spiritual knowledge were scripture and reason. That is, revealed truth contained in scripture could be reflected upon by employing reason, resulting in the knowledge necessary for Christian living. This kind of spiritual knowledge was inherently indirect revelation, with the corollary that God no longer revealed spiritual knowledge directly to individuals. In this circumstance, in which rational reflection and indirect knowledge were sources of spiritual knowledge, faith was understood to be an intellectual assent to scripture and doctrine.[17] This perspective could not account for the certainty of faith that Wesley witnessed in the Moravians, but it did influence Wesley as he considered, articulated, and defended his own epistemological views.

The second group of thinkers who influenced Wesley was within the intellectual movement of the Enlightenment, in particular, empiricism. John Locke and Peter Browne were two of the most influential empiricist philosophers, and they had a substantial impact on Wesley.[18] Empiricists rejected Platonic ideas of ideal form, thus moving intellectual work from metaphysical speculation to processes of experimentation. This stance arose from their belief that knowledge comes from observation and experience and that its end is descriptive. In other words knowledge does not explain connections to Platonic forms but describes mathematical and mechanical processes. The human mind, they contended, has no natural ideas or knowledge. Rather, ideas come from information

---

[16] Mitsuo Shimizu, "Epistemology in the Thought of John Wesley" (PhD diss., Drew University, 1980). 11–12.

[17] Ibid., 41–42.

[18] Randy Maddox, *Responsible Grace: John Wesley's Practical Theology* (Nashville: Kingswood Books, 1994), 27. Also, Theodore Runyon, "The Role of Experience in Religion," *International Journal for Philosophy of Religion* 31 (1992): 188.

gathered by the senses, and reason helps put them together in an orderly way.[19] This scientific, empiricist perspective, that valued experience, was crucial for Wesley as he thought about the purpose and sources of spiritual knowledge, though it was far from problematic.

This reliance on experience as the source of knowledge, particularly as related to spiritual knowing, was open to the charge by critics of "enthusiasm." Enthusiasm in the eighteenth century meant preference of personal experience, particularly in spiritual knowing, over scripture, tradition, or reason. It was one of the most dismissive critiques that could be leveled against people of faith in the eighteenth century, so it was important that any epistemological framework Wesley employed account for charges of enthusiasm. Wesley's reliance on empiricism to explain spiritual knowing and to develop his epistemology meant that he had to account for its ultimate conclusion, enthusiasm.

Wesley was a thinker working within an empiricist framework but seeking to explain the transformative nature of direct, personal spiritual experience.[20] To begin, Wesley accepted the distinction between two different types of knowledge, natural knowledge and spiritual knowledge.[21]

Consideration of the sources and outcomes of these types of knowledge must begin with an understanding of the origins of that knowledge. Natural knowledge originates from the sensory experiences of a visible, sensible world. This observation of the natural world is then subject to ordering by reason. The result is natural knowledge, which explains what is happening in the

---

[19] Rex D. Matthews, "'Religion and Reason Joined': A Study in the Theology of John Wesley" (ThD diss., Harvard University, 1986), 256–7, 259, and 271–2.
[20] Maddox, *Responsible Grace*, 40.
[21] Ibid., 34–35.

world and how natural processes are unfolding, both of which are helpful in improving human existence. Spiritual knowledge has a different origin, source, and result. Wesley's understanding of the origin of spiritual knowledge came from the testimony of scripture in Hebrews 11:1, which speaks of "the evidence of things not seen." This verse, along with other testimony about the work and promises of God found in scripture, indicated to Wesley that an invisible, spiritual world is unknown and unseen by human beings, because they cannot naturally see or discern that spiritual world.[22] As such, knowledge of the spiritual world can only come through revelation by God. This spiritual knowledge informs us about the invisible world and, most important, about God and God's work of reconciliation and healing in Jesus Christ.[23]

Spiritual knowledge has as its sources the revealed truth of scripture, the collective witness of tradition, and the direct testimony of experience, all of which are ordered by reason.[24] The result of spiritual knowledge is faith, which transforms lives and recovers friendship with God. This perspective on spiritual knowledge, based in scripture, set Wesley apart in the intellectual and philosophical context of the Anglican Divines, who rejected experience as a valid source of knowledge. However, he was also working in the framework of Enlightenment empiricism, which accepted evidence only from the physical senses as a valid source of knowledge; this meant Wesley also needed to develop an explanation for how evidence of spiritual knowledge is discerned and what prevented it from descending into the dreaded realm of "enthusiasm."[25]

---

[22] Matthews, "Religion and Reason Joined," 284.

[23] Maddox, *Responsible Grace*, 29.

[24] Shimizu, "Epistemology in the Thought of John Wesley," 33, 36.

[25] John Wesley, "The Witness of the Spirit II" *The Works of John Wesley*: Sermons, vol. 1, ed. Outler, 285.

Wesley had observed among the Moravians, himself, and the Methodist Movement that spiritual knowledge originated from the invisible world, shared by direct witness from the Holy Spirit, but a number of sources combined to reveal and evaluate that spiritual knowledge. First, Wesley never denied the validity of indirect spiritual knowledge that the Anglican Divines advanced based on scripture and reason, only that such knowledge was insufficient for a transformed life with God in Christ.[26] Wesley agreed that a person could apply reason in the practice of natural theology and discern evidence about God from the created world, though he felt this knowledge was limited and incomplete. Wesley referred to this as the "faith of the servant," because it was merely intellectual knowledge, which would never lead to the transformed heart that was necessary for authentic Christian life.[27]

Second, and more important, Wesley believed spiritual knowledge was shared by direct witness of the Holy Spirit. In support of this perspective, Wesley returned again and again to Romans 8:16, "The Spirit itself beareth witness with our spirit, that we are the children of God." The joint testimony of these two witnesses, the Spirit of God and the human spirit, was certain testimony, not only about the individual's relationship with God but also an opening to knowledge about the invisible, spiritual world. This belief is the "faith of the son," the assurance that one is loved and saved by Christ, but also "the evidence of things not seen" described in Hebrews 11:1.[28]

The concern of Wesley was always of clarifying that this witness of the Spirit was authentic, as a way of defending his

---

[26] Ibid., 287–8.
[27] A reference to Romans 8:15. John Wesley, "On the Discoveries of Faith." *The Works of John Wesley:* Sermons, vol. 4, ed. Outler, 35.
[28] Ibid.

views from charges of "enthusiasm" by the Anglican Divines but also as a way to explain to empiricist critics that spiritual knowledge was imparted by senses, just a different set of senses.[29] To address these criticisms Wesley seems to have drawn an idea from the philosophy of Francis Hutcheson.[30] Hutcheson, like Locke and Wesley, rejected that human beings had any kind of innate ideas and believed the human mind only gains knowledge from outside itself. Hutcheson proposed that human beings have a "moral sense" that helps locate moral knowledge and perceive virtues.[31] While Wesley disagreed with Hutcheson's application of moral sense (it was a means of excluding God from thinking about conscience and morality), he did adopt its form to his theory of "spiritual senses."[32]

Wesley explains spiritual senses by way of analogy: just as the physical senses gather knowledge from the visible world, the spiritual senses gather knowledge of the invisible world. The spiritual senses are dormant until the witness of the Spirit activates them, revealing knowledge about God, the individual's relationship to God, and other spiritual knowledge. Again, Wesley employs analogy, this time of an infant in the womb, to explain.[33] When a child is in the womb, the physical senses are useless and are not taking in any information. Since the senses of sight, smell, and touch are unable to gather knowledge, then the child is ignorant of the physical world, even though the physical world is all around. When the child is born, the

---

[29] Maddox, *Responsible Grace*, 31.

[30] Matthews, "Religion and Reason Joined," 293–4.

[31] Ibid., 292.

[32] Maddox, *Responsible Grace*, 31.

[33] John Wesley, "The Great Privilege of those that Are Born of God," *The Works of John Wesley*: Sermons, vol. 1, ed. Outler, 432–4. Wesley employed the analogy again in "The New Birth," in *The Works of John Wesley*: Sermons, vol. 2, ed. Outler, 192, and a similar analogy, the analogy of the toad, in "On Living without God," *The Works of John Wesley*: Sermons, vol. 4, ed. Outler.

physical senses are opened, the child can perceive objects the senses are meant to perceive, and knowledge begins to accumulate. This process is the same, Wesley teaches, with the spiritual senses. They are present in a person but are not "sensible"; that is, the spiritual senses do not perceive the invisible world they are meant to perceive. Receiving the witness of the Holy Spirit changes a person and the way the spiritual senses perceive the spiritual world. "His whole soul," Wesley writes, "is now sensible of God."[34] This flood of spiritual knowledge brings not just awareness of invisible realities, but also the assurance of a saving relationship with God in Christ. In "The New Birth," Wesley observes.

> By the use of [spiritual senses] he is daily increasing in the knowledge of God of Jesus Christ whom he hath sent, and of all the things pertaining to his inward kingdom. And now he may properly be said to live: God having quickened him by his Spirit he is alive to God through Jesus Christ.[35]

Even though science has documented that the world of the unborn child is much richer and complex than Wesley could have imagined, his analogy is still helpful. Spiritual knowledge that comes directly from God by the witness of the Spirit is transformative knowledge: not only imparting awareness of the invisible world but assuring the believer of his or her saving relationship with God in Christ.

While, the Christian believer might receive indirect spiritual knowledge through scripture and direct spiritual knowledge

---

[34] John Wesley, "The Great Privilege," *The Works of John Wesley: Sermons*, vol. 1, ed. Outler, 434.
[35] John Wesley, "The New Birth," *The Works of John Wesley: Sermons*, vol. 2, ed. Outler, 193.

by the witness of the Spirit,[36] spiritual knowledge also came to people of faith through the experience of the community of believers.[37] For Wesley, this living witness was Peter Bohler and the Moravian Christians, who, as a group, affirmed an experience of spiritual knowledge. However, the benefit of experience by the community of believers was not limited only to the present. Wesley also saw Christian tradition, the experience by the community of believers across time, as a source of spiritual knowledge. As a student and scholar, he had studied and consulted the Greek and Latin Church Fathers along with the homilies, doctrines, and theology of the Church of England. Finally, Wesley stood apart from the Platonic perspective of the Anglican Divines and did not see reason as a source of spiritual knowledge; however, he did honor the role of reason in ordering and evaluating the spiritual knowledge gained in scripture, individual experience, community experience, and tradition.[38]

Perhaps most important, in a religious landscape, which included both Anglican Divines seeking "rational faith" based on accumulation of evidence alongside so-called enthusiasts who uncritically accepted the alleged direct knowledge of an individual by the Spirit, Wesley needed to have a process for evaluating spiritual knowledge imparted by the witness of the Spirit. One important place for him to evaluate the witness of the Spirit was in the community of believers. As described above, in explaining the validity of the witness of the Spirit, Moravian leader Peter Bohler brought several other members of the Moravian group to Wesley to provide their

---

[36] Maddox, *Responsible Grace*, 31.

[37] John Wesley, "The Witness of the Spirit I," *The Works of John Wesley:* Sermons, vol. 1, ed. Outler, 271.

[38] John Wesley "The Case of Reason Impartially Considered," *The Works of John Wesley:* Sermons, vol. 2, ed. Outler, 587. Also, Maddox, *Responsible Grace*, 40.

own affirmation of the experience.[39] Not long after, Wesley's own experience of the witness of the Spirit at Aldersgate was another that happened in the company of fellow believers.[40] In addition, if experience can be evaluated by the living witnesses in the community of believers, it can also be subjected to tradition, that is, the witness of believers who have come before.[41] Wesley's own practice included frequently consulting the witness of tradition as contained in both early church and Church of England sources.

Finally, the witness of the Spirit is always consistent with scripture. Wesley was quite clear on the subordination of experience to scripture in his "Letter to a person lately joined with the people called Quakers." There he wrote,

> The Scriptures are the touchstone whereby Christians examine all, real or supposed revelations… For though the Spirit is our principal leader, yet He is not our rule at all; the Scriptures are the rule whereby He leads us into all truth.[42]

While the Spirit might be a guide, the direction of that guide was always held up against the witness of scripture to determine its validity. Through these important checks of the witness of the Spirit with the community of faith and scripture, Wesley sought to find a middle way between the rejection of experience by rationalists and its uncritical embrace by enthusiasts. However, the most important evidence for the valid-

---

[39] John Wesley, *The Journal of John Wesley*, ed. Nehemiah Curnock (London: Epworth Press, 1938), 492, quoted in Noro, "Wesley's Theological Epistemology," 62.

[40] John Wesley, "The Witness of the Spirit II," *The Works of John Wesley: Sermons*, vol. 1, ed. Outler, 290.

[41] Ibid. Also Noro, "Wesley's Theological Epistemology," 65.

[42] John Wesley, "Letter to a person lately joined with the people called Quakers," in *The Letters of The Rev. John Wesley, A.M.*, ed. John Telford (London: Epworth Press, 1931), 117.

ity of the witness of the Spirit is quite practical: a transformed life.[43] That is to say, the witness of the Spirit is to be accepted if it leads to particular characteristics in the internal life and external behavior of believers. One manifestation of the witness of the Spirit is the flourishing of the fruit of the Spirit (Gal 5.22-23). As Wesley instructed in Sermon 11, "The Witness of the Spirit, II," "let none ever presume to rest in the supposed testimony of the Spirit which is separate from the fruit of it."[44] He also explains that the fruit of the Spirit can be discerned internally, through rational reflection on one's spirit, and externally by the community of faith. In evaluating the reality of spiritual knowledge given by the witness of the Spirit, Wesley's most convincing evidence is found in the lives of believers who are transformed by that knowledge, showing forth fruit such as patience, faithfulness, and joy.

The outcome of this spiritual knowledge, this transformative knowing, is nothing less than the healing of broken, suffering lives.[45] The objective of the witness of the Holy Spirit is the restoration of the holy life with God that God always intended.[46] In "The Imperfection of Human Knowledge," Wesley names the outcomes of this relationship, which begins with the witness of the Spirit but continues as the believer grows in knowledge and love of God. The first is humility, because of the need for the Holy Spirit's intervention to help human beings see and live rightly.[47] The second is faith, trusting in God's wisdom because human knowing is so limited

---

[43] Maddox, *Responsible Grace*, 32.

[44] John Wesley, "The Witness of the Spirit II" *The Works of John Wesley:* Sermons, vol. 1, ed. Outler, 297.

[45] Runyon, "The Role of Experience in Religion," 192.

[46] Wesley, "The New Birth," *The Works of John Wesley:* Sermons, vol. 2, ed. Outler, 198. Also, Runyon, "The Role of Experience in Religion," 192.

[47] John Wesley, "The Imperfection of Human Knowledge," *The Works of John Wesley:* Sermons, vol. 2, ed. Outler, 585.

and cannot see into human hearts or intentions.[48] The third is resignation, by which Wesley means seeking out and obeying God's will.[49] Wesley would agree[50] with Nicholas Lash when he characterizes this attitude as "creaturely dependence relearned as friendship."[51] This renewed friendship is one in which God offers the continual gift of the Holy Spirit and the believer offers love, praise, and prayer in response.[52] This friendship with God, based in the knowledge and love of God, manifests virtues and the fruit of the Spirit in the internal and external life of the believer and validates the witness of the Spirit that sets in motion this growth in grace.[53] This life of grace begins in the transformative knowledge of the witness of the Spirit and forms the basis of the restored and reconciled community of believers.

Conclusion

Scriptural Reasoning is a practice that is consistent in principles, process, and outcomes with Wesleyan epistemology and can serve as a resource for United Methodist chaplains and campus ministers to engage in and lead interfaith conversation. Both SR and Wesley acknowledge and honor the roles of natural and spiritual knowledge, the significance of intellect and faith, for the fullness of human knowing and faithful action in

---

[48] Ibid.

[49] Ibid.

[50] John Wesley, "The New Birth," *The Works of John Wesley:* Sermons, vol. 2, ed. Outler, 189.

[51] Nicholas Lash, *The Beginning and End of "Religion"* (New York: Cambridge University Press, 1996), 13 quoted in Janet Martin Soskice, "Friendship," in *Fields of Faith: Theology and Religious Studies for the Twenty-First Century*, ed. David F. Ford, Ben Quash, and Janet Martin Soskice (New York: Cambridge University Press, 2012), 178.

[52] John Wesley, "The Great Privilege of those that are Born of God," *The Works of John Wesley:* Sermons, vol. 1, ed. Outler, 434–5.

[53] Runyon, "The Role of Experience in Religion," 192.

the world. The practice of SR and Wesley's epistemology share the same sources and evaluators of spiritual knowledge: scripture, experience, tradition, and reason. Sacred text is central for both SR and Wesley, but both also have space in their process for individual experience and reflection, including personal experience of divine revelation. At the same time, SR and Wesley recognize constraints around that individual experience, always measuring individual interpretation, reflection, and revelation by the experience of the community of living witnesses, by the tradition of witnesses who have come before, and always by the text itself. Finally, in their objective, SR and Wesleyan epistemology share the purpose of discovering spiritual knowledge for personal edification and social transformation. Evidence of the effectiveness of both SR and Wesley's epistemology is practical, in that lives are changed and manifest virtues like patience, faithfulness, joy, hope, humility, and friendship. As a practice that is consistent with Wesleyan epistemology. SR provides a method for United Methodist chaplains and campus ministers to engage in interfaith dialogue with authenticity and conviction for the healing of a broken, suffering world.

ALL FAITH CHAPEL OR NO FAITH CHAPEL?
CONTOURS OF DIVERSITY AND PLURIFORMITY IN
COLLEGIATE MINISTRY
Mark Forrester

Eighteen years before I became Vanderbilt's University's Chaplain and Director of Religious Life, I was appointed by my bishop to direct the Wesley Foundation at Vanderbilt University. This was the early 1990s, a time when Chaplain Beverly Asbury had leveraged his considerable influence to renovate a large lecture hall positioned directly under Benton Chapel, the old-line university chapel, into a catchall place of sacred gathering for an emerging diversity of religious groups. It was aptly, if not generically, named All Faith Chapel.

Soon the National Campus Ministry Association reached out to me to inquire if Vanderbilt University could host its next annual conference, which meant that, once confirmed, I would serve on the conference design team. The team met to establish a theme, secure plenary speakers and workshop leaders, and deal with logistics. Meanwhile, I conducted a walk-through at our projected host site, Vanderbilt Divinity School, to scope out the classrooms, dining area and, of course, the two chapels. When we approached the entrance of All Faith Chapel, identified only by a simple brass plaque next to a hardwood door with pewter hardware, I opened it outward and motioned to a senior peer to break the silence of AFC's passive, contemplative space. Our esteemed Jesus-loving colleague hesitantly entered, meandered all around and reemerged with a pensive demeanor. Raising the tip of her finger she traced the border of the plaque and, with gruff seriousness, jabbed at me and asked, "All Faith Chapel? Really? Don't you mean 'No Faith Chapel'?"

This is a true (and truthful) story meant to solicit our awareness of the delicate balancing act between being faithful and being hospitable to the faithful other. As religious professionals in the global world of higher education, we each come from a distinctive theological center as we extend ourselves—pastorally, pedagogically, and administratively—to a broadening range of others whose religious, spiritual, and philosophical leanings, established or newly emerging, define an ethos worthy of our engagement. The particular and peculiar ways we chaplains can, and should, entertain such diversity are myriad, so I will not presume to enumerate every best practice or exhaust the collective wisdom of a field that can yield its treasure only as one university context after another is mined, plundered, and shared by each with all. I will primarily examine and reflect upon my role as University Chaplain and Director of Religious Life at a private, nonsectarian, top-twenty national university with historic Methodist roots. It is to those roots that I briefly turn in order to frame this inquiry about the complementary, yet distinctive, forces of diversity and pluriformity in collegiate religious life today.

In 1873, progressive Methodists in Tennessee, led by Bishop Holland McTyeire, acquired a $1 million endowment from the shipping magnate, Cornelius ("the Commodore") Vanderbilt, to bridge the smoldering post-Civil War chasm between North and South. Sometimes diversity has its origins in disparity and disunion, so at this juncture in history our Methodist forebears were both wise and tenacious as they launched a new first-class university with a theological school attached. More than anything, they were convinced that the North-South division could be healed, and that the New South needed a school like Vanderbilt to keep up with the nation's rising middle class, meet the challenges of an industrial economy, and prepare clergy for a vastly different culture defined by modernism and urbanization.[1] Although these Tennessee Methodists lost control of the Board of Trust in 1914, their intent was to join academic excellence, grounded in reason and critical acumen, with a more holistic life of divine purpose that would promote unity in the midst of regional disarray (an excellent example of Wesleyan *vital piety*). Clearly, national differences along the lines of religion, race, gender, class, and privilege would persist throughout the twentieth century (and into the present), and yet the seeds of a religiously motivated vision extended roots into secular soil. Primacy of theological education gave rise to a general (liberal arts) emphasis that came, in turn, to serve and equip a greater diversity of people for a greater diversity of vocations.

Our Methodist benefactors did not create diversity, but spotted it on the horizon and sought ways to welcome, nurture, and explore its many facets. Likewise, we do not create diversity today. Although every university and college competing for higher and better enrollment will craft a diversity narrative into its mission and policy statements, school brochures and demographic charts, such laudable diversity outcomes are often, upon closer inspection, gifts given rather than prizes attained. The main thrust of this essay, therefore, will be to clarify my belief that diversity is a gift that we should honor, while pluriformity[2] is the ongoing work of achieving unity

---

[1] Ray Waddle, Chancellor Checkmates Bishops: One Hundred Years Ago, a Grand Schism of Ideologies Recast Vanderbilt's Future, *Vanderbilt Magazine*, https://discoverarchive.vanderbilt.edu/bitstream/handle/1803/5694/VMAG_Summer_08.pdf?sequence=1.

[2] I have chosen the term "pluriformity" instead of "pluralism" for two reasons. First,

within diversity without requiring uniformity. Diversity and pluriformity are interrelated, sometimes synonymous, and yet diversity is not unlike the gift of talents—in Matthew's Gospel (25:14-30)—that can be invested or squandered, engaged or ignored, loved only for its immediate value or valued for the intrinsic possibility of Divine love revealed relationally through, and in dynamic tension with, the other. I will return to the work of pluriformity later, but will now segue into a brief consideration of diversity, its connotations and contours taking shape in our midst.

The Gift of Diversity

Cultivating religious life and fostering the spiritual development of students is not ancillary, but central, to the mission of higher education. While chaplains and religious professionals are aware of more theologically nuanced commitments to mission that (can) orient us toward a campus community's transcendent purpose, many of us serve at the pleasure of secular institutions that are committed to a mission with a more imminent and practical, albeit transformative, purpose. These respective missions, the theological and the

---

I am drawn to the notion of an emerging pluriformity in the history of higher education—going from the Protestant era (1636 to the late nineteenth century), to the Privatized era (late nineteenth to late twentieth century), to the "post secular" Pluriform era (now underway)—as masterfully laid out in Douglas Jacobsen and Rhonda Hustedt Jacobsen's *No Longer Invisible: Religion in University Education* (New York: Oxford University Press, 2012), 16–30; secondly, when it comes to theology of religions, I don't find myself completely at home as an exclusivist or as an inclusivist (I lean toward calling myself a radical inclusivist), and certainly not as a pluralist (as coined by John Hick). Personally, I cannot abide the notion of a religiously neutral universe while, professionally, I operate as a religiously neutral advocate of all faiths. I have decided (for the sake of this essay) to use "pluriformity" as a term that embraces aspects of inclusivity, exclusivity, and plurality without settling on any single approach to religious life. For a wonderful synopsis of this theological conundrum see Aimee Upjohn Light's *God at the Margins: Making Theological Sense of Religious Plurality* (Winona, MN: Anselm Academic, 2014), 68–92.

secular, need not collide, but coincide, as we recognize the fact that we support many missions, or mission objectives, through which we create strategies for our own unique engagement with students in an academic context. The mission statement of our office implies that we give ourselves to multiple missions:

> [Vanderbilt University's Office of] Religious Life seeks to function in an educational capacity, not only for those students and groups who are traditionally religious, but by way of raising ethical questions and issues of value and character among the student body at large. Because we seek to educate the "whole person," we view ethical and spiritual formation as integral to the University's overall educational mission and religious life as an important dimension of the so-called hidden curriculum of the University. We therefore seek to integrate the programs and services offered by the chaplains and professional staff into the larger life of the University community.[3]

Along with our educational mission to impart holistic values of ethical reasoning, service learning and interfaith awareness, it is also evident that this shared educational mission dovetails with a seemingly larger mission of liberal American education seeking to align with the aims of democracy. Sixty years ago the landmark case of *Brown v. Board of Education of Topeka* saw the Supreme Court overturn an earlier ruling (*Plessy v. Ferguson*, 1896) of "separate but equal," and in 1978 the Supreme Court's decision in *Regents of the University of California v. Bakke* served to define diversity as a value superior to fairness because racial and gender diversity, in particular,

---

[3] Vanderbilt Office of the University Chaplain and Religious Life: Mission Statement, http://www.vanderbilt.edu/religiouslife/.

were seen to strengthen and inform the larger social and cultural context through which an educated citizenry of tomorrow could better thrive. The *Bakke* decision added a different rationale to the earlier arguments for inclusion and equality regardless of race by saying to universities, in effect: stop talking about quotas and about redressing the effects of past discrimination and start talking about the educational benefits of mixed-race student bodies. As the Harvard professor and acclaimed intellectual historian Louis Menand goes on to say: "The term (diversity) plainly connotes racial diversity...But "diversity" also means a variety of interests and abilities. . . . They (colleges) no longer want well-rounded students; they want a well-rounded class."[4]

Two perennial mission criteria of higher learning—liberal *educational outcomes* distributed more equitably among the masses through *democratic principles* of access and opportunity—have guided and mobilized the emerging twenty-first century university. And churning within the wave of this century is a third mission trajectory now permeating all others: the global. When I graduated from divinity school thirty years ago, I joined a generational cohort venturing boldly into ministry to be "change agents" in a world barely on the cusp of broadband technology and massive population migration. The cliché "think globally, act locally" had panache, and while it is still a fairly wise maxim to follow it is more accurate to say that many of our universities and colleges have taken yesterday's visioning a step further by linking global thinking *with* global acting in ways that are mind-staggering.

In 1873, Vanderbilt was a regional school courageously seeking to bridge Tennessee, and other southern states, with our far away, and quite alien, northern neighbors. Today Van-

---

[4] Louis Menand, *The Marketplace of Ideas: Reform and Resistance in the American University* (New York: Norton, 2010), 78.

derbilt, like many other schools, is bridging the northern and southern hemispheres of the world through student and faculty recruitment, multi-institutional research, and a robust study abroad component to undergraduate education that weaves global thinking and acting into a seamless garment.

We did not magically divine global diversity as an innovation to be factored into our mission, since long-established groups like the Association of American Colleges and Universities (AAC&U) have reshaped higher education's global purpose and mapped out its destiny decades before now. The AAC&U provides a rich menu of initiatives, campus models, and case studies that illustrate the seminal influence that chaplaincies, offices of religious and spiritual life, and campus ministries have made to advance religious purpose and identity within a holistic model of higher learning marked by global inclusivity and equity (which has its roots, I believe, in religious expressions of hospitality—a theme that I will touch on later).

One excellent example of how the educational, democratic, and global objectives of religious life have coalesced with a college's mission can be found in the AAC&U's online publication *Diversity & Democracy*. The Fall 2014 edition (vol. 17, no. 4) shows how Elon University and Wofford College used student assessment data to make evidence-based decisions relating to diversity and pluralism. Overall, it explains how campus climate could be improved by encouraging interfaith exchange. Some of the salient lessons they learned were: have a clear but evolving vision that aligns with defined areas of responsibility; establish academic avenues for interreligious understanding and exploration; support co-curricular learning for students and colleagues; and anticipate potential barriers to inclusion.[5]

---

[5] http://www.aacu.org/diversitydemocracy/2014/fall/felten-barnett-fuller.

Also essential to the sharing of educational, democratic, and global mission by creating a healthy religious climate is the Interfaith Youth Core's *Pluralism and Worldview Engagement Rubric* utilized by Elon and Wofford.[6]

While I have lifted up a best practice to illustrate how "diversity" is written into our shared missions and, in turn, how it prompts us to serve our schools by assessing and improving the religious climate through interfaith awareness, dialogue, and cooperation, I will now explain why it is that mere diversity, wonderful as it is, becomes a better thing when nurtured in the flexible, expansive, respectful soil of pluriformity.[7]

The Trouble with Diversity

"All Faith Chapel or No Faith Chapel?" When I ruminate upon my friend's query, the subject of diversity, when viewed through the prism of today's secular university, still remains as rife with hidden trouble as it is with positive potential. When it comes to religious identity, however, diversity within the American collegiate context pertains less to race and more to the waning of Christian hegemony and what to do about it. The questions I would like to explore in this section are: How does the university define and model diversity? How

---

[6] http://www.ifyc.org/sites/default/files/u4/PluralismWorldviewEngagementRubric2. pdf.

[7] As I differentiate diversity and pluriformity as being complementary, but not synonymous, ways of valuing religious difference, another important insight is that the broader objective of enhancing diversity on campus, via strategic admissions marketing and student affairs programming, pertains, in this instance, to what Interfaith Youth Core's Eboo Patel commends as the "science of interfaith cooperation." And yet, as Patel warns, the actual work of interfaith cooperation must press beyond the insight and analysis proffered by the social sciences into the realm of a religious, spiritual and ministerial "art" rooted in the genius of discernment that grasps how a plurality of people can be drawn together through the stories of their spiritual journeys openly shared. One's biography precedes, and then presses beyond, empirical approaches to interfaith cooperation. See Eboo Patel's *Sacred Ground: Pluralism, Prejudice, and the Promise of America* (Boston: Beacon, 2012), 65–103.

do chaplains invite and facilitate religious diversity? And wherein lies the rub?

The history of religion in higher education far exceeds the narrow scope of any essay, so I commend the excellent, tightly wrought overview given in Andrew Delbanco's *College: What It Was, Is, and Should Be*. Delbanco gives the sweep of the academy's religious roots and its subsequent secular state of embarrassment:

To anyone even glancingly acquainted with the history of American education, it is hardly news that our colleges have their origins in religion, or that they derive their aims, structure, and pedagogical methods mainly from Protestantism and, more particularly, from the stringent form of Protestantism whose partisans were called—at first derisively by their enemies, later proudly by themselves—Puritans.

Yet many academics have a curiously uneasy relation with these origins, as if they pose some threat or embarrassment to our secular liberties, even though the battle for academic freedom against clerical authority was won long ago. If you were to remind just about any major university president today that his or her institution arose from this or that denomination, you'd likely get the response of the proverbial Victorian lady who, upon hearing of Darwin's claim that men descended from apes, replied that she hoped it wasn't so—but if it were, that it not be widely known.[8]

While religious professionals have more than a plausible purpose to share in the educational mission of the university, how we relate to the democratic and global aspects of that mission is, at times, tenuous. More to the point, as today's research university has eclipsed yesterday's teaching college,

---

[8] Andrew Delbanco, *College: What It Was, Is, and Should Be* (Princeton: Princeton University Press, 2012), 64–65.

and as democracy's global mission is promulgated by the gospel of market capitalism, universities are becoming the engines of a new kind of progress that, out of practical necessity, embody tremendous zeal for STEM (Science, Technology, Engineering, and Math) focused fields, departments, and majors that are outpacing all others. Even among the most revered Ivy League schools, the relevance of the liberal arts still figures large in the grand narrative but less on the campus horizon where gleaming research towers are becoming the new spires of institutional self-transcendence.

Along with the emergence of the global university as a corporate multiversity operating under the oversight of a business, rather than academic, model of management,[9] comes now the question about the role diversity plays as it relates to student life and, by extension, religious life. The growing diversity of religious, racial, ethnic, gender and geographical diversity is clearly, on balance, a huge and remarkable stride forward into the only kind of learning environment that makes sense in the twenty-first century. All of what I have said above about the gift of diversity affirms the power of intentional interfaith engagement fostering a new dynamic of learning, and community building, in our respective milieus. Nevertheless, how we relate to the gift of diversity is one thing, but the how and why of corporate logic touting "diversity" for more selective enrollment gains is another issue altogether.

---

[9] Probing deeper implications of my point on how the business model impacts the way chaplains are constrained to view and implement change in order to realize greater diversity outcomes, I recommend Benjamin Ginsberg's *The Fall of the Faculty: The Rise of the All-Administrative University and Why it Matters* (New York: Oxford University Press, 2011). Ginsberg examines how, until recently, universities were mainly led by their faculties and, within the span of a generation, have now been eclipsed by ever escalating numbers of career administrators. This is especially relevant to many chaplaincies that, historically, supported an academic mission in natural alliance with faculty colleagues but have, of late, been collapsed under an administrative Student Affairs paradigm wherein diversity engagement and multicultural programming are often instruments of managerial power rather than theological conviction.

Several years ago I heard an admissions director refer to the "three in the tree" rule that goes like this: randomly search any college website and the homepage will flash at least three students before your eyes who are sitting in a tree, on a wall or inside a science lab—one Caucasian, one African American and one Asian, or some variation thereof. Granted, while displays of staged diversity might suggest a campus environment that is integrative, and might honestly represent the school's policies and aspirations, such symbolism is too often disingenuous, exploitative, and done for the sake of market appeal. The trouble with diversity is that it can be valued as a means to other ends rather than as a value unto itself.

Another troubling aspect to the corporate diversity narrative is that inclusivity and equity, key diversity descriptors, are not consistently followed when it comes to serving *U.S. News & World Report's* scoring formula. Anthony Marx, former Amherst president, assessed the *U.S. News* formula by saying, "the key driver is how much money does an institution have and therefore how much does it spend. And how many kids can it turn away."[10] Inclusivity is vaunted when it comes to students (if they are allowed inside the admission's gate), but exclusivity is the ultimate measure of institutional status that goes up as acceptance rates go down. William Shain, former dean of admissions at Vanderbilt, wrote:

> I have long believed that below a 30 percent acceptance rate, a class is not really getting better . . . Rather, test scores rise from the very high to the stratospheric, and more valedictorians are denied admission. To

---

[10] Frank Bruni, *Where You Go is Not Who You'll Be: An Antidote to the College Admissions Mania* (New York: Grand Central, 2015), 86.

my knowledge, no one has ever documented that this brings any improvement to the quality of intellectual discourse on campus. Institutions do not change as rapidly as guidebook ratings.[11]

While American higher education dances the inclusivity /exclusivity two-step, a more troubling economic trend is that equity, the quality of being fair or impartial, is often sidestepped when we consider the role that universities play, or fail to play, in an economy stymied by income and wealth disparity.

Georgetown law professor Sheryll Cashin argues that educational inequity is fueled by the illusion of merit as the great arbitrator of fairness. She examines standardized testing as the bargain we have bought into in order to maintain plausible deniability about the importance of rectifying "place" (class) over all other disadvantages.

As long as there are wealth inequalities, there will be socioeconomic achievement gaps on standardized tests. As with geographic segregation and the unequal allocation of high-quality K–12 education, intentionally or not, the SAT has become the tool for hoarding the resource of selective higher education, even as it is imbued with an aura of objective fairness. Those who don't score high, it appears, have only themselves to blame. And yet using standardized test scores as indicia of merit rests on the invalid assumption that all those who take the test have had the same educational opportunities, experienced teachers, and well-resourced classrooms.[12]

To reiterate Dr. Cashin's point, a recent report in the *Washington Post* compared SAT scores by family income, parental education,

---

[11] Ibid., 87.
[12] Sheryll Cashin, *Place, Not Race: A New Vision of Opportunity in America* (Boston: Beacon, 2014), 72.

SAT scores by ethnicity and SAT scores by PSAT participation, and all four charts indicate that the SAT favors rich, educated families.[13]

What does all this have to do with the relationship between higher education and religion? I believe the rub is between real diversity—which includes the religious other along with the economically dispossessed other—and the ruse of diversity all prettied-up inside the cultural model of identity. A more holistic and reputable form of diversity, in my opinion, is one that is naturally skittish about identity politics because emphasis upon identity of any kind defines the righteous struggle to be over cultural respect rather than today's deepening inequality that, while impacting disproportionately along the lines of race, ethnicity and gender, is an equal opportunity oppressor.[14] With lacerating dry wit, Walter Benn Michaels puts it this way:

> The true victims of the injustice of our educational system are not the students who have been made to feel uncomfortable on the campuses of Duke, Northwestern and Harvard but the ones who have never set foot on these campuses or on any other. What is surprising is that the battles over social justice in the university have taken the form of battles over cultural diversity, which is to say, of battles over what color skin the rich kids should have.[15]

---

[13] Zachery A. Goldfarb, http://www.washingtonpost.com/blogs/wonkblog/wp/2014/03/05/these-four-charts-show-how-the-sat-favors-the-rich-educated-families/.
[14] Not all universities are indifferent and unresponsive to the challenge of our economy's deepening economic disparities. Vanderbilt is among a small number of US universities to have a need-blind admission's process. "Opportunity Vanderbilt" is an endowment that has replaced all need-based undergraduate student loans with scholarship and grant assistance. https://giving.vanderbilt.edu/oppvu/.
[15] Walter Benn Michaels, *The Trouble with Diversity: How We Learned to Love Identity and Ignore Inequality* (New York: Metropolitan Books, 2006) 108.

When diversity is held captive to the cultural model of identity, religious life on campus, not to mention religious leadership, is sometimes collapsed into a morass of programs and interdepartmental initiatives that strangely tamp down true diversity of thought and expression in the name of getting along. Authentic religious diversity, what I prefer to call pluriformity, is most vital, real, and energizing when differences are allowed to be edgy, disorienting and sometimes a little discomforting. Matthew Charlton, offering a Wesleyan affection for "sharing sacred space amongst the religions," highlights this point well:

> I do not think we will, nor should we, end up with a version of a religion, or even no religion, that is universally communicable and universally understood. In part, this is a critique of how interreligious dialogue seeks to validate itself: find a common bond and then seek to eliminate tension by eliminating differences. To the contrary, the interreligious conversation that begins in the common bond of shared humanity receives its energy from the tension created by difference.[16]

For the university chaplain, this might mean that we become advocates in behalf of certain Christian constituencies and para-church groups who find themselves against the cultural grain of a more liberal ethos. Rev. Ian Oliver, Senior Associate Chaplain for Protestant Life at Yale, and Pastor of the University Church (Battell Chapel, where the legendary William Sloane Coffin preached), beautifully echoes my own sense of collegial calling in this regard:

---

[16] Matthew Charlton, "Sharing Space: Philosophical, Theological, and Wesleyan Resources for Sharing Sacred Space amongst the Religions," https://oimts.files.wordpress.com/2013/09/2013-6-charlton.pdf.

Another of my tasks is to work with the many evangelical Christian groups that serve Yale's students. Some might see this as a betrayal of Coffin's legacy. After all, this means occasionally supporting people whose religious forebears fought tooth and nail to preserve segregation and those who still today oppose equal rights for the LGBTQ community. But when no one religious group is in charge or one voice authoritative, the right of each group to exist and speak as citizens of the university depends on the right of all groups to do the same. What my work has allowed me to see is how many students are cared for and served by these groups and how many evangelical Yale students would never be comfortable in Battell Chapel. That doesn't mean I don't invite them, but it does mean that I don't presume my liberal Protestant voice is the only one on campus and that if students don't like it, they should have no other options.[17]

Religious life on many campuses, at least functionally speaking, can easily be associated and aligned with "intercultural awareness" and other sensitivity models of understanding that, nice and valuable as they may be, are juiceless substitutes for the messiness of lived faith. But the corporate university abhors messiness, especially religious messiness, and thus protocols are set in place to blunt controversy by domesticating "faith" as good and acceptable only if it never succumbs to the sectarian or the dogmatic. While a university chaplaincy should be nonsectarian as it seeks to dispassionately direct religious life (in a spirit of fairness) among a contending pluriformity of worldviews, we

---

[17] Lucy A. Forster-Smith, ed., *College and University Chaplaincy in the 21st Century: A Multifaith Look at the Practice of Ministry on Campuses Across America* (Woodstock, VT: Skylight Paths, 2013), 59.

should also seek to orchestrate interfaith understanding by encouraging the free and passionate expression of contending beliefs without becoming contentious. Ours is a balancing act that is rooted in exploring beliefs that transcend, yet impact upon, identity constructs. Michaels goes on to show how religious life gets the short shrift when defined as an identity-based rather than belief-based phenomenon.

This process has not only been applied to politics but even more vividly to the area in which the importance of belief should be the most obvious, religion, and it is in this area that the cultural model is exposed at its most vacuous. It's one thing, for example, to promote the virtues of religious tolerance. But it is a very different thing to celebrate religious diversity ("Theo-diversity," the Global Diversity Institute calls it), as if religion too could be transformed into an identity category along the lines of race and culture.[18]

In order to coax out the contours of diversity, and set the stage for a more fulsome description of pluriformity, I will draw a few sharp lines of contrast between its good and troubling dimensions to map out, if you will, the university's cultural topography. Our willingness to recognize and further diversity as a salient feature that helps gauge, quantitatively and qualitatively, the educational, democratic, and global objectives at the core of the university's mission is in keeping with the deep and abiding values of collegiate religious life as well. Whatever points of tension and disconnect that might arise as we pursue a more robust pluriformity should not be taken as disparagement of the secular academy or disregard for nonsectarian leadership. I simply propose that we appropriate the good inherent in mere diversity as a means of deepening our path to pluriformity.

---

[18] Ibid., 173–74.

Pluriformity: An Alternative to Mere Diversity

Let me restate my argument as I now take it further: diversity is a gift that we should honor, while pluriformity is the ongoing work of achieving unity within diversity without requiring uniformity.

The quandary posed by "All Faith Chapel or No Faith Chapel?" symbolizes the difficult, and yet sincere, task of accommodating religious diversity (all faith) without capitulating to just any garden-variety form of universalism that relativizes, minimizes or denies distinctive belief (no faith). Mere diversity, which is primarily identity-driven, seeks unity-within-diversity by placing emphasis on commonality to the near exclusion of difference, or at least differences that do not complement each other. Pluriformity, on the other hand, builds upon the complementary attributes that each religious, spiritual, or philosophical tradition brings to the emerging interfaith setting, thus establishing a modicum of comfort and trust, but then begins to explore, and risk, the tendentious and irreconcilable differences of each respective tradition that is belief-based. As Michaels cautions above, the cultural model of diversity stresses religious tolerance but is not willing to support a full-blown theo-diversity, since "tolerance" (a fairly elitist sentiment) becomes the means through which a happy, risk-averse culture of inclusivity prospers. What hinders us from pressing beyond the peaceful (but bland) civility of religious tolerance, into a more respectful, discerning, and nuanced appreciation of pluriformity, is that inclusivity and exclusivity have become oppositional binaries when, in my opinion, they need not be construed in such a way.

The inclusivity/exclusivity binary is played out in the all faith/no faith question concerning religious space, a resolution that winds up honoring everyone in general and nobody in particular. To be fair, there are countless ways that the all-faith paradigm serves us, mostly under the auspices of interfaith learning and general community assemblies that support educational, social, and multicultural purposes central to a thriving religious life program. And yet the burgeoning of religious minorities, once marginal and virtually nonexistent, summons an alternative to (but not replacement of) an all-faith with a more pluriform multi-faith paradigm, a paradigm that might better inform how we provide appropriate space to each emerging community while, at the same time, maintaining common space for kumbaya gatherings that are anything but passé. Allow me to present a case study that captures the way VU's All Faith/No Faith dichotomy gave rise to a multi-faith resolution.

The all-faith/interfaith attempt to accommodate the religious other at Vanderbilt worked reasonably well in the early 1990s, but by the year 2000 it was apparent that our Jewish students, who comprised 2 to 3 percent of our student body, were not persisting and our retention rates with them were lackluster. Our (then) Hillel director and his board of directors soon gained approval by the development office to proceed with a capital campaign to establish a Jewish life center. In 2003, VU opened The Ben Schulman Center for Jewish Life and, by 2010, our Jewish student population soared to 12 percent as retention rates dramatically improved. This is only one example of how a pluriform/multi-faith approach to religious life, which allows for exclusive space to exist in tandem with inclusive space, empowered the otherness of the religious other to thrive and gain a distinctive appeal.

The pluriform/multi-faith paradigm, on one level, serves an institutional self-interest of recruiting and retaining a greater diversity of students. But it also serves to point us toward a theologically holistic awareness of how religious others cannot be welcomed, understood, or thrive in their unapologetic particularity if the occasional right to be exclusive and faithful—in ways contrary to the university's Western, modernist (and corporate) norms—are not supported. Below is another brief case study to illustrate the legitimacy of, and resistance to, the honoring of exclusive religious lifestyles.

This past year I was approached by women members of our Muslim Student Association to help them gain exclusive (women's only) access to the pool at the recreation center for only one or two hours per week. Because faithful living for these devout women requires complete gender separation in situations where their bodies are exposed, I became their advocate without hesitation. But because our commitment to coeducational student life is so enormous, and also because these traditional Muslim women are viewed by some with a modernist bias that deems them as aberrations, if not a threat, to a more progressive view of women, I soon discovered that trying to weave a pluriform exception into the larger inclusivity cultural fabric will be met with scoffing, disdain and yet another reminder that religiosity on campus is more of a liability to be managed than a gift to be cultivated. I do have hope that this request will soon be honored, but this otherwise routine administrative task suggests, in my opinion that the university will never fully realize its global aspirations if a more pluriform sensibility about religious diversity remains stalled and compromised.

Another theological description of pluriformity adding to a balanced appreciation for exclusivity, within a sustained vision of inclusivity, comes from Miroslav Volf who, lifting up the first creation narrative in Genesis (1:1-2:4), speaks of male/female differentiation as the creative activity of "separating and binding" that results in patterns of interdependence. Volf goes on to say,

> By itself, separation would result in self-enclosed, isolated
> and self-identical beings . . . The account of creation as

"separating-and-binding" rather than simply "separating" suggests that "identity" includes connection, difference, heterogeneity. . . The human self is formed not through a simple rejection of the other, but through a complex process of "taking in" and "keeping out."[19]

In order to bring to closer perfection a communal unity among religious others, the one-dimensional uniformity of mere diversity must be seen as incapable of creating real interfaith dialogue. Having an interfaith "connection" with one another first requires well defined and mutually understood points of "dis-connection" due to multiple, and sometimes disparate, truth claims not being capable of claiming all. Rabbi Abraham Joshua Heschel says it best:

The first and most important prerequisite of interfaith is faith. It is only out of the depth of involvement in the unending drama that began with Abraham that we can help one another toward an understanding of our situation. Interfaith must come out of depth, not out of void absence of faith. It is not an enterprise for those who are half learned or spiritually immature. If it is not to lead to the confusion of the many, it must remain the prerogative of the few. . .

The purpose of religious communication among human beings of different commitments is mutual enrichment and enhancement of respect and appreciation rather than the hope that the person spoken to proves to be wrong in what he regards as sacred.[20]

---

[19] Miroslav Volf, *Exclusion and Embrace: A Theological Exploration of Identity, Otherness, and Reconciliation* (Nashville: Abingdon, 1996), 65.

[20] Susannah Heschel, ed., *Moral Grandeur and Spiritual Audacity: Essays of Abraham Joshua Heschel* (New York: Farrar, Straus and Giroux, 1996), 241–43.

While the cultural model of religious identity might well ignore Heschel's key insight that (exclusive) faith development(s) must be the prerequisite for an (inclusive) interfaith outcome, a pluriform approach to religious diversity in higher education commends this as the best way to infuse knowledge *about* religion(s) with wisdom derived by a singular *lived* faith. Interfaith dialogue, literacy, and the prophetic transformation of individuals and movements quite often takes root in a grounded set of beliefs and, through exposure to and enrichment by the religious other, a greater clarity of calling and courage to act decisively as a steward of peace and reconciliation takes flight.

Martin Luther King Jr. was following faithfully as his father's pastoral protégé at Ebenezer Baptist Church in Atlanta, but when he read Mahatma Gandhi's autobiography, *The Story of My Experiments with Truth*, it captured his imagination and helped catapult him into a realm of prophetic vision and utterance that gave new expression to America's civil rights movement. Professor John S. Dunne of Notre Dame described this spiritual rhythm—moving from the particular into the universal and back to the local—in this way:

> What seems to be occurring is a phenomenon we might call "passing over," passing over from one culture to another, from one way of life to another, from one religion to another. Passing over is a shifting of standpoint, a going over to the standpoint of another. . . . It is followed by an equal and opposite process we might call "coming back," coming back with new insight into one's own culture, one's own way of life,

one's own religion.[21]

From Space to Grace

Welcome one another, therefore, just as Christ has welcomed you, for the glory of God. (Rom 15:7)

I will draw this discussion to a close by making explicit what I hope has become implicitly understood: Questions about religious space (All Faith/No Faith/Multi-Faith) point to the tangible—and intangible—ways we seek to be hospitable, nurture a sense of belonging and honor diversity without compromising religious particularity. Each university context will determine how it gives three-dimensional shape to space(s) welcoming the religious other. Emory University's Cannon Chapel is one of the best examples of a single multi-faith dwelling that allows everyone "room to breathe,"[22] while Penn State's Center for Spiritual & Ethical Development[23] has become the nation's largest university based multi-faith center lavishing alternative spaces to accommodate, all under one roof, approximately sixty religious organizations.

However we arrange, configure, or set aside sacred space(s) within the secular academy, a mere house will not feel like home unless the temporal finds reference to the Eternal—where grace transcends space, inviting inter-religious diversity to thrive amidst the ebb and flow of inclusivity allowing for exclusivity and, on the return side, inviting exclusivity to discover a vital, compassionate, and respectful awareness that many

---

[21] John S. Dunne, *The Way of All the Earth: Experiments in Truth and Religion* (Notre Dame, IN: University of Notre Dame Press, 1978), ix.

[22] See Rev. Dr. Susan Henry-Crowe's essay, "Room to Breathe: Nurturing Community by Creating Space," in *College & University Chaplaincy in the 21st Century*, ed. Lucy A. Forster-Smith, (Woodstock, VT: Skylight Paths, 2013), 157–69.

[23] http://studentaffairs.psu.edu/spiritual/director.shtml

worlds, for a time, can also cohere within *a* world of gathering, learning and serving that is greater than the sum of its separate parts. Miroslav Volf's theological probing into the duel quest for identity and otherness, as he explores countless biblical texts as foundational narratives of *Exclusion and Embrace*, says that both distance and belonging are essential ingredients: "Belonging without distance destroys. . . But distance without belonging isolates."[24]

My own Wesleyan embrace of this vital need to serve the religious other's need for "distance," including striking differences regarding his/her theology, eschatology, and soteriology, is best understood, according to Vanderbilt Divinity Professor Emeritus Douglas Meeks, as Practical Divinity:

> Practical Divinity would eschew the formal attempt to find what is universally true in each religion, an activity that takes place mostly in academic settings at some distance from the violence prone distortions of religion or from the marvelous expressions of peace in localities.
>
> Instead of agreeing on universal conceptions of God, start with concrete questions. . . This requires patience for hearing the story of the other and respect for the different conceptions of God and redemption that emerge from the other's story.
>
> Practical Divinity and sanctification as the love of God and neighbor are our reliable contributions to a common table with the other religions at which the peace we share with them is a religious experience.[25]

---

[24] Volf, *Exclusion and Embrace*, 50.
[25] M. Douglas Meeks, "Wesleyan Contributions to Life with Other Religions," 6–20, https://oimts.files.wordpress.com/2013/09/2013-3-meeks.pdf.

While it will remain a pressing concern to fairly accommodate the rising demand for religious space within our bourgeoning multi-faith campuses, *how* we dwell together-and-apart is far more important than *where* we dwell together-and-apart. We are smart to further the diversity initiatives that define many of our institutional job descriptions, knowing full well that most of these outcomes, good as they are, will be quantitatively valued only through an assessment metrics lens. So we would be wise to give presence, leadership, and voice to the cacophony of faith claims coming from all around, voices of church, synagogue, mosque, or mandir requiring the rich and paradoxical climate of pluriformity to transform mere diversity into a sustainable diversity. How we dwell together with the other, as Doug Meeks and others have made clear, has less to do with universal ties that bind than with the ethical and scriptural insights peculiar to the other that expand our visions of service and solidarity which, in a way, keep us from becoming blind.

Finally, while pluriformity supersedes mere diversity as the best way to realize, at any given moment, unity within diversity without requiring uniformity, and while the ethics of *how* we dwell together in harmony better approximates practical moves we should make toward authentic community (from shared space to experienced grace), ultimately the perfection of our souls requires that we aim beyond the consecration of space to the sanctification of time. How else can our good (holistic) works and tangible achievements bear witness to grace if they do not originate and find their doxology in the Holy? Rabbi Heschel describes better than anyone this move from diversity to pluriformity, from space to grace:

> The higher goal of spiritual living is not to amass a wealth of information, but to face sacred moments. In religious experience, for example, this is not a thing

that imposes itself on man but a spiritual presence. What is retained in the soul is the moment of insight rather than the place where the act came to pass. A moment of insight is a fortune, transporting us beyond the confines of measured time. Spiritual life begins to decay when we fail to sense the grandeur of what is eternal in time.

Our intention is not to deprecate the world of space. . . Time and space are interrelated. To overlook either of them is to be partially blind. What we plead against is man's unconditional surrender to space, his enslavement to things. We must not forget that it is not a thing that lends significance to a moment; it is the moment that lends significance to things.[26]

Collegiate ministry in the twenty-first century is at a telling moment where questions about space and place prod us thoughtfully and prayerfully to be stewards of a more generative grace. Many of our institutions would have us view religious and spiritual diversity as potential liabilities to be shrewdly managed and brought into alignment with a more palatable presentation of campus religiosity that is marketable and safe. Our missions as religious leaders, informed and energized by a vigorous pluriformity, could be to faithfully serve our institutions by engaging in educationally honest ways with the other, and relationally among all others, in order to foster and deepen each student's search for his or her place in the sun—protected by hospitable space and authenticated by a spiritual grace that gives meaning, purpose and Divine guidance in a world both woefully and wonderfully complex.

---

[26] Abraham Joshua Heschel, *The Sabbath* (Boston, MA: Shambhala, 1952), xiii.

Sunesis: Understanding via Interplay
Timothy Moore

Problems of authority and belief are certainly not uninteresting.
Nor are they ever likely to be, so long as christians (sic) *seek to reflect*
on the criteria according to which their beliefs are held and their
courses of action decided.[1]

Despite nearly four decades having passed since Nicholas Lash opened his reflection on authority in the Christian tradition with this observation, Lash's assessment remains both insightful and accurate. In particular, Lash's identification of a connection between beliefs, actions, authority, and the importance of establishing the criteria by which those beliefs and actions are evaluated persist. The topic endures—as Lash surmised—with such "centrality, complexity, and perennial urgency that one more attempt to throw a little light on it may not be entirely out of place."[2] Taking Lash's observation as sufficient warrant, I wish to offer my "one more attempt" at casting light on a way of understanding and living, expressly understanding and living with others who think and believe differently. Specifically, this project emerges from innumerable conversations with my students and others regarding how we speak with integrity with each other when we encounter and might even hold several truths simultaneously. Said another

---

[1] Nicholas Lash, *Voices of Authority* (Shepherdstown, WV: Patmos Press, 1976), vii.
[2] Ibid.

way, how do we come to understand clearly and to live truthfully with others in such a diverse and complicated world? More specifically, this project attends to the issue of these multiple truths and their interaction as we seek to understand well and faithfully. Yet, before engaging in this theoretical (and practical) exercise, a little more context is needed.

A Collegiate Conversation as Context

For more than a decade, I have worked on college and university campuses, frequently having conversations with students, faculty, staff, and others about very deep and often personal issues. One venue where these conversations occurred and, in fact, were intentionally cultivated was a Friday lunch-time gathering of students, faculty, and staff around a table in our college dining hall at an event we called The Hard Questions Study Group. The group was open to anyone who wanted to explore with others different penetrating, timely, and confounding issues. My task, typically, was to serve as the group's moderator.

The gatherings usually looked something like this: I presented a topic to be discussed for that day. I framed our conversations with a brief introduction to the topic and then focused our conversation by asking a specific question of that topic. For example, if the topic considered was to be climate change, then I supplied background via various bits of data related to climate change, offered a few quotations from influential persons representing different secular and/or religious reflections on that data, and, then, asked: "Taking into account this information, these observations, and his/her own convictions, how might or should a person's most fundamental beliefs impact how he/she engages our changing world?"

As you can imagine, an hour was never enough time. But, the conversations were regularly impassioned and weighty, pressing the lunchtime interlocutors to search themselves, their commitments, and their reasoning in ways that might have otherwise remained uncritically examined. However, regardless of the topics offered and the persons present, our conversations frequently stumbled into the overgrown yet fascinating field of truth and epistemology. In other words, almost without fail, our particular conversations on a given topic relied upon a subtext of unarticulated yet influentially present assumptions about what is true, how we know something is true, how we use truth in those conversations/convictions, and how we construct our arguments consciously and unconsciously from these assumptions. Practically speaking, this meant that regardless of the data, the theological arguments cited, or political affiliations held, or personal experiences interjected, we were, for the most part, each assembling this same information in different ways. The way we assembled this information depended, in part, upon the (unconscious) mechanisms at work when asserting a claim or making an argument.

For me, this observation was fascinating and a bit simplistic. It should have been obvious. I have studied epistemological theories. I was taught that when we want to state something we know that we rely upon an amalgam of sources, weigh those sources against and with each other, and can often produce divergent claims despite using the same information. Yet, rather than mere abstract possibility, our lunchtime conversations gave some flesh to those theoretical bones. Spurred by the needs on my campus, our conversations and my observations challenged me to engage those thoughts with a renewed interest, exploring how we generate knowledge from the complex interaction between different sources of information; the legitimate role that faith and sincerely held convictions, communities of origin, and fundamental habits, might have in shaping our knowing; and how different claims can interplay to supply something more than knowledge, a deep understanding. More important here, my interest lies in examining how and affirming why our Christian convictions fundamentally color deep understanding. Perhaps most important, I want to lift up how those convictions are faithfully and appropriately refined and not diminished through interplay with others of different commitments and convictions. In the end, I am not interested in exploring the entire field of epistemology and outlining various theories, or in attempting to identify the epistemological schema underlying different individual claims. Rather, I am more interested in helping to describe a way that accounts for how the different conclusions we draw when encountering the same information may be concurrently truthful while fundamentally disparate.

In this chapter, I will examine the pieces of our conversations and lives to propose an epistemological system—a way of understanding—that I see as vital to living, speaking, and thinking truthfully. That epistemology relies upon a robust attendance to the relationship between performance and understanding, the impact of our story and the stories of others, how we reflect on what is done and told, and the criteria for assessing the truth of our claims.

Utilizing three sources (performance, stories, and systems), my project points toward how these various sources interplay to account for a deep understanding. As a result, I name my epistemology Sunesis. *Sunesis* is a Greek term describing the converging interplay of several sources of information to produce a deep understanding.

A Previously Trod Path: An Aside into Epistemology

Christians do not know it all, however confident some appear to be that they do. Instead, they are called by our Lord to think. . . . and in a way conducive to that concern—in short, to think Christianly.[3]

As mentioned above, I have a particular interest in examining how our Christian convictions fundamentally color our deep understanding. For John Stackhouse, thinking is invariably shaped by our most fundamental practices and concerns. In the opening chapter of his book *Need to Know*, Stackhouse delineates his epistemology by establishing that "Christians are called . . . to think" and "in a way conducive to that concern." Wanting to challenge contemporary efforts at epistemological compartmentalization, Stackhouse considers how many conversations and rationales used by Christians tend to divide their reasoning into isolated spheres.[4] As an alternative to such compartmentalization, Stackhouse imagines a way to integrate Christians' thinking, connecting it to all aspects of their lives and merging previously presumed discrete spheres of thinking into a comprehensive whole through an overarching epistemology. Stackhouse is not alone in his assertion.

Linked to a long chain of epistemologies, presuming the influence of particularity on truth claims and proposals for what we know, Stackhouse sees his work as a direct heir to what he terms the *Christian* Quadrilateral.[5] Stackhouse borrows the term "Quadrilateral" from the Wesleyan Quadrilateral, which was coined by twentieth-century theologian Albert Outler, who used it to systematically describe John Wesley's epistemological method. The schema, as described by Outler, has four parts: scripture, tradition, reason, and experience. Although, following Wesley, scripture is weighted more significantly than

---

[3] John G. Stackhouse, *Need to Know: Vocation as the Heart of Christian Epistemology* (Oxford: Oxford University Press, 2014), 4.
[4] Ibid., 4–5.
[5] Ibid., 10.

the other three. According to Outler, the Quadrilateral works together in multiple configurations to supply a kind of understanding that is both complex and particular in character. Its complexity comes from multiple sources acting together in a myriad of ways, while its particularity results from an understanding that it always bears the distinctive mark of the community, vocabulary, and context that produces it.

While many believe that we have moved past the Quadrilateral's relevance, both strengths and weaknesses to Stackhouse's and Wesley's (according to Outler) methodologies are evident and worth evaluating.[6] I am interested less in incorporating or rejecting their work than in recognizing that an epistemology, certainly one rooted in the Christian tradition, may possess a distinctive character and rely upon multiple sources interacting with each other in order to produce understanding. I am suggesting that Sunesis is an epistemological system that can account for (Christian) particularity and a refining interaction that both embraces particularity

---

[6] For a presentation of Wesley's epistemology, see Randy Maddox's work *Responsible Grace: John Wesley's Practical Theology* (Nashville: Kingswood Books, 1994). There, Maddox offers a critical reading of Outler and Wesley and the presence of the Quadrilateral in Wesley's work and the Quadrilateral's usefulness in theological discourse. For contemporary utilizations of the Quadrilateral as the basis for theological reasoning, see Lesslie Newbigin's and Thomas Langford's work, especially Lesslie Newbigin, *Truth and Authority in Modernity* (Valley Forge, PA: Trinity Press International, 1996) and Thomas A. Langford, *God Made Known* (Nashville: Abingdon, 1992). In his text, Stackhouse offers a significant reworking of the traditional quadratic elements as he expands the number of sources and incorporates modes for processing those sources into his epistemological accounting (Stackhouse, 127ff.). For an alternative to the fourfold structure of the Quadrilateral, look to David Brown's efforts to reconcile a possibly unnecessary distinction between scripture and tradition, suggesting that the two sources might be better described as a single source, a source he names *revelation* and one that I capture in my category of stories. See specifically, David Brown, *Tradition and Imagination: Revelation and Change* (Oxford: Oxford University Press, 1999) and Brown, *Discipleship and Imagination: Christian Tradition and Truth* (Oxford: Oxford University Press, 2000).

and comfortably assumes the presence of multiple truths and competing claims.

Undeniably, while in the end helpful, this journey takes us into the complexities of epistemological philosophy and theology. Certainly making it difficult to navigate, the trek is worthwhile. This trek supplies us with helpful language to differentiate what we might actually be claiming and not claiming when we assert that we know, understand, or have the truth, especially when we encounter multiple truths in our own reasoning and engage those truths asserted by others.

At the outset, I turn to define and mark those places along this intellectual journey needed to give my epistemology its direction.

1. First, I will provide a brief survey of the relationship between performance and understanding, specifically noting performance's constructive contributions to knowledge formation.

2. Then, having detailed this role of performance in knowledge, I will examine what it means to speak of different species of knowledge and what these different species signify for an epistemology.

3. Next, I will explore the possibility of testing the justifiability of our knowledge and their connected truth claims. This exploration of testing our knowledge and truth claims requires a brief consideration of truth, distinguishing between the various types of truth claims operative in reasoning.

4. Finally, I draw together the last pieces of my epistemology, thinking more directly about how performance, stories, and systems work together. This final turn delivers additional structure and essential cohesion to my epistemology—one suited to account for the complexity of understanding our often disparate expressions of what we know and our

native and necessary ability to manage and retain multiple truths simultaneously.

With the goal established and the trajectory plotted, I turn, now, to the task of identifying the important landmarks along this epistemological trek.

An Epistemological Landmark: Performance

Rightness becomes a necessary condition for the possibility of truth, just because what corresponds to ultimate reality is the religious form of the life as such, not minds or sentences independent of that form of life or in conflict with it. A kind of social coherentism seems to be the result. The coherence of linguistic usage with behavior in accord with communal norms (rightness) is a condition for the possibility of using a sentence to refer accurately to the external domain of ultimate reality (truth).[7]

In his assessment of Karl Barth's and George Lindbeck's articulations of truth, George Hunsinger notes, in both theologians, two major assumptions: (1) a direct connection between a community's *primary* enacted story and (2) the necessary coherence between that enacting, subsequent speech and *secondary* intelligible truth claims. That is, truthfulness precedes truth.

"Truth," for Hunsinger, designates a correspondence between (external) reality and the (internal) coherence, which is enacted in the primary (cultural-linguistic) practices of the community, and the subsequent (truthful) descriptions rendered as a result of those practices. Following Hunsinger's lead, I maintain that a latent theory of performatives resides in

---

[7] George Hunsinger, "Truth as Self-Involving: Barth and Lindbeck on the Cognitive and Performative Aspects of Truth in Theological Discourse," *Journal of the American Academy of Religion* 61, no. 1 (1993): 44.

many epistemologies, i.e., the idea that performance somehow substantively relates to knowing. In what follows is a short examination of that theory, and especially, the notion that performatives may be divided into complementary theories: performative utterances and performative acts.

Performative Utterances—J. L. Austin, in his well-known account of the role speech plays in constituting specific states of affairs, describes what he terms "performative utterances." Performative utterances are not merely statements that describe something simply as it is but are statements essential to the act being described.[8] Austin's classic example is the speech uttered in a wedding ceremony, when what is spoken does not just depict an account of what is taking place but actually assists in constituting the new state of affairs. While not assuming that the simple statement of a few words always renders something true, Austin recognizes that some kinds of speech are always part of and essential to substantive actions. Taken together, this type of performative speech and associated actions generate a new state, a state that is socially located in appropriate circumstances to help make that state intelligible. This new state would be fundamentally altered and diminished without that speech. Moreover, speech is frequently the "leading incident," initiating the act and the new state.[9] As such, actions create a new condition, which is spoken into existence and comprehended in the speaking. These performative utterances link describing, acting, and knowing tightly together.

Performative Acts—Related to this notion of performative utterances is the concept of performative acts. Much like performative utterances, performative acts are actions that help

---

[8] J. L. Austin, *How to Do Things with Words* (Cambridge: Harvard University Press, 1962), 5.
[9] Ibid, 6.

constitute new states of affairs that, without those particular actions, such states would remain absent. Judith Butler, in her analysis of various kinds of performative theories, says that some actions produce the environs and the actors engaged in the action.[10] Specifically interested in how language and action create notions of gender, her understanding of performative acts also has broader implications. Butler's argument—that actions help to produce the environment and the actors—suggests that a reflective analysis of that environment, those actors, and any subsequently reasonable claims concludes that formative actions have logical priority over secondary and derivative reason.[11] Further, the reason that emerges from those contexts mirrors those contexts and, thus, indirectly, the original constructing actions. In other words, actions may be primary in the formation of intelligible and reasonable claims.

The implications of performatives are manifold. Here are four.

1. Speech and acts appear essential to certain types of knowing and truth claims appropriate to certain circumstances.

2. Storytelling (narrative speech) and story-performing (narrative practices) just might be those kinds of speeches and acts.

3. Such speech and acts help render certain states of affairs and are fundamentally prior and indispensable to reasonable claims because reasonable claims seem to require those prior performances.

4. Finally, the telling of narratives, the preforming of practices, and reflecting on the world describe related

---

[10] Judith Butler, "Performative Acts and Gender Constitution: An Essay in Phenomenology and Feminist Theory," *Theatre Journal* 40, no. 4 (December 1988): 519.
[11] Ibid., 520.

yet distinct kinds of knowledge. As I will argue, these distinct kinds of knowledge produce related types of truth, suggesting that we regularly and necessarily (and without soteriological consequence) hold and negotiate multiple kinds of truths simultaneously.

It seems to me that the connection between performances (actions), stories, and systems preserves a tension between multiple truths, granting priority to actions and stories over reflective systems within a mutually informing/correcting matrix. This priority, however, is not an exclusivity. Reflective systems are vital to the kind of understanding Sunesis supplies. Ultimately, the *sunetic* understanding presupposes a variety of sources that fittingly produce related kinds of truth claims *and* species of knowledge appropriate to those distinct, originating sources. But what are different kinds or species of knowledge?

An Epistemological Landmark: Species of Knowledge

N. T. Wright, in his essay "How the Bible Reads the Modern World," discredits the Enlightenment's reintroduction of ancient Epicurean philosophy, an introduction that splits existence into two discrete realms with discrete accounts of knowing.[12] Rather, he embraces a value of balancing distinct modes of knowing that, then, produces various species of knowledge. Wright offers an account of knowing that describes different species of knowledge working together to produce a robust version of understanding.[13]

Wright further considers brain research, which suggests that the right hemisphere, i.e., the imaginative side, initiates engaging with new data and experiences, while the left side,

---

[12] N. T. Wright, "How the Bible Reads the Modern World," in *Surprised by Scripture: Engaging Contemporary Issues* (London: SPCK, 2014), 132–33.
[13] Ibid., 136.

i.e., the analytical side, follows up by assessing those initial for-mulations.[14] While research also suggests the brain cannot be quite so easily divided in this way,[15] Wright's argument still has merit. He says that, because of modernity's bias for data over everything else, its epistemology is unable to account for the fact that imagination might have the potential for greater accuracy and depth of knowledge given the inherently more expansive and elastic capacity of narrative, metaphor, art, etc. compared to the more rigid and limited potential couched in "a list of facts or a string of formulas."[16]

Wright indicates that there are several species of knowledge,[17] preferably operating together to supply an "integrated mode of knowing."[18] Those species or types of knowledge include a per-formative type suited to *knowing how*, a reflexive type suited to *knowing that*, and a relational type suited to *knowing who*. This di-vision of understanding into discrete species of knowledge might explain why some truth claims appear contradictory. Claims may appear contradictory when we fail to recognize their different originating sources or that different sources point toward distinct sets of knowledge and descriptions. That failure is compounded when we assume that different sources represent exclusive and/or competing claims that are to be perpetually held in isolation. This means that understanding is more complex and integrated than one particular species of knowledge.

Looking to expand Wright, I suggest that identifying and engaging with these types of knowing helps substantiate and explain the diversity and complexity inherent to understand-

---

[14] Ibid.
[15] http://www.livescience.com/39373-left-brain-right-brain-myth.html. Accessed 9/17/15.
[16] Wright, "How the Bible Reads the Modern World," 147.
[17] Ibid., 143–47.
[18] Ibid., 148.

ing. Yet, how do we know that what a source produces might not be justifiably called knowledge or truth and, therefore, reliably used? Before working with these different sources and their truth claims, let's briefly consider what it means to assert that species of knowledge produce justifiable and reliable information.

An Epistemological Landmark: Justifiable and Reliable Claims

Justifiable Claims

John Frame, in his reflections on Christianity and epistemology, describes how John Pollock catalogs the varieties of theories of knowledge.[19] Pollock's distinction between *justifiable* beliefs and *justified* beliefs shapes his project.[20] While technical, this distinction is important. Justifiable beliefs are beliefs that someone has every reason to hold true, given what he or she knows or believes that they know. Justified beliefs are beliefs resulting from use of some external standard to determine that those beliefs are irrefutable. Pollock supports the former while remaining suspicious of the latter, because he is uncertain of any legitimate ability to secure an external standard.[21] As a result, Pollock classifies justifiable (and useful) knowledge into two classes, doxastic and nondoxastic. Doxastic knowledge is justifiable knowledge that relies upon an internally consistent continuity of a particular belief with other beliefs others hold. Justifiable nondoxastic knowledge does not require other beliefs we might hold to have continuity with each other to make

---

[19] John Frame, "A Review Article: An Article Reviewing John L. Pollock's Contemporary Theories of Knowledge," *Westminster Theological Journal* 52, no. 1 (Spring 1990): 136.

[20] Ibid.,135.

[21] Ibid.

each claim legitimate.[22] Proceeding from these general categories, Pollock then goes on to explain several theories.

Preferring the subjective justifiability of doxastic theories, Pollock advocates an internalism to knowledge.[23] This internalism operates on the assumption that what is justifiably known ultimately rests on some original, primal, untestable belief, i.e., on some accepted "given." All other beliefs must conform to this original one, making those beliefs "subjective," relative to their derivation from this originally trusted given.[24] Affirming much of what Pollock offers, Frame seeks to move beyond Pollock's contentment to only having subjective justifiability via internalism. Frame looks for a way to test beliefs from both the inside and outside.[25] But Frame also concedes that he might be describing a kind of subjective justifiability via externalism—i.e., relying upon bits of information/knowledge found outside the system of thinking that he wants to test, because Frame resists firm demarcations between doxastic and nondoxastic. In other words, Frame wants to allow different species of knowledge to interplay with each other. Thus, his externalism allows for other species of knowledge—i.e., knowing how, knowing that, and knowing who—to engage directly with each other. Frame, sounding like Wright, wonders if a more integrated knowing is possible.[26]

A similar assumption of internal and external subjective justifiability functions in Sunesis, advancing the formation of claims internal to a particular species of knowledge and externally between these species in the generation of deep understanding. Such a notion of integrated theories of knowledge and an

---

[22] Ibid., 136–37.
[23] Ibid., 140.
[24] Ibid.
[25] Ibid., 140–41.
[26] Ibid., 141.

internal and external kind of justifiability of that knowledge suggests a regular and necessary interplay between what we know and our justifiability of holding that knowledge.

Reliable Claims

In a similar yet distinct way, Philip Hefner advocates for a knowledge that is testable and integrated. Hefner describes what he sees as a false tension between the opposite poles of revealed and natural knowledge.[27] Assuming knowledge's extensive overlapping mutuality, Hefner seeks to subject Christian theological theories to the same testing that scientific theories endure.[28] He hopes to substantiate certain theological claims and to refine those claims while simultaneously exposing the unconsciously assumed *givenness* underlying many presumed scientific "facts."

His process includes identifying the "hard core" of a position (i.e., a belief, idea, theory, and so on), assuming that position is true and then attempting to falsify that position via testing.[29] Such a procedure, as in all scientific inquiry, does not begin with nothing and then attempt to make a claim. Rather, inquiry, even scientific theory, begins with something (i.e., a hard core) and tests that something's claims. The resulting tests either confirm, reject, refine, or prove inconclusive. Thus knowledge is not constructed from nothing but refined from some original unsubstantiated belief that is subsequently tested.

Hefner's commitments to a mutuality in knowledge and the legitimacy of testing and exposure of knowledge to other's claims and inquiry is intriguing and useful for Sunesis. Like

---

[27] Philip Hefner, "Theologies Truth and Scientific Formulation," *Zygon* 23, no. 3 (September 1988): 266.
[28] Ibid., 270.
[29] Ibid., 170–78.

Hefner, I assume that different species of knowledge do produce different claims, yet those claims are testable *while* necessarily particular *and* not exclusive. Methodologically, Sunesis pays attention to Hefner's insistence on testability and interplay, Frame's insistence on justifiability, and Wright's insistence on diversity and mutuality.

When some source claims to supply knowledge, we should designate the kinds of knowledge that source is best suited to supply. For example, a relationship with a concert pianist might not supply us with good knowledge about how to play the piano personally or how a piano functions mechanically, but it might supply us with knowledge about what good piano playing is. That particular source of information supplies an appropriate kind of knowledge. Such a designation helps remove tension between different sources of knowledge, as we recognized that those sources are best suited to do different, complementary yet not necessarily competing things. Furthermore, if there are different species emergent from the diversity of sources for knowledge, then the potential that these species point toward different notions of truth appears more plausible. In the next section, I will look at how two theologians describe truth, especially as they illustrate how truth relates to Christian knowledge.

An Epistemological Landmark: Theories of Truth

Bruce Marshall, in *Trinity and Truth*, insists that Christians must have an accounting of truth. Yet, that accounting of truth should not simply borrow from other disciplines for its justification nor operate in exclusive isolation from other truth proponents. Rather, Christian accounts of truth need be particularly Christian and always committed to interlocution.[30]

---

[30] Bruce Marshall, *Trinity and Truth* (Cambridge, U.K.: Cambridge University Press, 2000), xi.

However, to speak intelligibly, first that speech needs context (i.e., enacting community) and vocabulary (i.e., formative story) for those truth claims to make sense. Framing his work using grammatical syntax, Marshall says that storied-practices shape knowing in the most fundamental and primary ways, supplying the subject (i.e., God) and object (i.e., belief) to faith utterances.[31] Marshall seeks something distinctively Christian, something that renders the speaker and the speaker's speech distinctly Christian. Since practices and story supply speech and substance, and because speech gives truthful utterances meaning, Marshall looks for those speech-acts that are central, enduring, and indispensable for shaping Christian identity, speech, and beliefs. He finds what he is looking for in Christian baptism and Eucharist.[32]

Looking to justify the truth claims issuing from these primary practices and speech, Marshall considers five theses for the justification of truth.[33] The first three (interiority, foundationalism, and epistemic dependence) he dismisses— interiority because it relies on immediate experience without recourse to descriptions of those experiences to give them meaning;[34] foundationalism because it subordinates God-consciousness to object-consciousness when rendering religious experiences valid;[35] and epistemic dependence because it assumes that a sentence's meaning might be established precisely and independently from its truthfulness.[36] As an alternative, Marshall advocates for both pragmatic and correspondence theories.

A pragmatic theory holds that beliefs are justified by the practices of a community and its members who maintain that

---

[31] Ibid., 10.
[32] Ibid., 19.
[33] Ibid., 50.
[34] Ibid., 51–54.
[35] Ibid., 56–59.
[36] Ibid., 60–61.

they are true.[37] Such a notion requires a robust accounting for the internal consistency of practices[38] and commitment to the meaning-making function of virtues.[39] A correspondence theory, on the other hand, argues that true beliefs, regardless of their particularity, are true relative to their correspondence with ultimate reality.[40] Marshall notes that correspondence theories may be parsed into two types: (1) those that claim that forms in reality conform to concepts in the mind and (2) those that claim that the semantics of truthful sentences bear truth.[41] Marshall leans toward this latter formulation of correspondence theory.[42]

Articulating a nuanced notion of correspondence theory that seeks relationships internal to sentences and their inherent beliefs, Marshall resists asserting that sentences speak to some form or idea outside the mind but, instead, points to the fact that sentences should logically be assumed to correspond to what really is without our ability to observe independently or adjudicate that external correspondence. Such utterances are publically spoken and, therefore, regularly tested against experience.[43] His public testing clarifies their truthfulness. Much like Hefner's assertions above, Marshall operates out of an assumption that truthful practices relate to truthful speech that produce truth claims, which may be tested for verification or falsification. Truth claims do not emerge independently from "midair," only to be adopted. Truth claims are "given" and then tested and refined.[44] Moreover, Marshall's parsing of correspondence theory into

---

[37] Ibid., 182ff.
[38] Ibid., 182.
[39] Ibid., 185.
[40] Ibid., 217.
[41] Ibid., 217–19.
[42] Ibid., 222–25.
[43] Ibid., 225–26, 234.
[44] This notion of refinement concurs with the account of deep understanding.

two parts is useful, because it involves a distinction that might allay concerns that truth as correspondence presumes deference to philosophical foundationalism.[45]

Robert Scharlemann articulates a different accounting of truth. However, what he shares is an assumption that truth, at least how it may be apprehended, is multiple. In his *The Being of God*, Scharlemann seeks to connect experience and truth to understandings of God, with a particular concern for how truth is acquired.[46] Offering an account of knowledge that resists conducting evaluative exercises from outside the system that seeks to know, Scharlemann's discussion of truth situates

---

[45] Deliberately moving away from correspondence theory, Andrew Schwartz advocates for what he terms a pragmatic theory of truth. Motivated by an impulse toward interreligious corporation, Schwartz seeks to eliminate a superfluous theological commitment to philosophical exclusivism, replacing exclusivism (and correspondence theory) with complementarity. His complementarity maintains that two statements, which on the surface may seem contradictory, might actually function in mutually beneficial ways. As such, he turns to Buddhism's notion that truth functions not as an end but as a means. That is, truth becomes truthful to the degree to which it leads to a religious "end." For both Christians and Buddhists, Schwartz names that end as liberation/salvation. According to Schwartz's pragmatic theory, truthful claims are truthful if they lead to liberation/salvation. Truths are not fixed ideas, as he presumes that they are in correspondence theories. Rather, having a disposable nature, truths are utilitarian utterances and practices that result in the end sought. Moreover, he identifies both a plurality and gradation in truth: (1) more than one truth may be held simultaneously as long as each truth possesses a functional benefit in achieving the religious end and (2) one truth might be truer if that truth is more expedient in leading to liberation/salvation. Both qualifications may be held concurrently. Importantly for his pragmatic theory to hold together, a determination as to what constitutes liberation/salvation is vital. Following his Wesleyan tradition, he recommends holiness or perfect love of God and others. In this formulation, Christian truths are those practices, utterances, and determinations that move the community toward that end. Schwartz's functional concept of truth is intriguing for Sunesis, particularly since his theory requires looking past truth as the goal of the religious intellectual enterprise. Truth becomes a servant to more practical ends, removing some pressure from an epistemological enterprise to bear truth. Such a pragmatic notion, it seems, shifts attention toward performing truthfully, c.f. Andrew Schwartz, "How 'Truth' Limits Inter-religious Dialogue: What Wesleyans Might Learn from Buddhism," *Wesleyan Theological Journal* 48, no. 1 (Spring 2013): 99–105.

[46] Robert P. Scharlemann, *The Being of God: Theology and the Experience of Truth* (New York: Seabury, 1981), vii.

those claims within the language, practices, communities, and systems of knowledge elemental to what is known. In other words, certain systems of knowledge are better able to describe particular notions of truth because of the inherent nature of those systems and the reason they supply.[47] As such, he endeavors to examine those distinctive notions of truth, stating that "truth has three senses: (1) the correspondence between what is thought (or said) and what is really so; (2) the manifestation of being in what is there; and (3) the constancy of being."[48]

As correspondence, truth is established to the degree to which what is stated corresponds with how things really are, i.e., "between what is said and what is so, between *intellectus*— how it appears in our minds—and *res*—how it appears in reality.[49] That correspondence may be ascertained empirically, experientially, or experimentally.[50] As manifestation, truth shifts. Here, rather than describing truth, Scharlemann notices truth. Using the ancient notion of *aletheia*, he introduces a category that understands truth as a focal clarity emerging from cluttered obscurity.[51] Such aletheian statements render what was previously undifferentiated from its surroundings into a new state of conspicuousness. This notion of truth carries a sense of truth as prophetic utterance, i.e., speaking the truth. Such speech makes apparent what was previously unnoticed.[52] As constancy, truth moves from descriptions or emerging notification to truthfulness of experiences discovered through engaging with persons, words, objects, etc., Scharlemann uses friendship to illustrate this third notion of truth. Truth is experienced

---

[47] Ibid.,11.
[48] Ibid.
[49] Ibid., 12.
[50] Ibid.
[51] Ibid., 13.
[52] Ibid., 14.

over time, as a kind of endurance and continuity in the midst of changing circumstances, i.e., one is a true friend.[53]

Ultimately, Marshall and Scharlemann provide conceptualizations of truth that demonstrate diversity and the complexity of attempting to establish what it means to assert that a claim is true. These accounts, minimally, suggest a plurality and mutuality present in notions of truth. In a rudimentary way, this plurality and mutuality is expressed in the variety of avenues available to lead to an apprehension of truth. While even more radical, this plurality and mutuality expresses the necessary existence of different kinds of truth.

In developing Sunetic epistemology, it is helpful to keep in mind the nuanced understandings of truth offered in these profiles. Additionally, it is useful to incorporate the implications presented above related to asserting that (1) understanding results from convergences of the several species of knowledge; (2) the internal and external justifiability of knowledge may be discovered through reciprocal exposure to other claims; and (3) there is a legitimacy to testing what is offered as known. Holding these implications in the forefront of my theological imagination, I turn to consider the sources that those different species of knowledge and notions of truth require.

An Epistemological Landmark: Sources of Knowledge

Throughout this project, I have suggested that an epistemology should take into account—in deliberate ways—the importance of performance as a vital factor in shaping interpretative lenses and the significance of additional interlocutors from other communities and disciplines of knowledge, interlocutors whose claims both compete with

---

[53] Ibid., 12.

and complement the epistemological and hermeneutical work of the Christian faith. Lying behind these assertions about the multiplicities of knowledge and notions of truth related to those different claims is the implication that there are different sources of knowledge. With this final epistemological landmark, I turn to consider, more intentionally, those sources, namely (performed) stories and systems (for reflection).

In Stanley Hauerwas's and David Burrell's estimation, "All our notions are narrative-dependent, including the notion of rationality."[54] Hauerwas and Burrell maintain that we describe the world we come to see and those descriptions are reliant on a community's grammar. This reliance invests those descriptions with value-laden assessments as to what is good. Consequently, narrative provides a vocabulary resulting in conditioned vision.[55] And that this narrative conditioned vision is seminal to the intellectual, moral, and rational life. Narratives allow for a continuity and integrity of a person's life. Therefore, persons are essentially social selves formed through a community's inhabited speech, while the self exists in a web of interlocution.[56] This socially and linguistically conditioned rationality depicts a vision of reality and of humanity's end and purpose within that reality.

The presence of narrative history provides the substantive context from which our descriptions emerge and in which those descriptions find their meaning. Hauerwas and Burrell contend that no normative theory exists that can account for

---

[54] Stanley Hauerwas and David Burrell, "From System to Story: An Alternative Pattern for Rationality in Ethics," in *Why Narrative? Readings in Narrative Theology*, ed. Stanley Hauerwas and L. Gregory Jones (Grand Rapids, MI: Eerdmans, 1989), 168.

[55] Emmanuel Katongole, *Beyond Universal Reason: The Relation Between Religion and Ethics in the Work of Stanley Hauerwas* (Notre Dame, IN: University of Notre Dame Press, 2000), 70.

[56] Stanley Hauerwas, *The Peaceable Kingdom* (Notre Dame, IN: University of Notre Dame Press, 1983), 96.

the varieties of histories and complex stories which shape our notions.[57] Since it is only within the framing structure of particular narratives that intelligible claims may be made, the integrity of those claims require testing against that narrative's dramatic telling across time and space.[58] This recognition that narrative supplies a structure to render intelligible the events of our lives—drawing epistemology, rationality, hermeneutics, performance, and truth together—is vital.

Taking this line of reasoning one step further, David Ford argues that an added dimension is needed. Ford claims that there must be more than just a connection to rationality and the provision of grammar to erect a coherent matrix for our actions. In his estimation for narrative adequately to supply our rationality and grammar, narratives require enactment. This coherent matrix is a balance, according to Ford, between (1) systems (i.e., philosophies, theologies, higher criticism, sciences, etc.); (2) stories (i.e., the narrated traditions of our lives); and (3) performances (i.e., the cutting edge action of our lives).[59] The first two dimensions of this construction are reflexive, addressing past actions, while, conversely, the third dimension is presently active, "hot" in character, as it performs the narrative in real-time, testing and adjusting the narrative into the future.[60] This performance of our narratives, Ford states, "helps to orient one within what one is actually living, and it is the assessment aspect of evaluations and decisions leading to response and action which is more prominent than

---

[57] Hauerwas and Burrell, "From System to Story," 169–70.
[58] Ibid., 170.
[59] David Ford, "System, Story, and Performance" in *Why Narrative? Readings in Narrative Theology*, ed. Stanley Hauerwas and L. Gregory Jones (Grand Rapids: Eerdmans, 1989), 191.
[60] Ibid., 203.

the realism of descriptions . . . "[61] So, for our lives to have intelligibility and for our rationality to form and prove meaningful, there must be an intersection of our storied existence
with our present living of those stories. Ford summarizes his
point about the necessity of the enactment of our narratives
by claiming that performance is "a process in which *lexis* and
praxis are the main focus and in which dramatic and narrative
content is taken seriously."[62] In the end, it appears, as Ford sees
it, that our lives become a kind of illocutionary speech-act on
a grand scale.

Lash anticipates the concerns many will raise when confronted with an epistemology dependent upon narrative in the
way Hauerwas, Burrell, and Ford offer. Preemptively, Lash
warns that our story telling "is threatened by 'self-indulgence
and even dishonesty.'"[63] This observation leads him to ask if
there are "countervailing influences to hand which might discipline and purify [our] tendency to construct a significance
which, *as* constructed, is at best distorted and, at worst, illu-
sory?"[64] He identifies two potential corrective influences, one
internal and one external, to the narrative community engaged
in the performative telling of its story.

Internally, Lash insists, we must remember to distinguish
between practice and reflection, between storytelling and
criticism of our stories, between the "hot" living of our stories
and the "cool" consideration of them. Insisting that narratives
must be tested against time (i.e., tradition) and experience
(i.e., other narratives), Lash maintains that powerful "*internal*

---

[61] Ibid., 202.
[62] Ford, 202–3.
[63] Nicholas Lash, "Ideology, Metaphor, and Analogy," in *Why Narrative?: Readings in Narrative Theology*, ed. Stanley Hauerwas and L. Gregory. Jones (Grand Rapids, MI: Eerdmans, 1989), 121.
[64] Ibid.

correctives to [our] own anthropomorphism" persist [65]. Any claim made by our narratives that diverge too radically from storied-experience (i.e., history) and performed-experience (i.e., present action) will rightly be drawn into question when confronted by the stark reality of our lives. Such a failed claim will be cast "as self-indulgent construction of satisfying narrative."[66] Moreover, this claim "inexcusably ignores the silent witness of the simplicity and realism, which has sometimes been the fruit of a practically sustained 'alertness to limits.'"[67] This observation leads Lash to state that we must "prove the truth, i.e., the reality and power, this-sidedness of this believing practice."[68]

Externally, Lash concludes that the claims of our stories must correspond with lived reality.[69] According to Lash, such a claim is not just the result of present experience, but the practical discipline developed over time through regular application of our stories to describe our lives.[70] This method of external verification proves more an art than a science and more about *truthfulness* than *truth*. Thus an accounting for the sources of our knowing suggests a diversity of sources, interaction, testability, and particularity. Again, this accounting helps explain how our claims might use the same information/experiences to produce different conclusions, appreciating that information/experiences are processed through different performances, stories, and systems, while also affirming that the particularity of those claims should be regularly refined through external interaction.

---

[65] Ibid., 122.
[66] Ibid., 123.
[67] Ibid.
[68] Ibid., 134.
[69] Ibid., 135.
[70] Ibid., 130.

Sunesis: Understanding via Interplay

While cursory, this chapter has supplied a framing outline of an epistemology. More specifically, an epistemology that takes into account the importance of performance as the primary way that we come to know through speech and acts. Also we have seen how different species of knowledge originating from different sources of information are necessarily and appropriately distinct. Moreover, these distinct species of knowledge lead to different claims that we are justifiable in holding and, then, tested against each other to refine what we know without obliterating each claim's unique assertions and points of origin. These different claims have different origins and might comport with different theories of truth given that truth is not one thing but may be understood to represent many kinds of claims to certainty. Finally, since different claims and truths rightly emerge from different sources of knowledge, those claims and truths bear the distinct character of their originating sources.

More specifically, the sources of knowledge identified through Hauerwas, Burrell, Ford, and Lash are well suited to the epistemology I propose. In particular, the three sources of performance, story, and system align with a threefold account of truth borrowed from Scharlemann and the species of knowledge pinpointed in Wright. *Performance* creates a distinct set of knowledge acquired through practices. Its species of knowledge is *knowing how*, a species of knowledge acquired over time by doing. This enacted kind of knowing fits well with the notion of truth as *constancy*, a notion of truth characteristically experienced over time as a kind of endurance and continuity in the midst of changing circumstances.

Stories designate those reflective narratives that labor to bring creative order to our lives. Its species of knowledge is *knowing who*, a species of knowledge understood to result from direct/shared relationship with what is to be known. Such a conceptualization of knowledge fits well with the notion of truth as *manifestation*. Manifestation or *aletheia* introduces the idea that truth is a focal clarity emerging from cluttered obscurity. Here, rather than experiencing truth, we notice truth. Aletheian statements render what was previously undifferentiated from its surroundings into a new state of conspicuousness.

Systems are removed from the hot living of our lives into the cool detachment of critical thinking. Acting at a secondary level, these systems of reflection are deliberately distant from daily living, given a vantage for evaluating and appraising. Its species of knowledge is *knowing that*. Knowing that describes a kind of knowledge that conveys facts and data. This knowledge fits well with the notion of truth as *correspondence*. As correspondence, truth is established to the degree to which what is stated corresponds with how things really are, trusting that the semantics of truthful sentences bear truth.

Lastly, incorporating a mode for refining knowledge through mutuality also proves useful. The kind of interplay between the various sources, species, and truths necessary to produce deep understanding requires a kind of mutuality similar to Frame's dual notion of internal and external subjective justifiability. This dual notion allows for the testing of a claim's internal constituency while subjecting that claim to external examination by other species of knowledge, producing a kind of hermeneutic spiral that presses onward towards (epistemological) perfection. This internal and external exposure and testing echoes the kind of assessment that Hefner maintains is required for deep understanding to issue. As such, other species of knowledge may and should engage directly with each other, moving from distinct types of knowledge to a deep, integrated understanding, or, Sunesis.

Conclusion: A Warranted Excursus

Ultimately, while this is a specific accounting of Christian epistemology, Sunesis seems well suited to explain why our truth claims are often different and to designate how claims made by others outside the Christian tradition and interactions with those claimants are unavoidable, even necessary and enriching. Sunesis presumes the value and necessity of interplay with others if we are to assert an authentic understanding. Further, Sunesis, while supporting the essentiality of (Christian) particularity, does not assume uniformity. On our campuses and in our work and world, knowledge is never formed or held in isolation. It could not and should not. Christian understanding, if it is to be faithful and effective, must boldly engage with the broader spectrum of knowledge and be willing to change and be changed. Moreover, this kind of processing of information and experiences through an amalgamating refinement toward a deep understanding is happening all the time, in every community and conversation. Regardless of the particular performance enacted or story embodied or reflective system deployed, understanding emerges and shifts when these three sources are intentionally subjected to each other. Vitally, there is frequent overlapping with other actors, stories, and systems, as these sources and different communities share common information and space and experiences and these communities meet and mesh. As Sunesis suggests, understanding is particular, composite, evolving, and involved. This realization is especially helpful in a world of increasing diversity and conscious possession of multiple truths.

The chapter began by describing Lash's account of beliefs and actions and his evaluations of those beliefs and actions. Like Lash, this is "one more attempt" at casting sufficient light on living in and interacting with the world. Such a task is difficult. The solutions suggested are complex, but such is our world. Lash, too, recognized the enduringly difficult nature inherent in laboring to articulate any epistemological schema. Yet, such difficulty demands humility, identifying the necessity of a rigorous attempt. In the end, that is what Sunesis is—a claim not so much of certain knowledge but of a certain eagerness to engage in trying to understand.

A Particular Ministry in a Pluralistic Context

Stephen W. Rankin

Introduction: Limning the Scope of the Chaplain's Role

In 1739 John Wesley famously wrote, "I look upon all the world as my parish; thus far I mean, that, in whatever part of it I am, I judge it meet, right, and my bounden duty, to declare unto all that are willing to hear, the glad tidings of salvation."[1] While Mr. Wesley made this statement to defend his ministry's geographic irregularities, it serves well as a metaphor for United Methodist higher education, especially for those serving as chaplains in colleges and universities. As chaplains, we find "all the world" coming to American schools to study—students from all Christian denominations and from the world's great religious traditions. At our colleges and universities, we find the "nones" and the "dones," skeptics and seekers alongside believers. We find Christians, Jews, Muslims, Sikhs, Hindus, Buddhists, and Wiccans. In this cultural and religious diversity, the chaplain's role becomes fraught with challenges and possibilities. So we ask, "What is the role of chaplains in this complex culture? Where are our conceptual boundaries that help us navigate our work?"

How, then, does a chaplain think of her or his ministry? As ordained clergy appointed to extension ministry (*Book*

---

[1] John Wesley, *The Works of John Wesley*, vol. 19, ed. W. Reginald Ward and Richard P. Heitzenrater (Nashville: Abingdon, 1990), 67. While the phrase, "The world is my parish" is often used (incorrectly) to talk about world mission, Wesley used it as the justification for preaching in another person's territory.

of Discipline, para. 332 and 337.2), we are called to take the mission of the church—to make disciples of Jesus Christ for the transformation of the world—into the academy. How do we understand the term *disciples*? What are the envisioned goals for world transformation? Are we essentially pastors assigned to fill a slot beyond the local church but otherwise like our parish colleagues? Are we frustrated academics trying to find a way into the academy short of a faculty appointment? Are we church relations functionaries helping to build good will with ecclesial stakeholders? Given current pressures on higher education and the complexities of this environment, it seems a propitious moment to ask these questions and to consider how chaplains contribute to fulfilling the church's mission. Otherwise, for those of us in extension ministry, especially in higher education, The United Methodist Church's mission statement, to make disciples for the transformation of the world, serves as little more than an empty slogan.

In an attempt to answer these questions, I will consider a number of critical topics. First, we need to look at the larger context of higher education—historical and contemporary— and reflect on the kind of institutions that nonsectarian, church-related schools are. These schools are different, for example, from confessional Christian universities in which certain—as I call them—control mechanisms stand in place: compulsory chapel, required courses in Christian doctrine or the Bible, and possibly lifestyle covenants requiring students (and sometimes faculty and staff) to uphold certain moral stances associated with that school's particular understanding of Christian identity.[2] At the same time, they are not secular

---

[2] Among the best-known examples of such schools are Wheaton College in Illinois, Seattle Pacific University, and Gordon College. Baylor University and Notre Dame exemplify this same quality at the research university level.

state universities. So which way do these nonsectarian, church-related schools lean, more toward openly confessional Christian schools or secular ones? How do leaders of a school think about that school's religious identity? What sources and norms guide this thinking? How do the leaders' views of a school understand the school's position relative to the general higher education culture as it affects the institutional expectations for the chaplain? How, then, do we embody and bear witness to our church-related identity? What role does the chaplain hold in fostering that institutional identity?

These same questions surface especially when thinking about the clientele of a school. What is the make-up of our student populations? What are their religious preferences? Here we look at demographics of religious preference among students, which likewise provokes thought and challenges us to integrate practical and theological commitments. The academy, looking at the same trends among students and in view of certain powerful academic values, has adopted programmatic strategies, such as including spirituality in wellness classes to meet this need among students. While offerings on spirituality may find their way into a school's curriculum in this manner, this move seems to open the door to the work of chaplains as teachers, at least, in some settings.[3] What resources, then, can a chaplain find to assist in this teaching ministry? Of course, students can still study religion(s) in a traditional academic way, but there, in many cases, they must maintain that familiar (to

---

[3] To be sure, many college and university chaplains teach already, so in one sense, my observation seems pointless. However, I am trying to ask a fundamental question about the role of the chaplain broadly within the academic institution. It is the rare chaplain, particularly at schools seeking for national prominence, who is seen as an educational leader giving shape to curriculum rather than filling important, but limited slots in the already-existing curriculum. I am aware of exceptions to my generalization but confident the generalization holds.

academics) detached, third-person stance. In wellness courses, on the other hand, students are encouraged to be personally engaged. Does a chaplain's work fit best there? Is it appropriate for the chaplain to operate from the standpoint of her or his own religious particularity or must the chaplain stick to the assumptions grounding the secular wellness material?

Two possible strategies emerge for conceiving the chaplain's role. One follows a now well-known path blazed by student development leaders such as Sharon Daloz Parks. This strategy focuses primarily on the dynamics of individual student faith development, with "faith" defined formally as "convictional commitment,"[4] a particular way of knowing, by means of which students envision and engage the world. This way comports well with wellness material by sharing its (largely Kantian)[5] assumptions regarding the limitations of religious knowledge. More broadly, a second strategy emerges as one ponders recent literature on post-secularity. This strategy challenges colleges and universities to rethink their basic understanding of the role religious faith plays in public life and, regarding the interest of this paper, in pedagogy. Post-secularity opens the door for religious particularity, with implications for the role of chaplain.

These reflections bring me to the thesis I wish to offer in this paper and to which I have already tipped my hand in the

---

[4] Sharon Daloz Parks, *Big Questions, Worthy Dreams: Mentoring Emerging Adults in their Search for Meaning, Purpose, and Faith*, rev. ed. (San Francisco: Jossey-Bass, 2011), 79–80.

[5] By "Kantian" thinking, I mean his emphasis on practical reason that limits warrant for theological knowledge claims and shifts emphasis to ethics and away from theology per se. A number of important thinkers on the subject of interest in this paper, such as Sharon Daloz Parks and her PhD advisor, James Fowler, admitted their indebtedness to Kant. With regard to political and cultural contexts, the democratic liberalism of John Rawls also stands within this Kantian influence. Rawls sought to develop a theory of justice that provides the grounds on which diverse peoples could come together for deliberation, which meant marginalizing or eliminating from public discourse all religious claims. This tradition of thought has come under serious scrutiny.

previous paragraph. I am convinced that the role of chaplain at a United Methodist college or university—in order to keep faith with and in strong support of the church's mission—should widen and deepen in order to claim a fundamental leadership role in shaping a school's basic vision for its educational mission and its pedagogy. The chaplain can, and should, become once again a theologically informed and driven, strategic thought leader, who operates from an expressly Christian framework. This work can be pursued quite well within the nonsectarian identity that, so far as I know, all United Methodist schools embrace. In other words, chaplains need not couch or mute their Christian beliefs in order to provide warm welcome and enthusiastic support to all members of the college or university community. Rather, chaplains should operate from a position of strong particularity. To some, this stance may seem obvious, given our ordination vows, our appointments, and the kind of schools in which we work. To others, it appears as an inappropriate and worrisome attempt to return to an age of ecclesial dominance that should be left dead and buried. In my view, however, it offers the best kind of education that a United Methodist-related school can offer.

The Significance of the Nonsectarian Character of United Methodist Schools

As George Marsden has indicated in his influential history of American Protestant universities, United Methodism has been very successful at establishing significant, nationally regarded schools. He also notes that this success provides an especially powerful illustration of the struggle that all such universities had walking the line between the expectations of their sponsoring denominations and the secularizing forces of early twentieth-century higher education.[6] On the one hand, these schools were expected by denominational leaders to contribute to and represent the church's beliefs and mission. On the other hand, higher education as an industry was coming into its own and demanding independence from denominations in order to further the advancement of knowledge. By the beginning of the twentieth century, higher education leaders were working to limit doctrinal restrictiveness in order to expand academic freedom for their faculty. During this period, a number of national professional organizations developed to improve, advance, and in many ways standardize practices in higher education. The Carnegie Foundation for the Advancement of Teaching was founded in 1905,[7] the American Association of University Professors in 1915. Both of these organizations have been strongly committed to academic freedom, which, in the twentieth century especially, meant loosening ecclesial controls. The American Council on Higher Education began in 1918 and the Association of Governing Boards of Colleges and Universities began in 1921. These organizations have stated missions to develop senior administrative leaders and "citizen trustees"[8] to guide colleges and universities.

Virtually all the major professional organizations for anyone working on college campuses originated in the first quarter or third of the twentieth century and fell under the

---

[6] George M. Marsden, "The Perils of Methodist Success," in *The Soul of the American University: From Protestant Establishment to Established Non-Belief* (Oxford: Oxford University Press, 1994), 276–87.

[7] Ironically, the son of a Missouri Methodist preacher, Henry Smith Pritchett, became president of the Carnegie Foundation in 1905, and worked tirelessly to free schools from denominational control.

[8] See the AGB web site for reference to citizen trustees, http://agb.org/about-agb.

influence of the burgeoning notion of public as secular. This history of the roughly one hundred years past in American higher education continues to shape higher education culture, with implications for how college or university chaplains perform their tasks. The tendency has been increasingly to loosen denominational involvement. For example, the practice of finding presidents for Methodist schools among leading Methodist clergy has largely passed out of practice. At the school where I serve, only two positions require the holders to be United Methodist clergy—the senior chaplain and the Dean of the School of Theology.

Another set of influences contributes to the same secularizing trajectory. A number of recent books have explored in compelling detail the power of market forces to shape higher education.[9] It is an alarming story that shows clearly the extent to which students and parents have become consumers of educational products, a phenomenon encouraged by college rankings and the pressure to raise money through securing grants from both the public and private sectors. The pressure is on schools to conform to a set of assumptions and values about higher education that generally marginalize religious identity and mission. A school's affiliation with the denomination and its institutional identity likely will weaken unless a core group of leaders from among trustees and senior administrators

---

[9] See, for example, Martha C. Nussbaum, *Not for Profit: Why Democracy Needs the Humanities*, The Public Square Book Series (Princeton, NJ: Princeton University Press, 2010); Anthony T. Kronman, *Education's End: Why Our Colleges and Universities Have Given Up on the Meaning of Life*, (New Haven, CT: Yale University Press, 2007); Jeffrey J. Selingo, *College (Un)Bound: The Future of Higher Education and What It Means for Students*, (Boston, MA: New Harvest, 2013); Andrew Delbanco, *College: What It Was, Is, and Should Be*, (Princeton, NJ: Princeton University Press, 2012); Harry Lewis, *Excellence Without Soul: Does Liberal Education Have a Future?* (New York: Public Affairs, 2007).

take into account the church affiliation and the church's mission for a school's direction.[10]

These observations reveal the need for United Methodist academic leaders to undertake fundamental thinking on the role of the chaplain and the questions raised in this chapter. Is the chaplain's role primarily pastoral and administrative, while leaving the pedagogical questions to others, mainly tenured faculty? If so, who in the institution bears responsibility to engage in sustained deliberation about the value and role of the school's affiliation with the church? If the role goes beyond conventional understandings of pastoral ministry to include some input into a school's mission, to what extent does the church's mission statement guide the chaplain's thinking?

Changing Demographics and Attitudes about Religion

According to a report produced for the General Board of Higher Education and Ministry in 2011, Kenisha Cantrell and Michele Pedersen indicate that 174,000 students attend United Methodist postsecondary schools.[11] We also know that, within that number stand a substantial proportion of international students. At the school where I work, within the new first-year class, nearly 8 percent come to us from outside the United States.[12] The world, by fits and starts, is becoming more culturally diverse within traditionally mono-cultural geographic areas and more complicated to negotiate for educated, world-aware people.

---

[10] For the importance of a core group of leaders to hold a church related school to its ecclesial identity, see Robert Benne, *Quality with Soul: How Six Premier Colleges and Universities Keep Faith with Their Religious Traditions* (Grand Rapids, MI: Eerdmans, 2001). See chap. 7, "Keeping the Faith," especially p. 182.

[11] http://www.gbhem.org/sites/default/files/documents/publications /PUB_STUDENTRELIGIOUSAFFIL2010-2011.pdf.

[12] Taking just two nationalities as an illustration, SMU hosts more than 300 Chinese students and more than 100 Indian students. We also have a large number of students from Saudi Arabia.

That diversity can be illustrated a number of ways and one of the most recent and compelling comes from the Pew Research Center's report, "America's Changing Landscape," published in May 2015. Whereas most Americans still identify as Christian (70 percent), nearly 6 percent of adults in the United States claim a faith tradition other than Christianity, which, as the report says, is a "small but significant" increase over the percentage in 2007.[13] The categories, "atheist" and "agnostic" have grown in proportion to religious believers. "Atheists and agnostics now account for more than 31 percent of all religious 'nones,' up from 25 percent in 2007."[14]

The Pew study reveals that, of the major categories, mainline Protestants, of which United Methodists are part, are shrinking the most rapidly. United Methodism has shrunk from 5.1% of the population in 2007 to 3.6% in 2015.[15] Explanations as to the cause vary, of course and, from one perspective, these numbers stand as a separate and largely irrelevant concern for colleges and universities, since only a small fraction of students at most United Methodist schools are actually United Methodist. But when one considers again that the chaplain is engaged in extension ministry on behalf of the church and when one remembers that one of the church's major missional strategies is the development of young, principled leaders, then the Pew research indicates work to be done.

Alongside the statistics regarding religious identity, the research of Alexander and Helen Astin reveals strong interest

---

[13] Pew Research Center, "Growth of Non-Christian Faiths" in the report, "America's Changing Religious Landscape," http://www.pewforum.org/2015/05/12/americas-changing-religious-landscape/.

[14] Ibid., http://www.pewforum.org/2015/05/12/chapter-1-the-changing-religious-composition-of-the-u-s/. Of course, the research on the "nones" has become well known though, in my view, generally misunderstood because of the increase of atheists and agnostics. Most "nones" still express belief in God, still pray and still read the Bible and even attend worship on occasion.

[15] Ibid., under the section, "The Shifting Composition of American Protestantism."

in spirituality and religion among college students. Their research has shown that, whereas students generally are eager to explore these topics with their professors, the faculty, in contrast, express the general feeling of uneasiness and hesitance to engage in these kinds of conversations.[16] The Astins offer a list of possibilities, such as contributing to new faculty orientation on questions of spirituality and religion, creating interfaith dialogues and collaboration, using living/learning communities (at schools who use this method, obviously) to facilitate awareness of spiritual questions, and hosting guest speakers and forums.[17]

The lingering gap between student interest and faculty willingness remains a challenge but also provides impetus for thinking about the role of the chaplain. It also raises the question of where the chaplain is located in the school's organization and how the chaplain's role is perceived by college/university community members. Depending on the institutional posture toward religion and a school's religious affiliation, a chaplain may serve in some capacity as an educational leader, have good relationships with faculty, and even hold faculty status herself or himself. Or the chaplain may be seen as limited to a role in Student Affairs, providing pastoral and administrative oversight to religious life organizations and being available for individual conversations, but little more. I speak somewhat stereotypically at this point, but it certainly is the case that a chaplain's profile may affect how all people concerned imagine the scope of possibilities for guiding a school's educational mission.

---

[16] Alexander W. Astin, Helen S. Astin and Jennifer A. Lindholm, *Cultivating the Spirit: How College Can Enhance Students' Inner Lives*, (San Francisco: Jossey-Bass, 2011), 37–39, 150.
[17] Ibid., 152.

When we step back and look at the aforementioned statistics, we can see how two major competing narratives shape what people consider appropriate for developing a strategy of engagement with religious faith in the academy. First, what I will call, somewhat contentiously, the modernist narrative—that higher education is about the public domain of knowledge for the common good, while religious faith is a private concern better left at the margins[18]—still exercises considerable influence, though perhaps on the wane. From this perspective, opinions that can be identified as emanating from religious beliefs are considered illegitimate for discussions on matters pertaining to the public good.[19] I hazard the guess that, on campuses where this viewpoint still shapes the ethos, the chaplain will have (to be sure) significant work to do through conventional means of religious life activities and other essentially extracurricular ways, promoting student spiritual development but steer clear of basic and far-reaching pedagogical concerns that shade into faculty prerogatives.

As I understand the work of Sharon Daloz Parks on faith development, it seems to me that it fits well within this first narrative of the modernist framework. In her well-known book, *Big Questions, Worthy Dreams*, she describes faith in ways that emphasize the dynamic psychological processes in emerging adults while seeking to limit the role of religious dogma.[20] Although she recognizes the inevitability of

---

[18] On this point, the theory of justice developed by John Rawls is particularly relevant.

[19] Any topic of concern tied to concerns about justice illustrate the problem. Sexual violence is a matter of grave concern, for example. Discourse surrounding this topic is couched in social science, public health, and legal terms. Moral values overtly guided by religious beliefs rarely, if ever, come into the public conversation, though people may privately admit that they take such values into account at some level.

[20] Parks mentions religious dogma five times in the book, always in relatively pessimistic (and bordering on dismissive) terms. I have sought to evaluate her work on this point in a paper published as part of the proceedings of Taylor University's Higher

religious particularity (Parks is a Christian), it is a qualified and exceedingly hesitant particularity that tends toward an affirmation of religious pluralism along the lines of John Hick's description in *A Christian Theology of Religions.* There, Hick argues that all religions, in so far as they promote interaction with the transcendent Real (his term) that leads to compassionate and just relations to others, should be seen as legitimate.[21]

This purportedly humble approach to dogmatic religious claims seems to be just what colleges and universities—comprised as they are by diverse student and faculty populations—require. It often has been the case that college and university chaplains have accepted these limits, whether or not they agreed with them. This view has exercised considerable influence in the academy, but the time has come to challenge it. In retrospect, we can see that, because this view of religion does not have the strength to stand up against the market-driven individualism (a consumerist anthropology, as it were), the effect among college students has been to blend all religions into a kind of generic "spirituality" that renders college students inarticulate about their particular religious identity. It also very well may contribute to the rise of the "nones."[22]

Education Symposium under the auspices of the Association of Christians in Student Development. See Stephen. W. Rankin, "What's Wrong with 'Meaning Making' to Describe Faith? The Problem with Sharon Daloz Parks's Kantian Assumptions for Student Development," in *A Faith for the Generations: How Collegiate Experience Impacts Faith*, ed. Timothy W. Herrmann et al. (Abilene, TX: Abilene Christian University Press, 2015).

[21] John Hick, *A Christian Theology of Religions* (Louisville, KY: Westminster John Knox, 1995).

[22] I realize the contentious tone in this statement. Two sources lead me to risk making such a strong claim. First is the empirical fact that mainline Protestant denominations, The United Methodist Church included, hold their young within the denominational fold at a much lower rate than churches that emphasize more doctrinal clarity and rigor. The Pew Research shows this fact very clearly. Second, the longitudinal research and publication led by sociologist Christian Smith also observes in lamenting tones that American young people are largely susceptible to (that now overused) "moralistic ther-

Toward the Post-Secular

The second major narrative, in contrast to what I have called
the modernist one, which is beginning to emerge relates to
dialogue and publication associated with the term *postsecular*.
It offers an intriguing opening for fundamental reflection on
the role of chaplaincy in church-related higher education.
Most notably associated with the evolving thought of Jürgen
Habermas, the term refers to a growing awareness among
philosophers, political scientists, and others that the supposed
neutrality toward religions that democratic liberalism claims to
offer turns out to be not as neutral as supposed. The allegedly
neutral stance of the secular actually impoverishes a society's
search for the common good—as I mentioned above—because
of an *a priori* out of court ruling of valuable ideas that come
from Christian theology or other faith traditions simply on
the grounds of their being religious ideas, makes them, as a
matter of principle, unfit for the public discussion.[23] Scholars
interested in exploring the possibilities of a "post-secular"
academy welcome the more open exchange of ideas, including
religious ones, with a widening variety of background beliefs.

The post-secular impulse illustrates a pluralism of a different sort than that generally founded on Kantian[24] principles. It
is what I might call a true pluralism, in which diverse peoples
with often competing belief systems bring their best arguments

---

apeutic Deism," with regrettable results. See Christian Smith et al., *Lost in Transition:
The Dark Side of Emerging Adulthood*, (New York: Oxford University Press, 2011),
especially chap. 1, "Morality Adrift," 19–69. For a United Methodist scholar who has
written eloquently about the same problem, see Kenda Creasy Dean, *Almost Christian:
What the Faith of Our Teenagers Is Telling the American Church*, (New York: Oxford
University Press, 2010).

[23] See, for example, Jürgeen Habermas et al., *An Awareness of What is Missing: Faith
and Reason in a Post-Secular Age*, trans. Ciaran Cronin, (Malden, MA: Polity Press,
2010). See especially chap. 2, "An Awareness of What is Missing."

[24] See n5.

to the table to help foster the search for truth and justice. In so doing, they need not mute their particular convictions, nor must they "translate" them into terms more fitting to a secular approach. Rather, their particularity is encouraged and the debates are open. It is the sort of pluralism exemplified in The Pluralism Project at Harvard University under the leadership of Diana Eck[25] and a project by the same name at the University of Virginia.[26]

The emerging sensibility about post-secularity opens the door for a fundamental rethinking of the role of the chaplaincy at United Methodist colleges and universities. We can build on the provocative work of those philosophers and social scientists who are beginning to imagine once again how particular religious beliefs serve the common good. This refreshing openness challenges United Methodist schools to reconsider—if they have not done so for some time—how the affiliation with the church supports and advances the school's educational vision. One helpful resource is Douglas and Rhonda Hustedt Jacobsen's book, *No Longer Invisible*. In it they explore how religious faith contributes to a school's academic mission. Each chapter offers its own gem, but one especially deals with how the "framing knowledge" that those working in higher education bring to their work, whether professors or administrators or program directors, operate in the academic context. The authors describe two basic styles: "monist" and "pluralist," with some evaluation of the strengths and limits of each.

These terms are not limited to religious or theological topics. Thinking about framing knowledge helps people realize that, while certain kinds of empirical knowledge tend to dominate, all knowledge stands on assumptions that cannot be demon-

---

[25] See http://www.pluralism.org.
[26] See http://www.iasc-culture.org/research_pluralism_project.php.

strated empirically. We all bring assumptions to our work that cannot be demonstrated empirically. In light of this admission, theological ideas start to be regarded as acceptable points of departure, not just for shaping a person's privately held values and beliefs but also for engaging in public conversations about the common good. Recognizing this condition helps us realize the importance of bringing particular theological views into important discussions about what constitutes an excellent college education offered in United Methodist schools.[27]

The Jacobsens' book can be understood to operate from a post-secular viewpoint. Their argument helps us make the turn to our particularity as United Methodists. We can draw on our own theological tradition as a rich source for envisioning a robustly United Methodist approach to higher education. Taking this more explicitly theological approach will not make us narrow and sectarian or enmesh us in some effort at salvaging a brittle denomination. It will identify us, however, as offering a distinctive approach to higher education, much like many Catholic schools (such as Notre Dame) are doing. There is much good work to be done at this point, and I am able, in the brief space remaining, to provide only suggestive hints at the fertile possibilities. Perhaps surprisingly, John Wesley's theology turns out to be a rich and relevant source for contemporary reflection on this topic.[28]

Where the Church's Mission and the School's Mission Meet

Returning to the church's mission statement of making disciples of Jesus Christ: How does this mission relate to a school's

---

[27] Douglas Jacobsen and Rhonda Hustedt Jacobsen, *No Longer Invisible: Religion in University Education* (New York: Oxford University Press, 2012). See especially chap. six, "Framing Knowledge," 92–106.

[28] In other words, Mr. Wesley can be more than a slogan on a button proclaiming him as a campus minister.

educational mission? Educators often make reference to "pedagogy." When academics talk about "pedagogy," they generally mean the theories and practices of teaching and learning. On closer inspection, we recognize the long-term formational impact of good teaching practices on students. Those practices are based on the best thinking regarding how human beings are made and how they learn most effectively.[29] Not limited to the classroom, pedagogy is something that professionals in student development consider as part of their normal course work. In a variety of ways, then, we can recognize how formative the whole college experience is. *In other words, pedagogy is a type of disciple making or discipleship.* The best professors share a vision and a love for their disciplines that infects their students and imparts that love to them. It involves a combination of skillful intellectual work and a sharing of their affections for the objects of study. Some of their students fall in love with the subject too. In Student Affairs, educators work closely with students in ways that challenge values and develop leadership skills. Again, through the relationship with college professionals, students get a vision of the world and of themselves and their calling with effects that often do last a lifetime and set the enduring course for their lives. It appears, therefore, that there is notable overlap between the church's notion of discipleship and the academy's understanding of pedagogy.

This observation about discipleship and pedagogy helps us make the turn toward John Wesley's thinking on human nature and the Christian life as a rich and relevant source for thinking about United Methodist higher education. As a suggestion for how to bring our particular theological tradition to bear on this project, I offer Wesley's doctrine of Christian perfection.

---

[29] We can see here the relevance of a Christian theological understanding of human beings as critically important for how a school envisions teaching and learning.

What if campus leaders were to consider Wesley's description of the mature Christian life as framing knowledge for thinking about pedagogy? It will take some work to untangle Wesley's perceptive teachings from the various kinds of polemics afflicting this topic since even Wesley's own time. But if we consider this doctrine as one feature of a school's framing knowledge, then the picture of mature Christian discipleship the doctrine offers stands as a compelling vision for the kind of informed and holistically transformed students we hope to let loose on the world once they have spent four or five years on our campuses.

There is not space in this chapter to develop the ways in which this doctrine can serve a United Methodist school's educational purposes, but we can begin to see the possibilities by remembering how the Spirit of God works through sanctifying grace.[30] This aspect of Wesley's teaching helps us focus on the affective or attitudinal or dispositional dimension of education. Wesley's view of the renewal of God's image in humans reminds us that as students develop, their *attitudes* (affections, dispositions, tempers) change as well as their outward behavior.

Considering Wesley's thinking about maturity on this point helps in two ways. First, it reminds educators what we already know, but easily forget in the pressures of the current education environment that places so much emphasis on critical knowledge and skill development. That is, while we are providing content to students and helping them hone

---

[30] A qualification is necessary here. With students who are not Christian, in a Wesleyan framework, God's grace works preveniently. This point needs development to recognize the diversity of student beliefs and attitudes toward religion. Nonetheless, a Wesleyan framework provides very helpful guidance for thinking about the educational mission. Regardless of religious background, students need to develop at the level of the affections along with cognitive knowledge and skill development. Using Wesley's framework, we can shape good citizens across the diversity of religious background.

their skills, we are also shaping their attitudes and dispositions. We are contributing to the emotional tonality of their lives. A campus's ethos teaches by what we emphasize in our institutional self-descriptions and by what we rarely (or never) mention. The holistic view of human nature that the doctrine of Christian perfection envisions challenges us to remember that third dimension of education—the dispositional or affective—that the current education environment tends to overlook. On this point, Wesley's discourses on the Sermon on the Mount, especially the early ones that cover the Beatitudes in Matthew 5, are instructive.[31]

Once we recognize that we are already shaping students' attitudes, then the doctrine of Christian perfection helps further. One of the major scripture references Wesley used to summarize the doctrine comes from Matthew 22:37-40, in which Jesus summarizes the two greatest commandments, to love God and neighbor. In college we spend much time discussing justice, as we should. Pondering Wesley's explication of Christian perfection through this lens would enrich our conversations and provide guidance for programming.[32] In the post-secular environment, such programming would not be limited to individual student development or to campus ministry groups. It could prompt public discussion and collaboration.

The Chaplain: Shepherd to a Particular Faith in a Pluralistic Context Conclusion

What does all this reflection have to do with the role of the chaplain in United Methodist schools? It suggests that, while

---

[31] See John Wesley, *The Works of John Wesley*: Sermons, vol. 1, ed. Albert C. Outler (Nashville: Abingdon, 1984), 466–571.

[32] John Wesley, *The Works of John Wesley:* Sermons, vol. 2, ed. Albert Outler, 99–124. For specific references to Wesley's description of Christian perfection, see John Wesley, *The Works of John Wesley:* Sermons, vol. 2, ed. Outler, 97–124. For Wesley's full defense of the doctrine, see John Wesley, *A Plain Account of Christian Perfection*, in Paul Wesley Chilcote and Kenneth J. Collins, eds., *The Works of John Wesley*, vol. 13, Bicentennial Edition (Nashville: Abingdon, 2012), 132–91.

she or he continues to serve in the expected pastoral and administrative ways, the chaplain does have a broader and more basic educational role to fill, even though it may not mean conventional classroom teaching.[33] Regarding, for example, a school's strategic plan: the chaplain should play an advisory role to senior administrators and trustees to help them understand how the school's identity and theological tradition guide strategic planning. Through presentations and discussions, the chaplain teaches senior leaders how to engage in fundamental reflection on what makes a United Methodist school authentically United Methodist.

With faculty, many schools have new faculty orientations and professional development opportunities. These moments can become means for the chaplain to have input into how faculty think about their work. Even though some graduate programs include training in pedagogy, it still holds true that the vast majority of professors have little or no experience in purposeful reflection and practice with how students learn. They know their disciplines, but what they know about college student development usually comes willy-nilly through experience. The holistic view of the human person that attends to content knowledge, skill, development, *and* what Wesley called the affections—the emotional, moral tonality of learning—expands the palette of teaching tools that professors would bring to the classroom.[34] The chaplain has a significant role to play here. We can offer lunchtime conversations with interested faculty on teaching and learning from a Wesleyan perspective. We can ask

---

[33] However, I believe that chaplains should also teach in the classroom.

[34] Here I admit the friction this causes for professors. They have limited time to teach the content. The idea of changing their patterns to allow for more "student development" through their courses often feels to them like an irrelevant intrusion. Precisely in these kinds of situations chaplains as educators can help professors work through this frustration. The students will benefit, ultimately.

to be made part of the new faculty orientation process. If we think creatively and take initiatives, we can in relatively simple and nonintrusive ways begin to season a school's educational environment.

Chaplains also can teach via student development courses or more informally through relationships with Student Affairs staff. As John Wesley himself was something of a "conjunctive" theologian, synthesizing seemingly disparate systems of thought, chaplains can (and should) do the same. We take the best of student development theory, which is based largely in developmental psychology and supplemented by large-scale sociological research (surveys, inventories, interviews), and we frame it theologically. Again, Wesley's teaching on Christian perfection provides guidance.

These suggested areas of input from the chaplain reveal an ample range of opportunities for how the church's mission could provide guidance to a school's educational mission. In all these ways the chaplain operates from a particular (Wesleyan) theological framework. She or he does so in full view of the diversity of the college community. These possibilities call for a rethinking of the chaplain's role that embeds it more explicitly in the larger educational mission of a school. Where the chaplain already plays this role as an educational leader in United Methodist colleges and universities, we can rejoice. Where it has been limited to (only) certain sectors of the school's activities, we have work to do. By engaging this fundamentally important work, we will do our part in pursuing the church's mission to make disciples of Jesus Christ.

PRACTICAL DIVINITY: PLURALISM IN A LIBERAL ARTS COMMUNITY

Ron Robinson and Erin Simmonds

Introduction

The important work of interfaith engagement has become a context in which college chaplains, campus ministers, faculty, staff, and students are sounding their prophetic voices as they work for peace among diverse constituencies of people. Much of the daily news around the planet involves religious conflict or extremist manifestations of the most negative behaviors. Humans can do better. It is imperative that people of differing religious views find ways to engage each other positively and constructively.

As the religious landscape on college campuses becomes more diverse, religious professionals, faculty, and institutions of higher education seek to address both the needs of the campus and the larger public sphere. For many, the goal of this engagement has become pluralism, commonly defined as the "positive engagement of religious difference."

Those who work, study, and live out of a Wesleyan theological frame are not immune from these interactions. How, then, might those in the Wesleyan tradition—individuals, groups, and institutions—appropriate that tradition in a practical manner that has integrity as they interact across lines of religious difference and move toward healthy, pluralistic relationships?

We offer a two-part response to that important question. This work comes out of our experiences in an academic community at a national liberal arts college affiliated with The United Methodist Church. The first part of our project is to develop a foundation for interfaith engagement from a Wesleyan perspective. This foundation is grounded in an understanding of some of the broad themes articulated by John Wesley, particularly perfect love and true religion. From there we move to presenting tools for interfaith engagement. The first of two tools we offer is a rubric for advancing and evaluating worldview and interfaith engagement, and the second is a quiz that functions as a catalyst for discussions of interfaith literacy and capacity.

This quiz draws upon the developmental nature of the rubric and has been designed for our particular context at Wofford College. It may easily be adapted to other contexts. We seek to present here a practical divinity so cherished by John Wesley: grounded in theology and useful in daily living. We are cowriting this chapter to demonstrate the synthesis of the work of a chaplain and professor of religion (Robinson) and an undergraduate student (Simmonds). Our worlds overlap at both the curricular and cocurricular levels. The important tools found here rest upon a foundation that is both universally human and distinctively Wesleyan.

Wesley and Interfaith Engagement

In the subtitle to her essay "John Wesley as Inter-religious Resource," Rebekah Miles asks the provocative question, "Would you take this man to an interfaith dialogue?"[1]

---

[1] Rebekah L. Miles, "John Wesley as Interreligious Resource: Would You Take This Man To An Interfaith Dialogue?" in *A Great Commission: Christian Hope and Religious Diversity: Papers in Honor of Kenneth Cracknell on His 65th Birthday,* ed. Martin Forward, Stephen Plant, Susan J. White (Bern: Peter Lang, 2000), 61.

Far from being a stellar model for interfaith engagement, Wesley does not come off well if he is judged by twenty-first-century standards. Such a judgment is hardly fair. Judging him by eighteenth-century standards renders a different view. In fact, Wesley often refers to other religions, and speaks of them as using the light given to them. Still, it is important to remember that even though the Enlightenment influenced Wesley, thinkers like Marx, Durkheim, and Weber were not born and therefore would not become influential until as much as a century after Wesley's death. While Wesley critically read thinkers like Kant, Rousseau, Voltaire, Adam Smith, Hume, and others, Tex Sample rightly warns that "Wesley was a person of his time and we should not expect from him ideas and agenda that would come after his time."[2]

John Wesley lived in a time when Christianity ruled the day. There were, to be sure, significant debates among kinds of Christianity, but his worldview was rooted in an overwhelmingly Christian context. Therefore the religious diversity John Wesley primarily addressed had to do with his dealings with Catholics and various Protestants. His sermon on *The Catholic Spirit*[3] is among the most notable examples of this. His irenic disposition toward people of differing Christian communities is demonstrated in this sermon.

Wesley did meet some Jews in Rotterdam, and likely in other places in Britain. He encountered Native Americans during his short time in Georgia, though it seems he had little awareness that they might have had religious commitments of their own. While Wesley claimed to be a person of one book, he in fact

---

[2] Tex Sample, *The Future of John Wesley's Theology: Back to the Future with the Apostle Paul* (Eugene, OR: Cascade Books, 2012), 53.

[3] John Wesley, *The Sermons of John Wesley*, "Catholic Spirit," Sermon 39, http://wesley.nnu.edu/john-wesley/the-sermons-of-john-wesley-1872-edition/sermon-39-catholic-spirit/.

read many books and insisted that his pastors do the same. He knew of Muslims (he called them "Mohamatans") but likely never encountered any. The religious climate of Wesley's eighteenth century was changing, and Wesley addressed some of the changes he saw going on around him. He was oblivious to some others, as was typical of his era. Similarly, the current milieu is witnessing a changing religious landscape. Recent demographic studies note that "Christians decline sharply as share of population; unaffiliated and other faiths continue to grow."[4] The spirit of the time is changing and the times are changing spiritually.

Dr. Martin Luther King Jr. once described Rosa Parks as "victim of both the forces of history and the forces of destiny," and he maintained that she "had been tracked down by the *Zeitgeist*—the spirit of the time."[5] Similarly, anyone who finds himself or herself within the Wesleyan tradition will be aware that the spirit of the time continually tracks him or her down and calls for faithful yet often imaginative and creative interpretations of the theological foundations and commitments of the eighteenth-century Oxford don.

Some years ago, during a conference dealing with the Methodist contribution to the academic study of religions, four British Methodist theologians offered their reflections concerning Wesley and interfaith dialog. They used the term "creative hermeneutic," to describe their thoughts and speculations about Wesley and interfaith. One of the theologians present said she thought of what they were doing as, "inspired guesswork."[6]

---

[4] "America's Changing Religious Landscape." Pew Research Centers Religion Public Life Project RSS (May 11, 2015), http://www.pewforum.org/2015/05/12/americas-changing-religious-landscape/.

[5] Martin Luther King, *Stride toward Freedom: The Montgomery Story* (San Francisco: Harper & Row, 1986), 44.a

[6] Pauline Webbs, foreword to "John Wesley's Premonitions of Inter-Faith Discourse,"

The honesty in this approach is refreshing. To be sure, we don't know how an eighteenth-century John Wesley would behave in our twenty-first-century pluralistic context in which college chaplains, faculty members, students, and administrators find themselves. Beyond the campus, however, the workplace and the public sphere are both much more diverse today than they ever were during Wesley's time. Still, those who find themselves following in that tradition regularly look to John Wesley— and occasionally his brother Charles—for insight and inspiration.

In his tract entitled *Earnest Appeal to Men of Reason and Religion*, John Wesley defines religion as "no other than love, the love of God and of all mankind; the loving God with all our heart and soul and strength, his having first loved us— in the loving every soul which God has made, everyone on earth as our own soul."[7] When one engages in a creative hermeneutic appropriate for the twenty-first century, and when one exegetes the *Zeitgeist*—the spirit of *this* time—it seems incumbent upon that person or group of people to ground themselves in this statement of Wesley's. Of course, the statement itself is a paraphrase of the scriptures. While Wesley read many books, his views were all deeply rooted within scripture and within this particular understanding of the depth and breadth of the love of God. Religion—true religion—for Wesley, necessitates this inseparable love of God and love of neighbor. This statement alone would seem to indicate that a Wesleyan sensibility would include engagement with *all* people, including people of various religious groups or those of no religion at all.

---

in *Pure, Universal Love: Reflections on the Wesleys and Inter-faith Dialogue, Westminster Wesley Series*, vol. 3, by Tim Macquiban, (Oxford: Applied Theology Press, 1995).
[7] John Wesley, "An Earnest Appeal to Men of Reason and Religion," in *The Works of the Reverend John Wesley, A.M., Sometime Fellow of Lincoln College, Oxford*, (New York: J. Emory and B. Waugh for The Methodist Episcopal Church, 1831), 5.

Many have argued that Wesley should be seen not so much as a systematic theologian or an intellectual critic of the religions of the world, but rather as a pastoral theologian. Randy Maddox rightly shows that this characterization of Wesley does not mean that he simply ignored matters of doctrine and only dabbled in theology when it suited his pastoral needs. Still, Maddox is clear that, for Wesley, practical divinity meant that there was no place for a theology that "neglected or undercut the dimension of responsible Christian living."[8]

Miles suggests that Wesley's pastoral turn is both weakness and strength. If one is addressing issues of soteriology, this is true. However, we contend that the pastoral bent of Wesley's theology is indicative of his keen interest in how a Christian lives and brings a distinctive emphasis to the project of interfaith engagement. This way of living, grounded in love of God and love of neighbor, is what he stressed in his sermons and letters. It provides an important imperative for engagement with and treatment of others. Wesley does not ignore doctrinal issues, yet at the same time he stresses the importance of developing one's relational capacities. While much current interfaith work revolves around the practice of dialogue, which is often soteriological in nature, we maintain that the important nugget to be discovered in Wesley is that he strongly sought for—and admonished— people to live a life of love of God and neighbor, and his understanding of neighbor was broad. His was a theology that demanded that people relate in ways that was beyond simple coexistence or tolerance.

Gustav Niebuhr in his book *Beyond Tolerance* quotes Amir Hussein, professor of religious studies at Loyola Marymount University:

---

[8] Randy Maddox, "John Wesley—Practical Theologian?" *Wesleyan Theological Journal* 23 (1988): 133.

There are a great many stereotypes about Islam and Muslims and it is only through dialogue that these will, slowly, be dismantled...The stereotypes that one may have learned, for example that Christians worship three gods and are therefore polytheistic, fall away when one is invited to a Christian worship service and realizes that it is the same one God who is being praised and worshiped.[9]

Niebuhr suggests that the vital word in Hussein's statement is *invited*—made a guest and welcomed.

This kind of intentional work is, of course, vitally important; and the narratives, as Niebuhr observes, go "largely untold—again, especially by the news media."[10] We strongly endorse the continuation and expansion of opportunities where formal hospitality is expressed and where people may experience each other's traditions. Some of the most inspiring narratives and visions of hope come from these gatherings. Even more broadly, the admission of a student or the employment of a faculty or staff member may be understood as an invitation to be part of the respective college or university community. Offering the invitation would seem to presuppose the welcoming of that person's worldview or religious perspective to the institution.

While it is important to note that much interfaith engagement can and does happen beyond formal opportunities, the vital word here is *beyond*—extending into the residence hall, larger campus, workplace, Internet, and public sphere. It is in these arenas that contact may be formal *or* casual, occasional *or* ongoing. It is in these arenas where we seek to share our basic humanity. These are the arenas in which the violence we hear

---

[9] Gustav Niebuhr, *Beyond Tolerance: Searching for Interfaith Understanding in America* (New York: Viking, 2008), 107.
[10] Ibid.

about on the news occurs, arenas in which we make friends, raise our families, and cultivate our deepest relationships. These are the arenas into which we are not so much invited but into which we assert ourselves—arenas where we bump into all sorts of people. How can these opportunities be positive and productive? How can they be places of light and love? As Wesleyan Christians, how do we treat these neighbors whose names and worldview may or may not be known to us? How do we live in this *beyond?*

An ethic of engagement that follows from a welcoming theological footing is necessary not only for the planned meetings but also for the unplanned and uncontrolled environment in which much of life takes place. Further, pluralistic sensibilities—positive engagement with religious difference—may be taught, learned, championed, embraced, and employed without anyone losing the integrity of religious commitments. Indeed, persons can more completely express their own worldview, particularly if it necessitates love of *neighbor,* through opportunities for interfaith engagement. In that regard, it is not a stretch to say that, "Embrace pluralism and interfaith engagement," is a twenty-first century way of saying, "Love your neighbor."

A Rubric and a Quiz

A person, group, or institution with Wesleyan commitments might now ask, "How do we do this? What is our method? How might this be defined or measured? In response to these questions, we wish to present a rubric and a quiz.

We have found the *Pluralism and Worldview Engagement Rubric* to be helpful, (appendix A). The rubric was designed on our campus (Wofford College, a United Methodist-affiliated undergraduate institution) and at Elon University (a private secular university). Also available through the

Creative Commons, the intention is for the rubric to be used by professors as well as cocurricular practitioners. Rather than being narrowly sectarian, the rubric helps "faculty and staff members identify and measure students' learning, growth, and engagement across lines of religious, spiritual, and secular difference."[11] The rubric provides five categories of assessment:

1. Knowledge of own worldview
2. Knowledge of other worldviews
3. Attitudes toward pluralism
4. Interpersonal engagement
5. Interfaith interaction and reflection

The rubric was the result of a two-year collaboration among the two higher education institutions and the Interfaith Youth Core (IFYC) organization. In addition, consultations were held with staff of the Association of American Colleges and Universities (AACU). Each institution piloted the *Campus Religious and Spiritual Climate Survey*, the forerunner of the *Interfaith Diversity Experiences & Attitudes Longitudinal Survey* (IDEALS). In addition, Elon and Wofford participated in multiyear model engagements with the IFYC. The project was funded by a grant from the Teagle Foundation.

Each campus processed survey findings with students, faculty, staff, and administrators, and collaboratively developed the rubric as both a goal-setting instrument and a qualitative evaluative measure of interfaith engagement and pluralism. Like some rubrics, it is read from right to left. The rubric provides descriptions of four levels of achievement (benchmark, milestone 1, milestone 2, and capstone) for each of the five categories. Evaluators determine where an individual

---

[11] Elon University, Interfaith Youth Core, and Wofford College, "Pluralism and Worldview Engagement Rubric," Interfaith Youth Core, http://ifyc.org/resources /pluralism-and-worldview-engagement-rubric.

falls on the rubric in each of the five categories. The benchmark is to the far right and growth is shown as people move to the milestones and then to the capstone level. Already the rubric has been used at numerous campuses across the country to develop campus-wide strategies, assess campus climates and develop interfaith initiatives, develop opportunities for building competence and capacity, and to make interfaith cooperation identifiable and tangible.

We propose this rubric be a tool for professors and cocurricular practitioners to help students assess their level of engagement and their attitude toward pluralism. For those grounded in the Wesleyan tradition, we have shown that pluralism is an important way to love our neighbor. Further we see significant possibility in using this rubric as a guide for developing programming and curriculum that expands opportunities for congregations, communities, and institutions connected with the Wesleyan tradition to engage in positive, loving relationships in a manner that can be prophetic in the culture.

As the rubric shows, an important facet of the positive engagement of difference is knowledge of one's own worldview and the worldview of others, which we term religious literacy. In discussions of interfaith engagement on our campus, we noted that most scholars and students alike agreed that increasing one's knowledge of other worldviews is an essential part of religious pluralism. Thus, we have come to the conclusion that religious ignorance often breeds prejudice, while knowledge and familiarity of religion foment compassion and tolerance and often lead to positive engagement. However, our conversations and research led us to realize that literacy is nuanced: there is religious literacy and there is interfaith literacy. They may overlap, but they are not entirely the same.

One might ask, "What do I need to know in order to positively engage with difference? How do I navigate in this pluralistic society?" We suggest that the first step in fostering a pluralistic worldview is a cultivation of both religious and interfaith literacies. However, this raises several questions: What does it mean to have interfaith and/or religious literacy? How should these be measured? Literacy of a language, for example, can be measured through reading and writing tests. Can interfaith and religious literacy be measured through a similar set of metrics?

We will now turn to three arguments for interfaith and/or religious literacy using models from Stephen Prothero, the Interfaith Youth Core (IFYC), and our own model. We will examine Prothero's and IFYC's respective metrics for testing literacy in an attempt to identify the benefits and shortcomings of their assessment tests. Then, we will present our own model, which we believe to be a synthesis of the Prothero's religious literacy and IFYC's interfaith literacy. In addition, our model will add a new element that is designed to help students self-assess their openness to pluralism and their capacity for positive engagement with difference. Our model, the Interfaith Self-Assessment, can be found at the end of this paper and is intended for students to use to self-assess and to prompt discussion in a classroom or cocurricular setting. We believe that our Interfaith Self-Assessment harnesses the strengths of the quizzes presented by Prothero and IFYC and adds an important unique element to this type of assessment: an assessment of disposition.

Steven Prothero, in *Religious Literacy: What Every American Needs to Know—And Doesn't*, addresses religion in America. He writes, "One of the most religious countries on earth is also a nation of religious illiterates."[12] What he means

---

[12] Stephen Prothero, *Religious Literacy in America: What Every American Needs to Know—and Doesn't* (New York: Harper Collins, 2007), 2.

is that throughout his time teaching undergraduate students at Boston University, he has found that his students tend to be religiously devout but also disconnected from the truths and narratives of their faiths. He also found, through surveys given to his classes and from general discussion, that many Protestant students could not name the four Gospels, that many Catholics did not know the seven sacraments, and that many Jews could not identify the books of the Torah.[13] Thus, Prothero argues, given the prevalence of religious rhetoric in our national civic discourse,[14] Americans must have a basic religious literacy to be engaged citizens. Although Christianity heavily dominates American rhetoric, Prothero believes that a basic religious literacy in the major world religions is a critical skill for all Americans.

What, then, does Prothero identify as the knowledge necessary to be considered religiously literate? Let us turn to Prothero's "Religious Literacy Quiz," which condenses the basic facts Prothero believes a religiously literate person would know.[15] Since Prothero's requisites for religious literacy are based on a person's ability to engage in American public discourse, the majority of the questions on his quiz are related to the Judeo-Christian tradition. In fact, eleven out of fifteen questions are related to Christianity or Judaism. Hinduism, Buddhism, and Islam each appear in one question. One question asks about the religious freedoms guaranteed by the First Amendment. Thus, the quiz is primarily focused on a Christian

---

[13] Ibid., 1.

[14] To illustrate this point, Prothero points to, among other examples, the frequency with which biblical allusions are made in political rhetoric. Within the last ten years, there were four issues debated in Congress that included "Good Samaritan" in the title. Congress repeatedly refers to the "Golden Rule" derived from Christianity as well. See Prothero, *Religious Literacy in America,* 16 for further discussion of this subject.

[15] Prothero, *Religious Literacy in America,* 294–98.

literacy, so that it can determine if Americans are equipped to participate in American discourse, which has been, historically, based on the Christian tradition. Essentially then, Prothero's version of religious literacy is about being fluent in the various Christian references one might encounter living in America, as well as being somewhat adept at understanding basic facts about other major religions. Prothero's religious literacy is about effective citizenship.

We contend that such literacy may be an important aspect of citizenship, but it falls short of a literacy necessary for love of neighbor. A Wesleyan Christian might find this to be a minimal standard, hardly worthy of the deeper commitments Wesley expected of those who were truly religious.

The Interfaith Youth Core presents a different understanding of literacy, which it calls interfaith literacy. The purpose of this literacy is to make Americans better equipped to participate in interfaith engagement. IFYC's overall mission is to make religious pluralism and interfaith engagement a norm on college campuses. Like Prothero, IFYC offers a quiz that is published on their website, which sums up the type of knowledge IFYC considers necessary for interfaith literacy.[16] If Prothero's quiz is a general test of basic knowledge he thinks most Americans do or ought to know, then IFYC's quiz is more of an instructive tool for teaching things it does not necessarily expect Americans to know. The quiz, as creators Cassie Meyer and Carr Harkrader have acknowledged, is a little more difficult than one might expect. IFYC has received some pushback because the questions seem a bit obscure at times.

According to Harkrader, the hope is that the new information presented in the quiz, as well as the detailed

---

[16] Cassie Meyer and Cara Harkrader, "Interfaith Literacy Quiz" (Interfaith Youth Core), http://ifyc.org/quiz/literacy.

and instructional answers provided, "will encourage [quiz-takers] to keep reading more about [interfaith engagement]. Hopefully it will slightly challenge people to keep learning about it."[17] Thus, the purpose of IFYC's quiz diverges from that of Prothero. As Harkrader said, the quiz is designed to be an interactive learning and teaching tool rather than an actual measure of interfaith literacy. In addition, it focuses on the history of interfaith engagement in America and appreciative knowledge of other religions. As Meyer emphasized, the quiz demonstrates that interfaith engagement has precedence in American history and that people of diverse faiths have made positive contributions to American society.[18]

Accordingly, IFYC is committed to promoting a vision of interfaith literacy. Founder Eboo Patel and Cassie Meyer have worked extensively to define interfaith literacy, to advocate for its relevance, and to create basic curricula and tools for teaching interfaith literacy. They write in an article for *Journal of College and Character*:

> We understand interfaith literacy as the type of knowledge that builds positive attitudes and relationships and ultimately contributes to civic good. Within this, we see four main topics for exploration:
>
> 1. Theologies or ethics of "interfaith cooperation"
>
> 2. Appreciative knowledge of diverse religious traditions
>
> 3. Shared values between diverse religious traditions
>
> 4. The history of interfaith cooperation[19]

---

[17] Carr Harkrader, interview by Erin Simmonds, May 1, 2015.

[18] Cassie Meyer, interview by Erin Simmonds, April 29, 2015.

[19] Eboo Patel and Cassie Meyer, "Interfaith Cooperation on Campus: Teaching Interfaith Literacy," *Journal of College and Character* 12, no. 4 (December 2011): 2–6.

Given these areas of exploration, the IFYC interfaith literacy quiz is quite fitting. Its questions work to teach about these areas of knowledge, in particular the final three areas of exploration. Meyer said, in a personal interview, that the quiz on the website is intended to be a jumping-off point for people interested in interfaith engagement but do not know where to begin.[20] As Harkrader noted, IFYC was trying to create an interactive learning/teaching tool that had the same appeal as a fun Internet quiz but was also academic in nature.[21] However, the interfaith literacy quiz has also received some criticism since its publication. According to Meyer, some critics were dismayed by the lack of female representation on the quiz; only one question is about a female religious leader. Others have pointed out that the quiz works with a body of knowledge from a period in history (the 1950s–2000s) that does not seem to be effective for college students. Given that IFYC's mission is to create interfaith engagement on college campuses, choosing questions from a period through which current college students neither lived nor did they likely learn about in history, seems to be misguided or ineffective.[22]

Both IFYC and Prothero argue for different kinds of literacy based on different grounds. Prothero believes religious literacy is necessary to be an engaged American citizen. IFYC believes interfaith literacy is the first step in their normative goal of making religious pluralism a norm on college campuses, and in America more broadly. Thus, Prothero's quiz adequately addresses his take on the subject. For Prothero,

---

[20] Meyer, interview, April 29, 2015.
[21] Harkrader interview, May 1, 2015.
[22] This was my (Simmonds) criticism of the quiz, which I mentioned to both Meyer and Harkrader. Both acknowledged that this was a fair criticism, and one they had not previously heard. Harkrader did say that the quiz is also used by faculty and other educators, not solely college students, which may help explain this issue.

active citizenship requires certain knowledge; his quiz asks questions about that knowledge and would be a fair barometer for measuring a person's religious literacy as defined by Prothero. Conversely, IFYC's quiz is a bit more complicated. Although both Meyer and Harkrader have stated that the quiz measurement of interfaith is more a tool to teach interfaith literacy than a measure of interfaith literacy, the fact remains that quizzes are designed to test and assess.

The major flaw in both the Prothero and IFYC quizzes is that they fall prey to a criticism stated by Meyer and Eboo Patel in an article about religious literacy. They write, "It seems that doing well on a quiz that covers just the facts does not determine how one will interact with those of different backgrounds."[23] The writers of this paper, like Patel and Meyer support the notion that religious literacy or interfaith literacy—alone or together—are insufficient indicators of a person's disposition towards interfaith engagement. Interfaith literacy, knowing about interfaith engagement (the theologies and histories of pluralism, the shared values of religious traditions, and so on), is an important part of religious pluralism.

However, there is an additional step to religious pluralism, which we are calling interfaith capability. Literacy, on the one hand, is purely about knowledge—how much do you know? How fluent are you in this subject? It is a cognitive exercise. Capability, on the other hand, is about disposition and orientation—how open are you? How likely are you to engage effectively with others? Capability is relational, cognitive, and affective. By capability, we are not referring to an inherent, unchanging trait with which someone is born. Rather, capability is seen as a potential, which may or may not be altered

---

[23] Patel and Meyer, "Interfaith Cooperation on Campus: Teaching Interfaith Literacy," 3.

throughout the course of an individual's life. Capability, then, really refers to skill level and disposition. Although interfaith and religious literacy are important elements in effective interfaith engagement, interfaith engagement is about more than knowledge. Interfaith engagement requires empathy, compassion, and openness. Indeed, the Wesleyan emphasis on perfect love—the love of neighbor, is an important, if not primary, aspect of positive interfaith engagement. How can a quiz judge this? How could these traits be measured? We argue that the literacy tests proposed by Prothero and IFYC are limited in their ability to measure religious tolerance, compassion, or pluralism. Thus, we offer the *Interfaith Self-Assessment* (appendix B), which combines the work of some religious scholars and includes questions of our own making.

In creating our assessment, we used the *Pluralism and Worldview Engagement Rubric* as a foundation. The rubric is an effective method of measuring actual interfaith engagement, which is comprised of interfaith literacy *and* interfaith capability. However, the limit of the rubric is that it is, as some of our students have observed, not terribly interesting or interactive. Moreover, the rubric presents fairly abstract conditions required to fulfill each category and it would be at the discretion of the evaluator or the self-testing individual to make a judgment about the various criteria. This may work well for evaluators but is neither efficient nor memorable to students. Unlike the religious/interfaith literacy quizzes, there are not right and wrong answers, no way to score points, and no concrete examples. The rubric does provide a solid foundation for assessing the likelihood of an individual to engage in religious pluralism. Therefore, we used the rubric as the underlying framework of a new quiz that addresses both interfaith literacy and interfaith capability.

We offer a new quiz, based on Prothero's quiz, the IFYC quiz, and the *Pluralism and Worldview Engagement Rubric.*

Combining questions from Prothero and IFYC, as well as adding our own questions, we call this new quiz, the *Interfaith Self-Assessment*. It is an attempt to include both disposition and knowledge in one simple test. In the disposition question section, there are four responses, each of which corresponds to a category on the *Pluralism and Worldview Rubric*. Responses that align with the capstone category are worth four points, milestone responses are worth three and two points, and benchmark responses are worth one point. The literacy questions each have different point values, which are explained in the answer key.

The focus of this quiz, designed by an undergraduate, is on the experiences of college students; most of the disposition questions are geared toward college experiences. Further research could apply psychological testing to this type of quiz. The Interfaith Self-Assessment is intended to be a model or suggestion for a future, more researched option. The benefits of this quiz, we believe, are that (1) it includes both literacy and capability for positive relationships with difference, (2) it addresses theism and atheism, and (3) it mentions a variety of different religions. In addition, this quiz is not a personality quiz that identifies inherent, unchanging aspects of personality, like those of StrengthsQuest or Myers-Briggs. Rather, it is a developmental quiz that could be retaken at different points in an individual's life, with the distinct possibility that he or she would score higher as they progress through the categories of the Pluralism and Worldview Engagement Rubric and as they become more familiar with interfaith engagement and religious pluralism. It can be a good barometer for interfaith literacy and capability until a better metric is in place.

Conclusion

We contend that the current *zeitgeist* on a liberal arts campus calls for interfaith engagement with a pluralistic ethic. People influenced by the Wesleyan theological tradition have not only sufficient justification but also an imperative to be part of this movement. We are aware that there may be concerns to be addressed, particularly soteriological ones, but this in no way precludes the positive treatment of the neighbor. We are also aware that there are people of good will as well as people of devious intent. The former are candidates for positive engagement of difference and merit our reaching out to them as they may similarly be reaching out to us. As people who seek to love our neighbor, we seek to align ourselves with people of good will. In doing so we can, with Wesley, extend our hands despite our differences. Interfaith engagement, then, becomes an act of witness and an act of love.

As one veteran of interfaith work so aptly put it: "I am called as a Christian to stand in the witness box, but I am not asked to sit on the judgment seat."[24] This sensibility seems solidly Wesleyan *and* appropriate to the world of liberal arts. Accordingly, hermeneutics grounded in love of God and love of neighbor equips those who align themselves with the Wesleyan tradition to make quite suitable companions whenever and wherever the varieties of faiths are engaged positively.

---

[24] Tim Macquiban, "John Wesley's Premonitions of Inter-Faith Discourse," in *Pure, Universal Love: Reflections on the Wesleys and Inter-faith Dialogue, Westminster Wesley Series*, vol. 3 (Oxford: Applied Theology Press, 1995), 7.

APPENDIX A

PLURALISM AND WORLDVIEW ENGAGEMENT RUBRIC

Evaluators may assign a zero to any sample or body of evidence that does not meet the benchmark (cell one) level.

	Capstone 4	Milestone 3	Milestone 2	Benchmark 1
Knowledge of Own Worldview	Situates own evolving worldview within a pluralistic context.	Reflects upon and clarifies own worldview in pluralistic context.	Recognizes own worldview within context of external processes (e.g., personal history and social norms) and how processes shape life choices.	Articulates personal worldview and how it impacts own life.
Knowledge of Other Worldviews	Articulates knowledge of multiple worldviews with appreciative and nuanced understanding.	Understands that worldviews are dynamic and have multiple expressions.	Recognizes traditions, practices, beliefs, and values of other worldviews within cultural context.	Articulates basic traditions, practices, beliefs, and/or values of some other worldviews.
Attitudes toward Pluralism	Committed to navigating complexities, ambiguities, and contradictions among worldviews, including own, with the goal of fostering pluralism.	Willing to be vulnerable and uncertain when grappling with tensions among worldviews and inherent in pluralism.	Open to engaging differences among worldviews.	Open to exploring similarities among worldviews.
Interpersonal Engagement	Adept at interfaith dialogue among diverse participants. Able to navigate differences among participants to foster pluralistic ethos.	Thoughtful about asking and responding to questions to deepen understanding when conversing with those of different worldviews.	Sensitive to those who hold other worldviews while learning to navigate reactions of self and others.	Somewhat self-aware and empathetic when discussing own views with those who hold different views.
Interfaith Action and Reflection	Creates and sustains formal and informal opportunities for ongoing interfaith action and dialogue. Ongoing reflection yields new insights for overcoming challenges to pluralism.	Seeks out formal and informal opportunities for interfaith action and dialogue and readily reflects on the impact of such activities on self and others.	Engages in formal and/or informal interfaith action and dialogue and, when prompted, reflects on impact of participation.	Participates in formal opportunities to engage in interfaith action and dialogue when prompted (e.g., through requirement or extra credit) with little or no reflection.

The development of this rubric was supported by a grant from the Teagle Foundation. For more information please visit www.ifyc.org/teaching-interfaith or e-mail rubric@ifyc.org. Pluralism and Worldview Engagement Rubric by Elon University, Interfaith Youth Core, Wofford College is licensed under a Creative Commons Attribution.

The development of this rubric was supported by a grant from the Teagle Foundation. For more information please visit www.ifyc.org/teaching-interfaith_or e-mail rubric@ifyc .org. Pluralism and Worldview Engagement Rubric by Elon University, Interfaith Youth Core, Wofford College is licensed under a Creative Commons Attribution.

Pluralism, for the purposes of this rubric, involves a positive engagement with diverse religious, spiritual, and secular worldviews in order to gain understanding of differences. Pluralism requires neither relativism nor full agreement; rather, it requires understanding and meaningful interaction among people with differing worldviews.[25]

Worldview, for the purposes of this rubric, is a commitment to a religious, spiritual, or secular tradition that informs an individual's tenets, values, and meaning-making. While we recognize the expansive nature of the term worldview, we choose this term intentionally to challenge presuppositions of and to broaden the conversation in higher education about religion, faith, and pluralism. For example, in many cultures, the dividing lines among one's economic, political, and religious worldviews might be quite blurry or even nonexistent.

Rationale

Higher education often aspires to create global citizens. To that end, students must have knowledge and experience with diverse religious, spiritual, and secular worldviews in order to navigate effectively our increasingly pluralistic nation and world. Research demonstrates that when a diverse society finds ways to bring people of different backgrounds together

---

[25] See Diana Eck, "What is Pluralism." Available at http://pluralism.org/pages /pluralism/what_is_pluralism.

in intentional ways, the community is more resilient and strengthened by its diversity; in addition to social cohesion, creativity and productivity are likely to increase for that community.[26] Diversity initiatives in higher education tend to focus on key components of social location such as race, class, and gender; this rubric extends the conversations to another social indicator, that of religious identity. The ideas might be difficult, the terms might be contested, but the conversations are crucial.

Potential Uses

This rubric is designed to help faculty and staff members identify and measure students' learning, growth, and engagement across lines of religious, spiritual, and secular difference, and it is intended for use in curricular and/or cocurricular initiatives. The five criteria are not listed hierarchically, but movement toward a higher level in one area is likely to promote and encourage growth in the others. Further, all five criteria might not be relevant to every piece of evidence and several pieces of evidence together might be more effective in gauging student progress than individual assignments or experiences alone. The rubric is intended to stimulate conversation and is most effective when adapted to suit institutional context (e.g., graduate or undergraduate, private or public). This rubric is not intended as a grading tool, but instead as a tool for assessment of student learning and development goals. The rubric may also serve as a guide for thinking strategically about institutional goals and charting institutional progress.

---

[26] Robert D. Putnam, "*E pluribus unum:* Diversity and community in the 21st century," *Scandinavian Political Studies* 20 no. 2 (2007). Retrieved from http://www.abdn.ac.uk /sociology/notes07/Level4/SO4530/Assigned-Readings/Reading%209%20(new).pdf.

Glossary

The definitions that follow were developed to clarify
terms and concepts used in this rubric only.

Interpersonal engagement: Formal and informal interactions with people of different worldviews that foster appreciative knowledge, meaningful encounters, and conflict avoidance or resolution.[27]

Appreciative understanding: The accurate and positive knowledge one holds about a religious, spiritual, or secular worldview, in contrast to inaccurate or selective negative knowledge. Also called interfaith literacy.[28]

Interfaith: Inclusive term for the potential interaction among people representing the vast diversity of worldviews.

Interfaith action / cooperation: Meaningful encounters among people of diverse worldviews with a focus on civic action or issues of shared social concern.[29]

Interfaith dialogue: Conversation among individuals of diverse worldviews that reveals commonalities and real differences, increases understanding of each worldview, and builds relationships among participants.

---

[27] Ashutosh Varshney, "Ethnic Conflict and Civil Society: India and Beyond," *World Politics* 53 (2001): 362–98. http://muse.jhu.edu/journals/world_politics/v053/53.3varshney.html.

[28] Eboo Patel and Cassie Meyer, "'Interfaith Cooperation on Campus': Teaching Interfaith Literacy." *Journal of College and Character* 12, no. 4 (2012): 1–7. http://works.bepress.com/ifyc/.

[29] Eboo Patel and Cassie Meyer, introduction to "'Interfaith Cooperation on Campus': Interfaith Cooperation as an Institution-Wide Priority." http://www.degruyter.com/view/j/jcc.2011.12.issue-2/jcc.2011.12.2.1794/jcc.2011.12.2.1794.xml.

APPENDIX B

Interfaith Self-Assessment[30]

Erin Simmonds

Answer each of the following questions as accurately as possible. Refer to the answer key to calculate your score.

1. You are in a religion class and a heated disagreement arises. What are you most likely to do?

   A. Invite each person to speak one at a time and allow others time to respond respectfully.
   B. Weigh the options but be firm in your own opinion.
   C. Keep your own opinion in mind, but listen to everyone else also.
   D. Admit that you don't know the answer, but are willing to hear everyone out.

2. There's a new international student at your school and she's wearing a hijab. You hear someone make a comment about it. What are you most likely to do?

   A. You don't laugh along with the joke; you don't think it's funny, but you don't say anything to anyone about it.
   B. Criticize the person who made the joke. You don't approve of bullying, and it's not cool that someone would tease a person who looks different.
   C. Join in on the joke.

---

[30] This assessment is intended for distribution and use. Published by The General Board of Higher Education and Ministry, The United Methodist Church. "Interfaith Self-Assessment," Erin Simmonds.

D. Tell the person who made the joke how and why they are being offensive. Explain, if you know, what a hijab is and why Muslim women wear it.

3. Your athletic team wants to hold a weekly Bible study. Your faith is not the same as most of your teammates. What are you most likely to do?

A. Just go along to the Bible study so that you can be part of the team bonding experience. It will look bad if you don't join in.
B. Decline to go, but don't tell anyone why you don't want to be there.
C. Decline to go, but let everyone know that you feel this Bible study is not inclusive to everyone on the team.
D. Go to the Bible study but make it clear that you don't want to be there by picking fights and arguing with your teammates.

4. Your school's interfaith religious group is holding a multicultural event. Which of the following might describe your experience with the event?

A. You ran the event.
B. You went to the whole event, watched student performances, and visited all the multicultural booths.
C. You went to the event, but you stuck around for the free food and free T-shirts.
D. You didn't go to the event and you maybe joked with your friends about why it was kind of dumb.

5. Your friend tells you that she is an atheist. How would you respond?

A. You tell her she is a godless heathen and that she is going to hell.

B. You think she's just confused; she'll come around in the end.

C. You admit to her you don't know much about atheism and it's hard for you to understand.

D. You tell her that she is free to be whatever she wants to be and that you hope you'll continue to talk about your mutual beliefs in the future.

6. Have you ever attended a religious service outside of your own faith?

A. Often

B. Somewhat often

C. Seldom

D. Never

7. Do you have many friends who have different religious beliefs or worldviews than you?

A. Most of my friends believe different things than me.

B. Some of my friends believe different things than me.

C. A few of my friends believe different things than me.

D. All of my friends believe pretty much the same thing as me.

Literacy Questions

1. Name four of Jesus' disciples.

2. Name a country in which Hinduism is practiced.

3. What is the name of the holy book of Judaism? With which other religion does Judaism share that holy text?

4. With which religion is the Dalai Lama associated? With which country is he associated?

5. Name the German monk who began the Protestant Reformation.

6. Adherents of which faith celebrate Ramadan?

7. Adherents of which faith celebrate Passover?

8. Which American president once said, "Tolerance implies no lack of commitment to one's own beliefs. Rather it condemns the oppression or persecution of others."?

A. Jimmy Carter
B. John F. Kennedy
C. George W. Bush
D. Bill Clinton

9. Mother Teresa was an advocate for the rights of the poor and ill, especially in India. In her many hospices, people from a variety of religions were treated and the hospices were places of multifaith prayer and support. What tradition was Mother Teresa?

    A. Protestant
    B. Muslim
    C. Hindu
    D. Roman Catholic

10. Which tradition's core principles include beliefs in "the inherent worth and dignity of every person;" "a free and responsible search for truth and meaning;" and, "the goal of world community with peace, liberty, and justice for all"?

    A. Mormonism
    B. Scientology
    C. Universal Unitarianism
    D. Secular Humanism

11. Which modern religious leader once said, "The time has come for religious leaders to cooperate more effectively in the work of healing wounds, resolving conflicts, and pursuing peace. Peace is the sure sign of a commitment to the cause of God. Religious leaders are called to be men and women of peace. They are capable of fostering the culture of encounter and peace, when other options fail or falter."?

    A. Patriarch Bartholomew I
    B. Pope Francis
    C. Billy Graham
    D. The Dalai Lama

12. Mahatma Gandhi, a voice for interfaith harmony, once wrote, "I offer you peace. I offer you love. I offer you friendship. I see your beauty. I hear your need. I feel your feelings. My wisdom flows from the Highest Source. I salute that Source in you. Let us work together for unity and love." Gandhi was a leader of which religion?

A. Buddhism
B. Sikhism
C. Hinduism
D. Christianity

APPENDIX C

Interfaith Self-Assessment Answer Key

Score your answers to each question and then multiply your point value by 2. This will give you your score out of 100 percent.

1. You are in a religion class and a disagreement arises. What do you do?
   A. 4 points
   B. 1 point
   C. 2 points
   D. 3 points

2. There's a new international student at your school and she's wearing a hijab. You hear someone make a comment about it. What do you do?
   A. 2 points
   B. 3 points
   C. 1 point
   D. 4 points

3. Your athletic team wants to hold a weekly Bible study. Your faith is not the same as most of your teammates. What do you do?
   A. 1 point
   B. 3 points
   C. 4 points
   D. 2 points

4. Your school's chapter of IFYC is holding a multicultural event. Which of the following best describes your experience with the event?
A. 4 points
B. 3 points
C. 2 points
D. 1 point

5. Your friend tells you that she is an atheist. How do you respond?
A. 1 point
B. 2 points
C. 3 points
D. 4 points

6. Have you ever attended a religious service outside of your own faith?

A. 4 points
B. 3 points
C. 2 points
D. 1 point

7. Do you have many friends who have different religious beliefs or worldviews than you?
A. 4 points
B. 3 points
C. 2 points
D. 1 points

Literacy Questions

1. Name four of Jesus' disciples. (1 point per disciple, up to 4 points)

Simon Peter, Andrew, James, John, Philip, Bartholomew, Thomas, Matthew, James, Thaddeus, Simon, Judas Iscariot, Nathanael, Jude.

Note: The names of all the disciples are not consistent throughout the four Gospels, thus there are fourteen acceptable answers to this question.

2. Name a country in which Hinduism is practiced. (1 point if you named a country listed)

India, Nepal, Mauritius, Fiji, Guyana, Bhutan, Trinidad and Tobago, Suriname, Sri Lanka, Kuwait, United Arab Emirates.

Note: Hinduism is practiced in many countries throughout the world, including the United States. However, these are the countries in which at least 10 percent of the population practices Hinduism.

3. What is the name of the holy book of Judaism? With which other religion does it share that holy text? (1 point for each question, 2 points total)

The book is called the Torah or Pentateuch. It is shared with Christianity, comprising the first five books of the Old Testament.

4. With which religion is the Dalai Lama associated? With which country is he associated? (1 point for each question, 2 points total)

He is Buddhist. He is associated with Tibetan Buddhism.

5. Name the German monk who began the Protestant Reformation. (1 point)
Martin Luther

6. Adherents of which faith celebrate Ramadan? (1 point)
Islam

7. Adherents of which faith celebrate Passover? (1 point)
Judaism

8. Which American president once said, "Tolerance implies no lack of commitment to one's own beliefs. Rather it condemns the oppression or persecution of others."? (2 points)
B. John F. Kennedy

9. Mother Teresa was an advocate for the rights of the poor and ill, especially in India. In her many hospices, people from a variety of religions were treated and the hospices were places of multi-faith prayer and support. What tradition was Mother Teresa? (2 points)
D. Roman Catholic

10. Which tradition's core principles include beliefs in "the inherent worth and dignity of every person;" "a free and responsible search for truth and meaning;" and, "the goal of world community with peace, liberty, and justice for all"? (2 points)
C. Universal Unitarianism

11. Which modern religious leader once said, "The time has come for religious leaders to cooperate more effectively in the work of healing wounds, resolving conflicts, and pursuing peace. Peace is the sure sign of a commitment to the cause of God. Religious leaders are called to be men and women of peace. They are capable of fostering the culture of encounter and peace, when other options fail or falter."? (2 points)

B. Pope Francis

12. Mahatma Gandhi, a voice for interfaith harmony, once wrote, "I offer you peace. I offer you love. I offer you friendship. I see your beauty. I hear your need. I feel your feelings. My wisdom flows from the Highest Source. I salute that Source in you. Let us work together for unity and love." Gandhi was a leader of which religion? (2 points)

C. Hinduism

RACISM

Systemic Racism: Making Room for Emerging Narratives as the Spirit Gives Utterance

How Is It with Your Soul? Developing a Liberatory Consciousness through Dialogue in Campus Ministries

Systemic Racism: Making Room for Emerging Narratives as the Spirit Gives Utterance

Sheila Bates

Not everything that is faced can be changed, but nothing can be changed until it is faced.

—*James Baldwin*

Introduction

I have taken my time in writing my chapter of this book, feeling a bit silenced and powerless. I could blame it on procrastination, but that would only be partly true. The truth is, the recent media impact and blatant conversations around racial injustice have me pondering the significance of faith, power, and structure within an academic setting. I believe Wesley Foundation directors and college chaplains are on the cutting edge of ministry and, through their work and the lens of their students, have the ability to affect the future of a "united" United Methodist Church.

As I write, I am personally reminded of my own inability to express my voice without anger, disappointment, and frustration at a system that seems to be unwilling to acknowledge the narratives and voices of black and brown bodies that need to be heard. As I sit here pondering the 2013 statistical data, which states over 90 percent of the members of The United

Methodist (UMC) are white[1], I also consider how this impacts higher education. I am narrowly writing for those (chaplains, Wesley directors, student leaders, churches, and communities) interested in developing an ethnically diversified collegiate ministry, where the "shape of . . . different communities and the theologies that arise from them are not determined by [the] common affirmation that 'Jesus is Lord,'"[2] but instead seek to understand "story [as] the history of individuals coming together in the struggle to shape life according to commonly held values."[3]

Through the recent statistics and personal experience, I understand the need for the eleven Historical Black College and Universities and the Black College Fund of the UMC. But I also wonder about the students of color who chose to embark upon an education provided by PWI (Predominantly White Institutions) and the space these institutions create for the development of their students' faith and leadership. I have visited a variety of higher education institutions with Wesley Foundations. As I view the surroundings, I find very few students of color. I know they are on campus, because I passed a multitude while touring the grounds, but I ask myself, "Where are they in worship, within the pictures displayed for mission and community service projects, serving not being served?" Most important, I ask, "Where are they in leadership?"

This Is Not the Kingdom of God

As I write and prepare for pushback, I am also reminded of Rev. Dr. Kim Cape's[4] 2015 message on racial injustice, gun violence, and terrorist attacks, where she confidently summed up

---

[1] http://www.umc.org/gcfa/data-services-statistics.
[2] James H. Cone, *God of the Oppressed* (Maryknoll, NY: Orbis, 1997), 92.
[3] Ibid., 93.
[4] Rev. Dr. Kim Cape is General Secretary of the General Board of Higher Education and Ministry of The United Methodist Church.

our conflicted society by stating: "This is not the Kingdom of God."[5] The James Baldwin quotation that opens this chapter also speaks from a place of intellectual prowess and authority, emphasizing that emerging narratives can no longer be dismissed and relegated to "the back of the bus." So here I am, writing as someone who has personal experience with racial profiling and injustice. And this experience leads me to believe that by denying positions of power and access within our own Wesley Foundations and chapels to those of a different class, culture, race, sex, or gender, we, perhaps unwittingly, contribute to a cyclical narrative that continues to proclaim: "This is not the Kingdom of God."

So I write, while pointing a finger at those in power who do little to shape the academic environment, where college students have the opportunity to think outside the boundaries of their personal traditions and experiences to benefit their faith and leadership formation. I write, because the desire to tell one's own story is part and parcel of what it means to be human and because to deny students the opportunity to share their story in faith-based contexts robs them.

I believe within every United Methodist institution of higher education and within every Wesley Foundation, campus ministers and chaplains have the shared duty to provide a theological space for an array of diverse students to "express and participate in the miracle of moving from nothing to something, from nonbeing to being"[6] through sharing their own emerging narratives. This may be countercultural in some power structures, so it takes *courage*. I write for those who are willing to commit to the challenge of helping create a new system focused on racial inclusion.

---

[5] Rev. Dr. Kim Cape, "In Defense of the Inn Keeper" (lecture, Advent Worship, Upper Room, Nashville, December 15, 2015).
[6] Cone, *God of the Oppressed*, 93.

This chapter has three key points, beginning first with a discussion of diversity and inclusion, while touching on the importance of narrative theology characterized by the voices of people of color (POC) affirming the significance of Howard Thurman's "working paper," and the importance of telling "our" stories. Second, this paper will discuss systemic racism from a womanish perspective by utilizing narrative and womanist theologians to discuss how systems of racism hinder emerging voices from coming into existence. Third, this paper, through a variety of interpersonal narratives, will show the invisible culture that underlines the collegiate and religious framework and how it allows the voices of faith and the witness of leadership to remain unheard. This line of reasoning is not for the faint of heart, because this paper calls for considerable reflection and issues an invitation for readers to give serious thought to the theological, pedagogical, and ontological implications of the assumptions of how many of our collegiate systems, suppress the narratives, traditions, and experiences of ethnic minority groups.

Narrative Theology and Howard Thurman's "Working Paper"

According to the book *Faith, Morality, and Civil Society,* narrative theology promises to firmly connect Christian ethics to local congregations, where individual persons are shaped into the people of God by the stories they hear and retell.[7] When narrative theology is incorporated into systems and used to realign persons' lived experiences within a culture or community, it has the power to transition conversations from a "them" to "us" attitude, while dismantling political correctness.

---

[7] Dale McConkey and Peter Augustine Lawler. *Faith, Morality, and Civil Society.* (Lanham, MD: Lexington Books, 2003).

In 2012, worldwide consumers spent over sixty-two billion dollars on movies,[8] illustrating society's fascination with the power of story. Stories are recapped on the news, evident on social media, and shared daily at the water cooler; but storytelling is not narrative theology. As a Wesley Foundation Director, I and the students would host Testimony Tuesday every semester. This was one of the most widely attended events where students would share their narrative with their peers. Focused on God, students deeply connected through their shared experiences and through their openness discussed how God shaped and transformed their lives through the power of another. In these moments, students recapped joy and pain-filled experiences that had a divine influence on their purpose in life. This event helped guide students to create and develop other Wesley Ministries based upon the cultural context and needs of the campus community.

My experience shows that this type of dialogue and format can greatly impact students. Roger Schank, a cognitive psychologist, writes that we interpret reality through our stories and open our realities up to others when we tell our stories. It is only when others are willing to hear, respond, and be open to seeing society as a community of selves as it pertains to race relations; because, we do not only live among other selves, but they live in us and we in them.[9]

The rhetorical power of narrative is a part of our Wesleyan heritage and manifested itself at the beginning of the Methodist

---

[8] David Lieberman, *"Worldwide Consumers Spent $62.4B On Movies In 2012, Up 2.1%,"* January 21, 2013. http://deadline.com/2013/01/worldwide-consumer-spending-movies-409050/. IHS Screen Digest Cross Platform Movie Market Monitor. The increase indicates that global consumer spending for movies "is recovering after declines across 2008 and 2009, with spending forecast to continue to rise by 2 to 3 percent every year from 2013 to 2016," IHS says. North America is still the no. 1 region, accounting for 41 percent of worldwide movie spending.

[9] Richard H. Niebuhr, "The Story of Our Life," in *Readings in Narrative Theology: Why Narrative?* (Eugene: Wipf and Stock 1997), 34.

movement. John Wesley, along with his brother Charles, recognized and incorporated the rhetorical power of narrative:

> Narratives were built into activities of the Methodist communities. For example . . . John and Charles Wesley would travel around to different communities carrying with them letters of spiritual experience to inspire believers. The formal event for sharing letters was the letter-day service where reading letters replaced preaching [and] Thomas Albin describes letter-days saying: The noetic focus of the letter-day was the increased awareness of the variety of ways that God was at work in the world. The practice was simple and profound as the people heard new things. . . . The affective focus was to increase members' desire for a deeper relationship with God and their trust in God's providential work throughout the world. [10]

The focal point of the Methodist movement was salvation, but education, leadership, faith formation were closely linked to it. And I would argue that narrative *about* the Wesleyan movement was also responsible for the movement's success. John Wesley was keen to educate and train leaders to spread the message of salvation, but he also famously founded schools. As Melanie Overton, Assistant General Secretary–Schools, Colleges, and Universities, General Board of Higher Education and Ministry says:

> We in the United Methodist education network like to tell the story of how John Wesley founded the Kingswood School in Bristol, England, to give the children of local coal miners a quality education so that they could

---

[10] Amy Caswell Bratton, *Witnesses of Perfect Love: Narratives of Christian Perfection in Early Methodism*. (Toronto: Clements Publishing, 2014), 42.

aspire to Cambridge and Oxford. Indeed, the learners served by this school were not wealthy, nor did they have access to whatever cultural capital was the currency of the day. Yet, the Kingswood School endeavored to recognize and enlarge each student's genius. We often say that the animating vision for Methodist involvement in education was to serve disadvantaged students. Certainly, United Methodist-related institutions faithfully live out this vision today. But, the underlying value is really to provide a high-quality, church-related education to all people. All people.[11]

Wesley viewed education as access for *all* people, giving them the ability to open a door to a loving God with one's heart and mind. We, as his heirs, should also strive to live into that ethos, recognizing when people share their mutual faith traditions and experiences, all can see themselves in God's greater story. It seems clear that if some stories are excluded or silenced, because they don't coincide with a majority view, the fuller implications of God's story cannot be known. Homi Bhabha suggests:

> [In order] to reconstitute the discourse of cultural difference [it] demands not simply a change of cultural contents and symbols . . . it requires a radical revision of the social temporality in which emergent histories may be written . . . [and] cultural identities may be inscribed.[12]

The impact of narrative theology is significant as a means of finding oneself in God's story and our Christian family as

---

[11] Melanie B. Overton, *Fulfilling the Great Commission through Education* in *Conversations Leading United Methodist-related Schools, Colleges, and Universities*, ed. M. Kathryn Armistead and Melanie Overton, (Nashville: General Board of Higher Education and Ministry, The United Methodist Church, 2015).

[12] Homi Bhabha, *The Location of Culture* (London: Routledge, 2004), 246.

told by the church. Consider your family stories recapped and retold around the table during holiday dinners or other events. These family stories substantiate themes of hope, struggle, and success that we share as a part of our leadership and faith formation. But even if our family doesn't share stories, we, as individuals, all have at least one story to share, whether positive or negative, that gives substance to our goals, dreams, and accomplishments. We may not realize that we are "doing theology" when we tell these stories, but, underneath the plot, runs a current of God's activity in the world.

These stories are a part of who we are. In fact, as we tell them, we can say that these stories also shape us as they serve as an interpretation of our meaning, our being.[13] Narrative theology is a tool, which can be used to help build community, foster relationships, and create an environment where we can thrive together. For me, narrative theology, "taking into account its very wide borders,"[14] is a discourse about God in the setting of story. Narrative (in its narrow sense) can become the decisive construct for understanding and interpreting faith.[15] For example, in our faith communities, the church recounts the story of Jesus Christ throughout the year but more specifically at Christmas and Easter. The many shared narratives, rituals, and traditions that surround the miracle of Incarnation hold a significant part of our human history and continue to have a far reaching and global impact. The stories of John Wesley, Martin Luther King Jr., Sojourner Truth, Dietrich Bonhoeffer, and countless others

---

[13] Sharing stories is a well-known pedagogical device. See: Stanley Hauerwas, "The Story of Our Life," in *Why Narrative? Readings in Narrative Theology*, ed. Stanley Hauerwas and L. Gregory Jones (Grand Rapids, MI: Eerdmans, 1989), 23.

[14] Gabriel J. Fackre, *"Narrative Theology: an Overview," Interpretation* 37, no. 4 (1983): 340–52. *ATLA Religion Database with ATLASerials*, EBSCOhost, 343.

[15] Ibid.

have changed lives and stirred hearts to make a difference. Richard Niebuhr writes:

> It remains true that Christian faith cannot escape from partnership with history, however many other partners it may choose. With this it has been mated and to this its loyalty belongs; the union is as indestructible as that of reason and sense experience in the natural sciences.[16]

We as United Methodists are no strangers to the loyalty, union, and partnering with history or tradition of our faith. It helps make us who we are. The narratives that inspire us for mission, teaching, and service are some of the same types of stories that will provoke students to action, while encouraging space where meaningful conversations can take place, transforming lives and the world.

In another related vein, Howard Thurman understands a person's narrative as part of human history and history as part of an individual's story. For Thurman, narrative is indestructible, extending beyond the mundane and into the sacred. Thurman briefly examines our lives intellectually referring to them as "working papers."

> The life working paper of the individual is made up of a creative synthesis of [a person] is in all [their] parts as he or she reacts to the living process. It is a wide of the mark to say that a person's working paper is ever wrong; it may not be fruitful, it may be negative, but it is never wrong.[17]

There is transformative power in telling and listening to other people's stories, as we listen not for mere information

---

[16] Richard Neibuhr, *The Meaning of Revelation*. (Louisville, KY: Westminster John Knox, 2006), 31.

[17] Howard Thurman, *Jesus and the Disinherited* (Boston: Beacon, 1996), 110.

but to position ourselves for a closer, deeper relationship. Then, as we get to know one another, we are better able to equip and give leadership opportunities, which can create enough space to expand positive and meaningful encounters between people from various ethnicities and help facilitate conversation about racial injustice and inequality.[18] What if we considered our lives as a working paper and a synthesis of our faith tradition and life experience?[19] In order to favor real inclusion instead of optimal diversity, a stranger's story should be embraced by the community as shared history and not perceived from a safe distance.[20]

Real diversity and inclusion means developing a space and systems where the desire to change the world starts within our own organizations.[21] Pluralism tends to be a primary focus on many of our college campuses, and it needs to be; but, unfortunately, discussions around racial tensions, issues, injustices, or bias often do not receive the necessary attention to foster dialogue and change.

While many campus ministers and chaplains work toward this end and are having conversations around creating resources for new initiatives that will help further develop spaces that go beyond judgment and tolerance, a curriculum for racial diversity and inclusion is also needed. While funding for many Wesley Foundations is inadequate, the need for program money is clear. The future of our church depends on it.

---

[18] Eboo Patel, *Sacred Ground: Pluralism, Prejudice, and the Promise of America* (Boston: Beacon, 2012), 86.

[19] Also see Charles Gerkin's classic: *Living Human Document: Re-visioning Pastoral Counseling in a Hermeneutical Mode* (Nashville: Abingdon, 1984).

[20] Sheryll Cashin, *Place, Not Race: A New Vision of Opportunity in America* (Boston: Beacon, 2014).

[21] Stephen Frost, *Inclusion Imperative: How Real Inclusion Creates Better Business and Builds Better Societies* (London: Kogan Page Limited, 2014), 7.

Courage in the context of achieving an inclusive organization is keeping the issue on the table when so many people believe it would be more convenient to drop it.[22]

I believe, with the stirring of the Holy Spirit, we should embrace the development of faithful United Methodist clergy and lay leaders who will speak out of the courage of conviction to "confront, change, or improve difficult situations,"[23] as well as take full advantage of the programs that already exist. [24]

Collegiate ministers are charged with creating space for students to live out their faith in a multiracial and global community within the academy or campus environment. This unique context can allow students to explore narratives outside of the DNA embedded in the foundation of the institution which may be experienced through the eyes of some students as more exclusive than inclusive. Campus ministers are finding opportunities to bring together a diverse racial makeup of young minds, eager to learn and focus upon diversity and inclusion. Yet, more is needed. Eboo Patel writes:

> In a culture with continuing tensions between racial and ethnic communities, campuses are a unique place where people from different racial backgrounds can come together, commit themselves to. . . develop an appreciation for cultural narratives that are poorly represented in high school textbooks and in the media, and nurture relationships between people from different backgrounds.[25]

---

[22] Ibid., 10.
[23] Ibid., 8.
[24] For church resources see those offered by the General Commission on Religion and Race at http://gcorr.org/resources and the General Board of Church and Society http://umc-gbcs.org.
[25] Patel, *Sacred Ground*, 111.

United Methodist-related colleges and universities, in particular, have the opportunity to address these tensions by exploring "narrative as a critical tool," because narratives are not simply stories. Narratives have the ability to be shared histories, acknowledged within context and fostered within communities. [26]

But, how? What if we applied a similar strategy currently used for interfaith cooperation to teach racial diversity and inclusion within the extension ministries dedicated to collegiate ministry? There is a distinct opportunity to implement interfaith strategies to develop bold, sustainable conversations on college campuses through Wesley-led conferences, councils, and joint declarations developed and implemented by faith-based students. The Academy for Cultural Diversity writes:

> The term 'Interfaith Dialogue' refers to the positive and cooperative interaction between people of different religions, faiths or spiritual beliefs, it is an expression of the participants' lived faith lives, and therefore interfaith encounters form communities of awareness. Constructing dialogue between followers of different religions means understanding, through cooperation, the different religious principles and teachings that should benefit all of humanity through the promotion of mutual respect and tolerance. It means coming together and sharing aspects of their respective faiths and striving to understand that which is foreign.

> Interfaith dialogue therefore plays a vital role in the field of Cultural Diplomacy, as it can advance world peace by uniting faiths and by fostering reciprocal understanding, acceptance and tolerance amongst disparate religious communities. Inter-faith dialogue can in this way break

---

[26] Hauerwas, *Why Narrative?*, 9.

down walls of division and the barriers that stand at the center of numerous wars, with the objective of achieving peace.[27]

The church and the academy should design, develop, and encourage peer-to-peer conversations focused on faith, race, bias, and power structures, well beyond Martin Luther King Jr. Day community projects or Native American recognition month. Visibility on social media in January and February tends to be high times for service learning projects. This display of solidarity with those who are different runs the risk of creating an edifice of diversity but no real inclusion. The social commentary pictures are celebratory in nature and outwardly display what it means to make a difference through community outreach but stop short of embracing those same communities as their own.

There is an alternate side to these outward displays of service on social media. When there are editorials or blog posts outlining a person of color's negative experience with police, being followed in a department store, or accosted for no logical reason, social media channels tend to move in a derogatory direction. I have read deplorable comments from college-age adults ranging from "all lives matter" or "oh the drama" to "go back to Africa,"[28] yet in these same circles a "white knight" (we can help you from a distance) mentality is embraced. This is not to say that only one demographic is responsible for all racism, because all persons are part of America's racial story.

While more individuals in contemporary culture talk about race and racism, the power of that talk has been

---

[27] "Academy for Cultural Diplomacy." ICD. http://www.culturaldiplomacy.org /academy/index.php?en_historical-examples.
[28] These quotations are from comment sections of Facebook of racially charged police conduct and department store surveillance.

diminished by racist backlash that trivializes it, more often than not representing it as mere hysteria.[29]

When students are indifferent or ignore injustice or systematic issues, the destructive cycle continues, even with leaders we mentor. So I ask, can we as the church impact the attitudes of those who negatively or unsympathetically respond to another's lived experience?

Regardless of my station in life, I continue to learn it is never a "good" time to tell the stories of ethnic concerns. Recently, I experienced tension when I presented the draft of this chapter to my peers in Syracuse, New York. The conversation around my outline (among the persons charged with creating an open space for college students) proved to be challenging. The discussion around my chapter became heated. As it pertains to narrative theology, it was suggested to me to reference white ethicist Stanley Hauerwas, because James Cone and Cornell West were not received as reputable enough. And writing about my own personal narrative stirred the emotions of some of my peers, who voiced their own narratives because they felt they were not being heard.[30]

In that moment, the space reserved for intellectual conversation was compromised and my voice silenced. All did subside but the damage had been done. Later, I was discreetly pulled to the side and quietly told by one of the participants that it was easier to stand before people of color and talk about issues of race, but he could not do it in front of his white peers. How can we create a space for diversity and inclusion, when we, leaders

---

[29] bell hooks (bell hooks without capitalization is a pen name), *Teaching Community: A Pedagogy of Hope* (New York: Routledge, 2003), 27.

[30] There was a racially charged dialogue between some of the participants, bringing to light the power of narrative and how it has the ability to stir emotions and if the opportunity permits, lay the foundation for authentic dialogue.

of the church, are not challenged to live outside of our own comfort zones?

The hurt, frustration, and anger this encounter caused was not unexpected; race is an extremely sensitive subject. It takes time and courage for a group who is charged with having a prophetic voice to work through their own differences. The overarching message of diversity and inclusion is not about collegiate ministers, but it is about the space they provide. Ultimately, however, it's about faith-filled college students and how they develop as leaders and are sent out to advance God's realm.

Steve Foster, an inclusion expert, accounts the process of creating the 2012 Olympic Games in London with diversity and inclusion in mind. He writes:

> It is not a story of universal success. There were failures. But some of those failures were necessary to demonstrate the need to change strategy and move on from the policies of the past. And all of the failures taught us something. They were difficult conversations, normally avoided in traditional professional practice for the sake of remaining professional. There were workplace tensions, often avoided in more mainstream organisations by people associating with people like themselves. [31]

Sunday morning worship continues to be the most segregated hour of the week. Worship happens where Christians profess their love for God and community through music, liturgy, preaching, the sacraments, giving their time and service, but too often it is also a place where people associate with those who look like themselves and tell their stories only to each other. Is

---

[31] Steve Foster, *The Inclusion Imperative: How Real Inclusion Creates Better Business and Builds Better Societies* (London: Kogan Page Limited, 2014), 8.

this true of your context? What strategies do we have in place to make sure our chapels and Wesley Foundations are not segregated spaces and make room for all to be heard?

As a church we acknowledge and strive to put scriptural principles from the biblical narrative into our daily practice. Yet we are too easily satisfied with a scarcity of voices. We do not faithfully "ponder the path of one's own destiny"[32] through an array of modern and diverse voices that have also been shaped by God. Hearing others' stories as part of a grander narrative will help us create an environment where we challenge systems and central issues of our time that will be to the benefit of all.

For example, society has a tendency to turn a blind eye to movements associated with #blacklivesmatter and mass incarceration as well as other issues of racial injustice. It is through social media and the voices of college-age protestors that the church has collectively witnessed a global challenge to systemic injustice and a proclamation of the importance of access to people of color. By sharing their narratives and sparking heated conversations, students across the world are fighting for equity, access, and justice. Marching in solidarity within the #blacklivesmatter movement is commendable. But what can we do when students return to campus, to your Wesley Foundations, to the chapel, to you? Do you encourage students to post, write, or share meaningful narratives? Do you help them find ways to continue the "march" but in a different form? Perhaps we could find ways to partner with other groups on campus and make a deeper commitment to meet and grapple with these hard conversations, even though it is easier to high-five one another and return to the regularly scheduled programs.

---

[32] Hauerwas, *Why Narrative?*, 29.

bell hooks[33], a nationally recognized author, feminist, and social activist, presents a transformational perspective in her writings, which have the ability to realign how we teach within a college community. Touching upon the ethics of risk, she reveals the importance of narrative and how sharing stories is an empowering process. However, we cannot expect our students who come to be a part of collegiate ministry to risk their narratives when we as leaders will not do the same. Transforming the DNA of an organization begins with those who are committed to investing in taking a personal and communal risk. This has the ability to expand and illuminate the experiences of students as they are developed in their faith and leadership.

A Womanish Narrative

As an African American youth pastor for a prominent black church and former Wesley Director at Historically Black University, my personal narrative stems from a womanish perspective, as characterized by Alice Walker in the opening of *In Search of Our Mothers' Gardens:*

> *womanish.* (Opp. of "girlish," i.e. frivolous, irresponsible, not serious.) A black feminist or feminist of color. From the black folk expression of mothers to female children, "you acting womanish," i.e., like a

---

[33] bell hooks has written several books pertaining to this subject:*Teaching Community: A Pedagogy of Hope.* New York: Routledge, 2003 and *Teaching to Transgress: Education as the Practice of Freedom.* (New York: Routledge, 1994). Her writings view the classroom as a place of transformation, and she focuses on the interconnectivity of race, class, and gender and their ability to produce and perpetuate systems of oppression and domination. She has published over thirty books and numerous scholarly and mainstream articles, appeared in several documentary films, and participated in various public lectures. Primarily through a postmodern female perspective, she has addressed race, class, and gender in education, art, history, sexuality, mass media and feminism: http://www.goodreads.com/author/show/10697.Bell_Hooks.

woman. Usually referring to outrageous, audacious, courageous or *willful* behavior. Wanting to know more and in greater depth than is considered "good" for one. Interested in grown up doings. Acting grown up. Being grown up. Interchangeable with another black folk expression: "You trying to be grown." Responsible. In charge. *Serious.* [34]

It is through my own personal narrative that I have the opportunity to be *womanish:* courageous, audacious, acting grown up, and being willing to share my story regardless of the consequences or strange looks.

In many ways I have felt silenced when it comes to my own story and the significance of my history as a young girl emerging into womanhood. Though race injustice is a difficult topic, it cannot be ignored because of our own discomfort. We live in a society where persons of color continue to wrestle with embedded systemic evils within institutional walls. But I didn't recognize the power I possessed in my life, because it was not always easy growing up in a home where the male narrative overshadowed other voices. Even so, I was encouraged as a child ("You can be anything you want to be"), yet a conservative theological stance inhabited our home and seemed to counterbalance my family's hopes for me. Until my preteen years, I grew up having no religious affiliation but heard with the constant refrain: "God is good, all the time," continually playing in the background, even when I felt the opposite was true. Can I really be anything I want to be? Is God really good *all* the time? In a conservative household—dare I ask?

Throughout my school tenure the educational system pro-

---

[34] Alice Walker, *In Search of Our Mothers' Gardens: Womanist Prose* (San Diego, CA: Harcourt Brace Jovanovich, 1983.)

claimed, "Girls study education. Become a teacher, get married, and live happily ever after." "You don't want to be too smart dear." "You should major in theater and learn to play an instrument, dear." Secretly, I wanted to play soccer, ride my bike, and become a lawyer who gave criminals a chance at justice. But I listened to those voices, to an extent; I did have wild hair and I hated wearing dresses, but I conceded by learning to halfheartedly play the clarinet and violin, becoming a cheerleader, and studying English Literature.

I did not acquire my own voice until I met a professor in college. Dr. Lazalia Richardson was not a campus minister but performed the duties of one. She was a dynamic African American professor who taught me the value of *being* (competent, intelligent, and self-assured) through her faith-filled witness. Dr. Richardson wasn't a Methodist; she was an ecumenical soul who attended another traditional mainline denomination. She shared her own college stories with twenty of us. We were a multicultural and multiethnic group, and she explained how it took time for her to find her own voice many years earlier. Dr. Richardson introduced all of us to James Baldwin, Phyllis Wheatley, Nikki Giovanni, Marcus Garvey, as well as other black literary geniuses. We listened to each other and had controversial and pointed conversations around race, faith, justice, and God. This was Dr. Richardson's way to create a shared space and teach from the likes of a transformational narrative.

The space she created during those critical young adult years opened our hearts, minds, and souls to hear other voices in conjunction with our own. During this time in my life along with my peers, I learned the importance of a shared history with those who did not resemble my own socioeconomic status or cultural background. College was a liberating time; and through the leadership and faith formation of Dr. Richardson, a womanist professor in Virginia, I grew to understand the importance of leadership, emerging narratives, and the ability to find the power of voice, when I believed I had none. Dr. Richardson displayed professional courage and took a risk by investing in our multiracial group.

The exploratory nature of college, coupled with faith and leadership formation led me to the United Methodist tradition where systems of racism and injustice continue to exist. Throughout my career, I've witnessed and experienced ethnic and minority clergypersons as unwanted and unwelcomed because of systematic evils; congregations screaming. "No women! No blacks! And God forbid, *No black women*!" Patel reminds us:

> Colleges develop society's leaders and sets a country's, intellectual and cultural agenda, meaning that the attitudes and relationships nurtured on American campuses impact diversity issues in the broader society . . . to do this people need open attitudes, appreciate knowledge and meaningful multicultural [and multiracial] relationships. College provides the perfect environment to cultivate all three.[35]

As collegiate ministers, we nurture the call of students on campus to whatever places God has in mind. When our faith undergirds the spaces we create, miracles happen, and our attitudes and relationships can shift society. When systems are significantly realigned to represent our global community, leadership, and faith, formation is inevitable and college students act upon their ability to go beyond sharing their hope and visions for the world.

The Invisible Culture and the Unheard Narratives

From numerous discussions with students around the country, students of color have a difficult time fitting into the

---

[35] Patel, *Sacred Ground*, 111.

programs that are in place within Wesley Foundations or on United Methodist Related College and University campuses. The Foundation and student-led leadership, board representation, worship design or programming is not representative of the global church or at times the campus where the Wesley is situated. Despite some of our best intentions, an invisible culture of systematic racism exists in Wesley Foundations and college and university campuses that is oppressive in nature and disruptive to the discourse of marginalized groups. Therefore, we must do our part to make the invisible visible. As James Baldwin says, "Not everything that is faced can be changed, but nothing can be changed until it is faced."

In many ways, the rise in tuition cost is a hindrance for people of color to gain access to education. While rising costs affect all students, students of color are often more vulnerable. Like more and more students, some students of color are unable to attend universities without having part-time employment to help defray the cost of an education. This may interfere especially with the ability for people of color to serve as interns or in a leadership capacity, because funds are not readily available to subsidize one's involvement in a seat of influence.

Many times, inclusion and diversity surrounding POC will take place through conventional invitations to speak or entertain in worship or at events, but through the deliberate realignment of faith formation and leadership structures that represent the global community, the church has an opportunity to invest in what it truly means to be diverse and inclusive. What if Wesley Foundations created part-time student positions for POC's to aid in diversifying and growing these faith-based spaces. By making room for emerging faith and leadership narratives, this could expand extension ministries to include the voices of others. I have witnessed Wesley Foundation directors and chaplains who are intentional in making racial diversity and inclusion a priority. This level of intentionality takes time but it also means diversifying across the leadership platform of programming, including the Board of Directors.

Whenever I had the opportunity, I would encourage my Wesley students to apply for summer internships within the UMC. These opportunities involved serving within a majority white ministry aimed at people of color. Students would always come back with heartbreaking stories of racist remarks from lay people and other student interns. They often felt like outcasts but were glad to have the experience, because it gave them confidence and a voice.

Rarely is there an occasion to dialogue about what needs to change in order to be an inclusive and racially diverse ministry. If racial conflict isn't an issue in one's life, then intentional diverse and inclusive training should be offered to compliment all leadership roles. So what am I saying? Always include diversity and inclusive training on your student-led, staff, and Board of Directors leadership teams. As I explained above, it is through narrative experiences that new voices will not simply overlay old ones, because structural racist experiences, attitudes, and ideological concerns thrive underground. New voices will have greater opportunity to be heard.

As I reflect on the James Baldwin quotation, I remember that we must consider embracing new alignments across nations, borders, histories, and essences,[36] just as the church intentionally and routinely entwines opportunities for interfaith dialogue. We must make room for emerging narratives within our Wesley Foundations and Methodist-related colleges and universities. In particular, United Methodist Campus ministries have the power to undergird a radical revision of

---

[36] Edward W. Said, *Culture and Imperialism* (New York: Vintage Books, 1994), 24.

"social temporality" on college campuses as we provide space for young adults to question their identity—personal, social, intellectual, spiritual, and political—at a critical time in their life. As students explore their future vocation, relationships, faith, and leadership, narrative can connect and help transform a community hesitant or resistant to change.

But how can a community be shaped by narrative theology? Bhabha says: "It is from those who have suffered the sentence of history—subjugation, domination, diaspora, displacement that we learn our most enduring lessons for living and thinking."[37] As a society, if we find ways to hear the stories of all persons, but especially ethnic minority persons and peoples of color, we all will have an opportunity to dialogue, live, and think as a community created and shaped by God.

Conclusion

Diversity and inclusion discussions are difficult, but I dare say even more so when discussing ethnic concerns. Real inclusion is hard to achieve, because moving past token diversity means understanding it is superficial inclusion, as opposed to real inclusion; and many people do not want to be challenged by different people with different perspectives,[38] especially those with less power or social capital.

Real diversity and inclusion start with leaders who define a process for change, encourage transparency,[39] and are reflective about their own life—their own contributions for good or ill.

To commit ourselves to the work of transforming the academy so that it will be a place where cultural diversity informs

---

[37] Bhabha, *Location of Culture*, 246.
[38] Frost, *Inclusion Imperative*, 45.
[39] Ibid., 97.

every aspect of our learning, we must embrace struggle and sacrifice. We cannot be easily discouraged. We cannot despair when there is a conflict.[40]

It's not simple, and "it does require an appetite for risk and it does require courage as well as creativity."[41]

I continue to have a variety of conversations and listen to many statements as they relate to diversity and inclusion on college campuses and Wesley Foundations.[42] Some are surprising; others are not. Yet, I believe as part of a new systematic way to express God's story for a global society, these conversations must continue despite the difficult feelings, thoughts, and even personal consequences. Frost says, "Increased diversity can actually increase conflict. We know this because people, even us, like to associate with people like themselves"[43] and sometimes, it's easy to be inclusive without being diverse.[44] If our campus ministers do not mirror our campuses and if our campuses do not mirror God's intent for the world, then we have to ask ourselves: How can we make them different, and am I willing to take the risk?

As college ministers, we must face our own demons in order to create a space for all stories to be heard, particularly from students from other racial and ethnic groups. Bottom line: it is not enough to tell, write, or recall; narratives should connect and racially align persons of influence on campuses, thereby helping

---

[40] Hooks, *Teaching to Transgress: Education as the Practice of Freedom*, 33.

[41] Ibid.

[42] Collegiate Ministers, Wesley Board members, and student interns have asked questions and shared insights into their collegiate ministry. "How do we become more diverse?"; "We invested in this event, where are the people of color?"; "Shouldn't your board be all black?"; "The students said they will stop coming when I'm no longer an intern."; "If only you knew some of the things my students say about blacks, I don't know if they would want to do a joint retreat."; "I wanted to continue to go, but no one looked like me."; "I've noticed the blacks don't do much of anything on your board."; "We can't find qualified people of color."

[43] Frost, *Inclusion Imperative*, 50.

[44] Ibid, 44.

students who are willing to receive or "interpret new experiences and powerful emotions."[45] Why? Because systemic racism has the power to "entangle with the interests and agendas of various groups [who] provoke and challenge the fundamentally static notion of identity."[46]

Frost in his experience notes that "people are not necessarily opposed to change, but they are opposed to loss."[47] What are we opposed to losing? Our Methodist heritage says:

John Wesley broke conventional rules of church conduct, probed the causes of poverty, morally condemned slavery, and denounced social injustices marginalizing women and the poor, which contributed inspiration for the direction for the early Methodist movement.[48]

We need to emulate Wesley. We need collegiate ministers who are willing to be committed to struggle with conversations and implement action plans to serve students. After all, we only have four to six years to help their faith and leadership skills develop. I think it's worth the effort and the risk. Don't you?

---

[45] Rolf Jacobson, "We Are Our Stories: Narrative Dimension of Human Identity and Its Implications for Christian Faith Formation," *Word & World* 34, no. 2 (2014): 123–130. *ATLA Religion Database with ATLASerials*, EBSCOhost.

[46] Said, *Culture and Imperialism*, xxv.

[47] Frost, *Inclusion Imperative*, 23.

[48] Harold J. Recinos, "John Wesley" in *Beyond the Pale: Reading Theology from the Margins*, ed. Miguel A. Torre and Stacey M. Floyd-Thomas (Louisville, KY: Westminster John Knox, 2011), 95.

How Is It with Your Soul?
Developing a Liberatory Consciousness through Dialogue in Campus Ministries
Kimberly Williams Brown and T.L. Steinwert

Throughout the 2014–15 academic year the refrain, "Black Lives Matter" punctuated daily life as the stories of brown and black men killed by police finally rose to the nation's consciousness. And, while police brutality captured the country's headlines, campuses were embroiled in sensationalized scandals surrounding fraternity chants and student parties, highlighting the institutionalized racism endemic to higher education. Around the country students rallied and protested, not simply the ignorant acts of intolerance and bias associated with the white supremacist culture of their peers, but also the insidious vestiges of that system, including the declining retention rate of students of color in some colleges and universities, the reduction of financial aid and support services for students of color at many schools, and a cultural climate of pervasive micro-aggressions toward students from marginalized communities. The notion that millennials are the first generation in a "post-racial" society was shattered as campuses and communities alike were forced to confront the institutionalized racism that has plagued the nation since its founding.

In an academic year that began in Ferguson and ended in Baltimore, race became the most pressing social issue on campuses and around the country. Yet the proposals for this volume did not originally engage the issue, and we were struck by the utter silence. How could United Methodists publish a book about campus ministries in 2015 with no mention of race?[1]

As co-facilitators of a course on dismantling racism and privilege, we decided to break the silence. We set out to write a dialogic article on the intersections of the development of liberatory consciousness and the cultivation of holiness of heart and life in Wesleyan small groups on college campuses. The project was, in many ways, quite simple. However, we were committed to writing this as a dialogue, modeling for our readers the practice we hoped they might engage. As we tried to do that within the constraints of academic discourse, we realized the project was much larger and far more complicated than we imagined. Instead of writing the paper we envisioned, we found ourselves writing in the margins. Literally, proliferating the right-hand margin of the paper with questions and comments about each other's life and work, unpacking and exploring our shared and diverse experiences, riffing off of each other's ideas: questioning them, challenging them, and reframing them in a truly collaborative fashion. The margins were exciting, enlivening, and encouraging. But, the margins, simply did not fit into the main body of the paper. And so, we stopped, reassessed, and did something entirely different.

The chapter you are reading is not the one we expected to write. The chapter you are reading is not the chapter you expected to read. In fact, the chapter you are reading is not a traditional academic paper at all. This is a paper about trying to write a paper. The telling of this story matters. We must be honest about the pervasive nature of the social hierarchies of race, class, and privilege that infect and distort even the very process of dismantling them. As scholars whose work focuses on confronting oppression, we found ourselves constrained by

---

[1] As a result of this omission, Sheila Bates also wrote an essay on race that is included in the book.

the prejudices and power differentials we set out to unravel. We believe our story is not unique, but representative of the extremely difficult, time consuming, yet oh-so-life-giving nature of antiracist work. By focusing on the process (and not the product) of writing this paper, we hope to provide a template for others who wish to engage and dismantle systemic oppression on campus, congregations, and communities. Below are reflections on that process: the origins of our idea, the challenges we encountered, and the new directions we are exploring. We begin with our premise and then painstakingly detail the process. Giving space to our own individual narratives of the process, we lay bare the significant differences in perspective created through social hierarchies. We conclude by joining our voices in a shared reflection on possible, new directions.

The Premise

At the outset of this joint venture, we planned to bring our scholarship into conversation with one another in hopes of creating a way forward for United Methodist chaplaincies interested in confronting and dismantling racism on their campuses and in the world. Kim brought years of research and experience in antiracist pedagogy, while Tiffany brought a Wesleyan lens on religion in higher education. By bringing these distinct disciplines into conversation we hoped to forge a new model for campus ministries.

Antiracist work is a lifelong commitment to changing both inward attitudes and outward action. It requires an ongoing recognition and confrontation of the social sin of racism and the perpetual development of a liberatory consciousness as espoused by Barbara Love.[2] For Love, liberatory consciousness

---

[2] Barbara J. Love, "Developing a Liberatory Consciousness," in Maurianne Adams et al., *Readings for Diversity and Social Justice* 2nd ed. (New York: Routledge, 2010), 599–603.

is a critical consciousness regarding issues of injustice that must be intentionally cultivated by those who seek to disrupt and unravel systemic oppression. It is a continuous commitment to a process of recognition, analysis, and action in which individuals in community seek to dismantle institutionalized oppression. Liberatory consciousness mirrors, in many ways, the communal process of Wesleyan sanctification as a critical-reflective praxis, ongoing process, and communal practice.

Like the development of a liberatory consciousness, the cultivation of a holy life is a lifelong praxis aimed toward transformation of self and world. For both Love and Wesley, the development of a new way of being, committed to liberation or to holiness of heart and life, requires both an inward and outward transformation. It necessitates a movement from new ways of thinking to new ways of living. Theory and action are fused as communities gather to critically reflect on the systems that impede their growth in liberation or grace. The development of a liberatory consciousness and the journey toward sanctification are commitments to living and being differently in the world. Neither fixed nor static, both processes gradually unfold as a perpetual and unending practice.

Looking back, our own thesis ought to have foreshadowed the deep wrestling, personal introspection, and difficult conversations that emerged. After all, we were asserting that this antiracist work, like the development of liberatory consciousness and the Wesleyan cultivation of holiness of heart and life, is a lifelong process that requires sustained relationships, deep introspection, and renewed action. And, yet, we forged ahead with the naïve assumption that we could write about the process without ever experiencing it with one another.

Kim

Writing a paper on deeply personal issues is extremely difficult. When Tiffany and I decided to write about the intersections of faith, sanctification, race, and intergroup dialogue, I did not suspect that it would be as difficult as it was. We began the process of writing, but instead of feeling fluid, vulnerable, and dialogic, it felt mechanical, boring, and a little too prescriptive. In this reflection, I will describe the reasons I think our originally intended paper was not as successful as we thought it could be and attribute these causes to being hyper-aware of the power differential between us, trying to dialogue through writing, without being in the same space theoretically and physically, and writing against the constraints of time. The process of writing became more important than the academic posturing we do in papers of this kind. This reflection is important as a reflexive process that was necessary to move us both to being able to model not just a collaborative writing project, but also what it means to decenter power through dialogue, which is an ongoing and deeply important process.

When Tiffany asked me to cowrite with her, I was flattered and elated. Then the doubts and insecurities set in about being able to write the paper and to write with Tiffany. What would I say and would my expertise be overshadowed by Tiffany's perceived expertise? Tiffany, Dean of Hendricks Chapel and as someone with a PhD in theology, sat in a differential space than I did as a PhD student. The other difference between us was race. Tiffany is a white woman and I am a black woman from Jamaica. On the surface, a white woman from Cincinnati and a black woman from Jamaica have nothing in common. But through dialogue, we learned of our different journeys that helped us raise our consciousness about our privilege and oppression. To write a paper about race and not acknowledge the power differentials between us in every sense, especially as it relates to race, would be a missed opportunity to challenge our socialization process and the white supremacist systems within which we operate. We, of course, being conscientious about the operation of power, discussed these differentials and were honest about them, but I wondered if, in the end, we ended up reifying them through the process on which we originally embarked.

Tiffany asked me to join the project. Although we tried to come up with an organic topic, Tiffany led the efforts on what the project would be. It is also true, even though we discussed "centering" my voice in the article, because we recognized that having marginalized groups speak for themselves credits and acknowledges their expertise. But the content of the paper also had to connect with Wesleyan principles and traditions, because the audience is campus ministers who abide by Wesleyan United Methodist principles. Therefore, Tiffany's voice had to be centered, because she was the expert in that area despite my recent discovery that I am a descendant of the Wesleyan tradition—I am Pentecostal, but I am not formally trained in these traditions. The chapter could not use dialogic principles, because we could not talk to each other in a way that was fluid. That is to say, we were not fluent in each other's expertise. We were getting to know each other.

To dialogue, it is important to first get to know the other, create trust, and come to understand what collaboration looks like for two (or more) people who have immense power differentials between them. There is no formula for an ethical dialogue, and it is a process best explored with caution especially when race and power differentials are in play. Therefore, to sit in dialogue with Tiffany, as we thought about this paper, and to discuss my insecurities and struggles with my faith, was difficult. I know I am not interested in giving up any parts of my faith, but to be constantly critical of a space of which you are a part can be exhausting. It is, I suppose, much like examining racism in a society that just doesn't get it. You feel constantly on edge or, like the odd person out. However, my Pentecostal belief is the place from which all my strength comes.

That strength, however, has never quelled the quest for understanding, which I have had for a long time, concerning the role of women in the Pentecostal church. I learned through writing this paper and in conversation with Tiffany that the Pentecostal church was born in resistance to mainstream church standards. I recognized that there is power and privilege in my position as a woman of color enrolled in a PhD program. I have this privilege and power as a nonconservative Pentecostal living in contradiction and finding beauty and God's grace through those contradictions. Indeed, I have a calling to move my church in its thinking about the role of women as pastors and spiritual leaders. This awakening only came through many weeks of conversation with Tiffany, and I share it here, because, only through dialogue, can we access liberatory consciousness in any form. For me, the consciousness was about my faith tradition.

As a scholar in Wesleyan theology, traditions, and principles, Tiffany is positioned as expert in a way that I am not, because of the varied ways in which we have been formally trained. My epistemic traditions—the ways in which I am trained to know— are steeped in dialogic, antiracist, and feminist principles. Our epistemic backgrounds complement each other and overlap in many places, but they positioned us differently as we approached this paper. Although we were looking to create a paper centered on dialogue, writing it became difficult, because we were not in dialogue with each other about a particular topic (specifically Wesleyan sanctification), but instead were speaking at each other about our areas of individual expertise.

Using intergroup dialogue (IGD) skills to write and situate this paper became important, because campuses were engaged in racial strife and conflict.[3] IGD is also distinctive in its critical-dialogic approach to addressing issues of social identity and social location in the context of systems of power and privilege.[4] IGD is broadly defined as "a face-to-face facilitated learning experience that brings together students from different social identity groups over a sustained period of time to understand their commonalities and differences, examine the nature and impact of social inequalities, and explore ways of working together toward greater equality and justice."[5] Tiffany and I knew we had to get to a place of modeling these principles, and it took time, vulnerability, and patience to get us there. Dialogic principles do not only engage "expertise," which we understand in the academy as only an intellectual project, but the principles also include important affective knowledge(s), especially in communities of color where they have been marginalized.

Patricia Hill Collins asserts that scholars have various ways of knowing, but we scholars tend to privilege Eurocentric ways of knowing.[6] Dialogue requires participants to not solely rely on their intellect, but to also engage their heart and emotions. It assumes that everyone has experience with race, gender, and ability as it relates to systems of power and privilege, because we live in a world where power, hierarchy, privilege, dominance, and oppression are always in play in

---

[3] Ximena Zúñiga et al., *Intergroup Dialogue in Higher Education: Meaningful Learning about Social Justice* (Hoboken, NJ: Wiley Periodicals, 2007), 2.

[4] Ibid.

[5] Ibid.

[6] Patricia Hill Collins, "Toward a New Vision: Race, Gender and Class as Categories of Analysis and Connection," in *Inequality and Society: Social Science Perspectives on Social Stratification*, ed. Jeff Manza and Michael Sauder (New York: Norton, 2009), 673–81.

individual and systematic ways. It also assumes that because we experience our socially constructed identities, we are only experts in our own lived experiences.

For this chapter, because we were writing from two different places of expertise, which makes sense in academic forums, the paper did not work as a dialogic theoretical frame for campus ministers. It did not work, because we were not dialoguing in the context of the paper, and we were not employing an important dialogic principle—sharing our similar and different experiences around a topic. What became more important than the paper was what we were writing in the margins as we responded to each other's work. What was in the margin became important, because it demonstrated the dialogic principles we were missing in the paper. We indeed were sharing common experiences in the margins and asking questions that were necessary for a dialogue.

Finally, what was missing from our paper was time. We did not have enough time to write a paper that was thoughtful and dialogic. We each put a lot of time into the project, but again, because we were speaking at—and not to—each other, it became a frustrating experience. The pressure of time made it difficult to really understand what was missing from our efforts. It is in the writing of this reflection that I have become aware that what was missing was a deeper connection between us, which took time and many conversations. Dialogical work is relational work; relationship takes time. Only through shared conversations, conflict, collaboration, and understanding can one get to a place of deeper meaning and build a true relationship that allows for effectively talking across difference.

On its own the paper could work, especially if we were interested in playing by the rules and principles of the academy. We both realized that to act with integrity through our collaborative process, to write about race through dialogic principles, and to dismantle, through our writing, the pillars of white supremacy and privilege (both of which the academy is steeped in), we had to cease our efforts and take a step back. I was sad and disappointed because, as a PhD student, publishing is always one of my goals. This paper about writing a paper is not the way I wanted to begin my publishing career. Alas, I had to forego my selfish yearnings to be accepted as a scholar in the academy pushing at the margins of the academy to make space for the scholarship and the people who do not fit easily. The paper we currently have does not fit easily, and we are okay with it not fitting well.

Tiffany

When I received the invitation to participate in this volume, I immediately decided to write on interreligious pedagogy. For the past five years, I had focused on the role of faith and spirituality in higher education as a religious affairs administrator. The conference quickly filled up with scholars as excited as I. Some wanted to explore the burgeoning interfaith movement from a Wesleyan perspective; others were eager to tackle the contentious issue of sexuality; and a few more, at the margins, were interested in ecology and vocation. Not one on race.[7]

Not one on race? How could that be?

Why didn't anyone want to write on race? Why didn't *I* want to write on race?

As a white woman I was hesitant to allow my voice be the only voice on race. I did not want to usurp space for people of color, positioning myself as "the great White savior"[8] or the

---

[7] Eventually one other participant chose to write on race.

[8] Much has been written about the "white-savior industrial complex," particularly in relation to film and entertainment. In 2012, writer, Teju Cole brought the conversation to Twitter in the aftermath of the controversial Kony 2012 video. Discussing the problems associated with privileged, white activists advocating for those on the margins, Cole

"guilty White liberal"[9] who writes over the voices of others simply to fill the void. But, now, how could I not write on race?

As I struggled for far too long to envision how I could contribute to the conversation without doing more harm, I remembered the power of cofacilitation used in Intergroup Dialogue (IGD), an intentionally antiracist pedagogy developed at the University of Michigan. This model is designed to cultivate a critical consciousness and communal action aimed at dismantling systemic oppression. Much like Wesleyan small groups focused on supporting members' cultivation of holiness of heart and life, IGD classes foster the development of liberatory consciousness. I wondered if IGD might address my concerns about writing alone and might actually provide the foundation for a renewed praxis of "holy conversations" or "means of grace" among Wesleyan campus ministries. Could the development of liberatory consciousness be part and parcel of the pursuit of holiness of heart and life? Making disciples for the transformation of the world might mean focusing attention in campus ministry on the intentional process of acknowledging, confronting, and dismantling racism.[10]

---

tweeted, "The White Savior Industrial Complex is not about justice. It is about having a big emotional experience that validates privilege." (Teju Cole, "The White-Savior Industrial Complex," *Atlantic*, March 21, 2012, http://www.theatlantic.com/international/archive/2012/03/the-white-savior-industrial-complex/254843/. My first sentence in this paragraph illustrates his point in many respects. My immediate framing of the dilemma in moral and spiritual language begs the question for whose benefit did I imagine myself writing. Allyship requires an ongoing critical consciousness of one's own attitudes and actions. Writing this paper has made me even more aware of the ways in which the white-savior complex continues to permeate my work and has challenged me to address it.

[9] Beverly Daniel Tatum, *"Why Are All the Black Kids Sitting Together in the Cafeteria?" and Other Conversations about Race* (New York: Basic Books, 2003), 106.

[10] I worry that, more often than not, the wider denomination understands campus ministry as UMYF 2.0 or a holding ground to ensure students return to their local congregations after college. For many working in the field, we know that is simply not true. Yet our funding (and in that way our merit and future) continues to be tied to traditional ecclesial statistics as metrics for ascertaining the success and saliency of

In some ways, this chapter was an idea, a thought experiment. In other ways, it was a real call for action. But, in either case, I already had my thesis in mind. Of course, academic discourse in many ways necessitates that approach to a paper. And, so when I invited Kim to write with me, I already had the frame of the paper in my mind.

So, let's just stop here.

I invited a colleague of color into a process to write a paper that I had already outlined in my mind with a predetermined thesis, argument, and conclusion. Let me say that again. I invited a colleague of color into a process to write a paper that I had already outlined in my mind with a predetermined thesis, argument, and conclusion.

I thought I was conscious of the dynamics that often happen between white activists and colleagues of color in which the privileged colleague dominates both process and product. I took note of these differences and tried to be honest and open about them. I pledged that we would work against this dynamic. Yet, in setting up the project, I had already done it. It could never be a dialogue when the script was already written.

Kim notes we only had one month to write. That is because I wrestled with the proposal for some time before inviting her into the process. The socialized identity of being white demands silence and complicity on race. Daring to speak can often be fraught with insecurities, questions, and hesitation. While I did not want to be the "great white savior," I confess I felt it was my responsibility to tackle this issue. As a member of the dominant social group that benefits from racism, I felt it was my duty to act. Yet, in doing so I ended up replicating the oppression I sought to confront. White guilt is a dangerous

---

campus ministries. What if the denomination reframed campus ministry to focus on the intersections between faith and social justice in an ongoing, deliberative way?

tool of the system that does little, if anything, to dismantle racism. Sometimes it only perpetuates it.

As I write this, I want to be clear that this is not intended as a public moment of self-flagellation, but a stark example of how the best intentions are always wrapped up in layers of socialization and institutionalized oppression that inhibit the work we seek to do. Antiracist work, like that of Christian sanctification, is never done. It is a renewed way of living and being in the world that requires constant attention, reflection, evaluation, and change. Indeed, the discovery of this dynamic made the writing of this narrative ever-more-important to me. In antiracist work (as in the Christian journey) we must often stop, recognize where we have strayed, regroup, talk it through, and start again.

As the clock ticked and the deadline approached, we contemplated giving up. Yet, something in us said we could not quit. At first, our commitment to deliver a paper to the conference bound us to one another, but the longer we worked together we found ourselves more deeply committed to the process and each other, discovering that the work we were doing was transformative for us.

I found as we worked together, I noticed race much more often. Although I consider myself aware of the dynamics of race in America, I find that in my daily life it is hard to keep my racialized identity front and foremost. Yet, as I worked with Kim, I found myself awake to the world in ways I have not been for some time, and I found my behavior shifting in response to what I was seeing. In parks with my children, I recognized how parents interacted and children played, and I initiated conversations with families of color. In lines at stores, I noticed how clerks attended first to me instead of families of color, and I moved back in line. In these seemingly small and insignificant moments, I noticed my privilege and tried to deconstruct it.

Of course, privilege can never be erased or given away entirely, but it can be acknowledged and leveraged. At work, I noticed how students of color were left out of professional networks, and I used my institutional privilege to connect students of color to influential staff and faculty. In the community, I noticed those recommended for job openings and committee appointments were predominantly white, and I used my privilege to recommend people from marginalized identities. In working with Kim, I came to understand the depth of commitment needed for this work. As Kelly Rae Kraemer wrote, "Only by recognizing and acknowledging the operation of cultural violence at work in our everyday lives and ordinary circumstances can ignorance of our own privileged status be explained and challenged."[11]

Through this process, I came to a critical awareness of my own limitations and confronted once again my privilege. In seeking to be collaborative, I discovered both the internal and institutional barriers my privilege had built up. I tried to construct an "easy" process to provide voice for our joint work. Yet, the reality is that dialogue is never easy. It is messy and complicated and requires both vulnerability and time. Kim and I had worked together over the past five years in a number of different projects, but we didn't truly know one another. The marginal conversations excited us because they drew us to one another through an exploration of our similarities and differences. You cannot presuppose the foundations of shared experience, you must build them.

Moving Forward

We could simply not write this paper within the academic frame with which we began. To push at the margins of this publication and to produce a paper that challenges both cur-

---

[11] Kelly Rae Kraemer, "Solidarity in Action: Exploring the Work of Allies in Social Movements," *Peace and Change* 32, no. 1, (2007): 20–38.

rent scholarship and the way in which campus ministries operate, we needed more time to be in dialogue with each other.

In this spirit, we set aside time to have the dialogue we planned to write about. Using a series of questions[12], we took time to do the relational work we found seeping and pressing on us from the margins and through our conversation discovered three distinct movements necessary for conversations on oppression and privilege. To nurture communities where members might acknowledge, understand and disrupt systemic oppression, we must craft intentional space for dialogue that helps participants: (1) re-member moments of coming to consciousness regarding their own identity and the identities of others; (2) wrestle with their multiple and shifting identities as a young adult; and (3) understand the systemic nature of oppression and pathways to liberation.

These three central tasks for dialogue mirror key movements in Love's development of a liberatory consciousness and the Wesleyan cultivation of holiness of heart and life. For both Love and Wesley, the commitment to liberation and holiness of heart and life each requires an inward and outward transformation as individuals and communities move from new ways of thinking to new ways of living through sustained awareness, analysis, action, and accountability.

---

[12] We framed the dialogue with the following series of questions: (1) What is your first memory of racial tension? How old were you? (2) What Christian tradition did you grow up with? If you deviated from the way you were raised why? (3) What keeps you connected to the Wesleyan/Pentecostal traditions? (4) How did you come to dialogue? (5) What about dialogue is interesting to you? (6) Have you facilitated dialogues? Why do you facilitate? (7) What is challenging about the dialogic method for engaging others around oppression and privilege? (8) What is rewarding about the dialogic method for engaging others around oppression and privilege? (9) How do you understand the intersections of faith and social justice? (10) Thinking about dialogue in the context of communities of faith, what similarities and differences do you see? (11) What strategies would you recommend for campus ministers if they were interested in using Intergroup Dialogue to develop liberatory consciousness to cultivate holiness of heart and life in Wesleyan small groups on college campuses?

"Re-membering" Ourselves

"Reading Black women's intellectual work, I have come to see how it is possible to be both centered in one's own experiences and engaged in coalitions with others. In this sense, Black feminist thought works on behalf of Black women, but does so in conjunction with other similar social justice projects." [13]

The quotation by Hill Collins is illustrative of what we as authors set out to do. Together we worked to build coalition by discussing not only our own intellectual journeys, but also our own personal journeys in coming to understand and confront systemic oppression. Through "re-membering" critical moments in childhood and young adulthood that revealed our own sense of privilege and oppression, we constructed narratives of awakening that propelled us into a liberatory consciousness.

In sharing our stories of coming to consciousness, we learned more about each other and ourselves. These retellings were difficult and liberating, requiring both vulnerability and courage. Listening to the conversation, you can sense in the pauses and pace the intimacy and exhilaration of the conversation. Tiffany's verbatim is peppered with "ums" and "ahs" which convey the slow, deliberate, and hesitant pace that characterized her recalling. Yet, as we retold our stories, we bore witness to one another evoking new self-revelations and shared understanding. Often sentences stopped mid-thought with what was unsaid being mutually understood by both without finishing the sentence.

In listening to one another, we cultivated a heightened sense of awareness regarding systemic oppression in our own histories and daily lives. Not only did we discover new connections

---

[13] Patricia Hill Collins, *Black Feminist Thought: Knowledge, Consciousness, and the Politics of Empowerment* (New York: Routledge, 2002), 11.

and insights about our personal journeys but also we noticed instances of institutionalized prejudice and discrimination in our lives that we had previously not seen. The process of dialoguing with one another woke us up to systems of oppression all around. For both Love and Wesley, this process of noticing is the first step in cultivating a new consciousness and way of life.

While the two of us have in the course of our academic careers had to think critically about the development of liberatory consciousness in ourselves and others, there was something distinct about doing this in conversation with another. The dialogue itself fostered healthy vulnerability that allowed us to touch our own truth perhaps a little more deeply than we might have as instructors in a classroom or colleagues in a department. This was not a rehearsed conversation with predetermined answers or theses waiting to be validated. By allowing ourselves to dialogue, we could retell our stories to one another and ourselves in new ways. In the words of feminist theologian, Nelle Morton, we heard each other to speech.[14] In the listening, we enabled one another to articulate truths about ourselves and our experience of systemic oppression in ways we had not fully understood before.

Antiracist work, as sanctification, must be done in community. Liberationists and Wesleyans alike recognize the pervasive nature of systemic oppression and human sin create barriers to transformed lives that cannot be individually overcome. Both processes require a community of accountability to resist injustice and sin. We needed to write in community—real community and not simply a predetermined academic process. We needed to listen to and respond to each other. We needed to be open to changing what we thought and where we imagined we

---

[14] Nelle Morton, *The Journey Is Home* (Boston: Beacon, 1985).

might go together. We needed to be held accountable for the ways in which we allowed privilege to go unchecked and oppression to silence us into a consent we did not give. We needed to practice what we theorized in a more integrated, holistic way and we could only do that in community.

Community is essential in antiracist work and in the cultivation of holiness as it holds individuals accountable for their own progress in the development of a liberatory consciousness or their growth in grace. Community fosters a sense of allyship that ensures individuals remain actively engaged in the journey whether in dialogue circles or Wesleyan small groups.

We discovered that it is indeed in the active listening and presence of another that we came to apprehend most fully those critical moments in our own development. For us to do this we needed to take time to know one another beyond our collegial relationship. We needed to establish trust by being vulnerable with one another. We also needed to re-member for ourselves these moments of awakening. In retelling them to someone with different identities, we came to understand our stories in a new way. It is the encounter with another person that often sheds the most light on who we are ourselves. The presence of another provides a new perspective from which we can see ourselves again for the first time.

Just as we, Kim and Tiffany, needed each other to listen to our personal stories in order to discern and understand our own moments of awakening, students also need the presence of each other to evoke and frame their moments of awakening. Campus ministries interested in engaging in this type of work must craft intentional communities of students who will listen deeply to one another as they critically reflect on their own experience. These communities must be formed with concrete communal covenants or ground rules that help establish a community of trust where students are able to be vulnerable with themselves and one another. This means the task of group formation is key. Students must come to know one another personally and have a structured environment that encourages personal sharing with clear boundaries that shape a container for the ongoing conversation. This type of community requires a stable, ongoing, committed group of students. Through ongoing dialogue, campus ministries have the potential to engage and resist systemic oppression in the context of faith formation. Dialogues on race and ethnicity become integral parts of students' spiritual journeys.

Intersectionality: Exploring Our Multiple Identities

My focus on the intersections of race and gender only highlights the need to account for multiple grounds of identity when considering how the social world is constructed

—*Kimberly Crenshaw*

Intersectionality is a concept coined by the black feminist Kimberly Crenshaw to describe the complexities with which we enact our social identities. She articulates that it is not possible to think that at any given moment only one social identity may influence our experiences as we move through the world, although at particular moments, some identities are more salient than others. She argues that identities are interconnected and intersected so that they are working together at all times. Through our conversation, we discovered again how our multiple identities simultaneously gave us access to privileges and highlighted our oppressions. We came to an understanding of our race, gender, sexual orientation, class positions, abilities, and religious identities together. They could not be separately experienced because they are not separate in their manifestations in our lives.

In our first attempt to write this paper, we found ourselves bumping up against these multiple identities. While Kim and I were both co-facilitators in IGD, the power differential between us included more than our racial identities. Kim is a doctoral student and I am a dean. Kim is a layperson and I am clergy. Kim is Pentecostal, a Wesleyan tradition often marginalized by the mainline, and I am United Methodist, inheritors of the dominant Wesleyan tradition. We found the layers of inequity in identity created barriers to having the conversation we so desperately needed to have.

When we let go of the predetermined thesis and allowed the conversation to happen, we discovered that both of us experienced an awakening to our multiple identities during college. Developmentally, young adulthood is a time of tremendous change and transition. Examining, exploring, breaking down, and reconstructing who they are and want to be, college students are open to and eager to think critically about their identities and those of others. Campus ministries interested in fostering dialogue circles to address issues of social oppression and liberation must create a frame that helps students acknowledge and articulate their own multiple identities along intersecting lines of race, gender, sexuality, age, ability, and class.

Students in campus ministries must be given the space to explore all their identities not just Christian identities. Dialogue circles should help students see the way in which their multiple identities overlap and intersect and how some may be privileged while others targeted. This process engages students in analysis, which for Love and Wesley fosters critical reflection on why and how systemic oppression functions. Understanding intersectionality requires careful analysis. By seeing themselves as both privileged and targeted, students not only begin to see the systemic structures of oppression but also increase their ability to empathize, moving them from an either/or categorization of social identities to a both/and frame in which they see the ways in which they simultaneously benefit from and are harmed by systems of oppression.

Engaging the intersections of their identity, students are able to see the dynamics of oppression at work and come to a fuller understanding of their own multiple identities. That is to say, one may not understand white privilege until one understands one's privilege or oppression as male. We are often inclined to rank oppression instead of thinking of them as parallel and interlocking systems.[15] Race, gender, class, and Christian identities are always present for a student although at any given moment one of those identities may be more salient than the others. Campus ministers must recognize these both/and occurrences to help students make sense of all their identities including their spiritual identities.

Dismantling Systemic Oppression

It is learning how to take our differences and make them strengths. For the master's tools will never dismantle the master's house. They may allow us temporarily to beat him at his own game, but they will never enable us to bring about genuine change. And this fact is only threatening to those women who still define the master's house as their only source of support.

—Lorde, 1984

These interconnections between our identities highlighted for us the way in which our experience of who we were in the context of a wider world was shaped and determined by systemic structures. As we re-membered our coming to consciousness in college we both noted how we believed this process to

---

[15] Collins, "Toward a New Vision," 673–81.

be normative for all college students. Yet, as Kim, asserted, "Very quickly I learned that that wasn't true." The systemic nature of oppression and privilege creates a seamless mask that is difficult for individuals alone to remove. It was only through conversation and community that both of us began a process of coming to consciousness.

Both in classrooms and campus ministries, those seeking to dismantle oppression can often reinscribe it. We did when we began this project and even, perhaps, in the course of the dialogue encountered it in ourselves and each other. Liberatory consciousness, like sanctification, is an ongoing process that is never complete. It requires a tireless, incessant striving to become and stay awake to the webs of oppression that seek to imprison and separate us from ourselves and one another. Dialogues on oppression and privilege must constantly attend to the systemic nature of the problem. Individuals cannot undo systems, but together communities of liberation and love can make progress toward that end.

As students come to understand the intersections of their identity, they will also be able to see more clearly the systemic nature of oppression. Moving students from engaging with oppression as an individual/person to person and to a systemic understanding of oppression and privilege requires deliberate and authentic conversations. Hill Collins asserts that oppression must be understood as institutional, symbolic, and individual.[16] Dialogue circles must help students see the way in which oppression is systemic and come to understand and imagine collective ways of fostering liberation through the dismantling of those systems. In this way dialogue moves from awareness and analysis to action as individuals and

---

[16] Collins, "Toward a New Vision," 676.

communities begin to see ways of dismantling the system together. For Love and Wesley, action is absolutely necessary to further the development of liberatory consciousness and the journey of sanctification. If dialogue circles do not move beyond the individual identities of the students participating, they risk reinforcing the notion that racism or other forms of oppression are personal problems or moral failings of individuals. The solution must go beyond confronting isolated incidents of prejudice or hatred and move toward a systemic dismantling of oppressive institutions and structures. College ministers must dispel the myths that oppression is interpersonal and only enacted in bad people. Campus ministers must be clear that oppression is systemic and that these systems work together to sustain oppression.

Conclusion

As educators and campus ministers we are called to help students make sense of all their identities. In the era of Ferguson, Baltimore, Cincinnati, and countless other US cities where racial violence is rampant, we must be willing to speak against this violence and create spaces for students to make sense of the world. If these issues are not important to our students in our ministries, we should be concerned and should ask ourselves why that is. What is our role in making connections for students between racism, faith, and salvation? It is not enough to say they do not care or it does not matter. It matters. People are dying nationally and internationally because of discrimination, oppression, and nationalism. Now more than ever, we as campus ministers must engage with our students on issues of systemic oppression.

We are convinced of the urgency and necessity of dialogues on race and ethnicity among campus ministries. As United Methodists we believe, "Racism plagues and cripples our growth in Christ, inasmuch as it is antithetical to the gospel itself."[17] For those committed to a faithful life, confronting racism is absolutely necessary. It is not an ancillary outgrowth of our faith commitments, but rather central to it. Without confronting and dismantling racism, Christians cannot proceed in their journey of sanctification.

If campus ministries take seriously their role to accompany and encourage students in their spiritual journey of sanctification they can do nothing less than engage students in intentional and sustained conversations on racism in America. Our students navigate this racism and these racialized spaces on our campuses every day. There are never enough opportunities for students to discuss how they do so. If we allowed them to simultaneously explore their faith, and other complex questions of identity, we would help them answer the question, "How is it with your soul?" We would give them the tools and the skills to see more clearly, interlocking systems of oppression such as race, class, gender, sexuality, and religion because what is literally at stake is their soul.

---

[17] The United Methodist Church, http://www.umc.org/what-we-believe/the-social-community.

SEXUAL ETHICS

Christian Sexual Ethics:
Accountability and Compassion
with LGBTQ College Students

CHRISTIAN SEXUAL ETHICS: ACCOUNTABILITY AND COMPASSION WITH LGBTQ COLLEGE STUDENTS

Brittany Burrows

Issues, People, and Intersecting Narratives in the Church

The battle over inclusion of lesbian, gay, bisexual, transgender, and queer/questioning (LGBTQ) individuals has raged for many decades in The United Methodist Church (UMC).

Too often, amid heated debates over the denominational stance against same-sex marriage and the ordination of persons in same-sex relationships,[1] the word *issue* is uttered too often. While meetings convene to discuss the *issue* of homosexuality, the *issue* of same-sex marriage, the *issue* of ordination, and the future of a denomination that cannot agree on these *issues*, the humanity of LGBTQ persons is often lost in the crossfire. Though their identities are at the center of this debate, the actual narratives of LGBTQ persons are seldom heard in the institutional dialogue.

In contrast to this prevalent institutional narrative, it is nearly impossible to reduce the conversation around sexuality and gender identity to *issues* in the context of collegiate ministry. LGBTQ college students are present on every single campus on which we serve. We know their faces, and we have heard their stories. LGBTQ students in United Methodist collegiate ministries are often unaware of the institutional

---

[1] *The United Methodist Book of Discipline* does not mention transgender individuals.

struggle of the UMC around LGBTQ inclusion, and yet they are deeply affected by it. This chapter will share narratives too seldom heard in midst of the institutional battle—the stories of LGBTQ students who are part of our United Methodist collegiate ministries—while providing a framework for a Christian sexual ethics that provides both accountability and compassion with LGBTQ college students.

"Friends of Ben" to Resurrected Belovedness—A Collegiate Ministry Narrative

During my first year as a collegiate minister in 2011, a senior student from the Wesley Foundation came to me and said that he was interested in starting a weekly small group for LGBTQ students and their allies. We shared this idea with a few students we thought might be interested and set a date for the first meeting. Held in the back classroom of our campus ministry building on a Monday evening, the meeting was attended by a small number of students, mostly heterosexual, cisgender[2] allies. After gathering, the students introduced themselves, shared what they hoped to offer and receive from meetings, and developed a group covenant. Of those in attendance, there was only one student who was "out of the closet," or open about his sexual orientation. Ben[3] says this about his experience:

> It took me awhile to come out at the Methodist campus center, but I found that everyone was extremely supportive of me, and that my identity wasn't a big deal to them. It was fantastic. But there weren't very many LGBTQ people yet, or at least they weren't open. In my final year, we formed an LGBTQ Bible study

---

[2] Meaning not transgender.
[3] Name and significant details have been changed to protect anonymity. Excerpt from interview in May 2015.

group. When I first started going, I didn't know that it was something that had been missing from my life. In the group, we could be open about ourselves—we could be both Christian and gay or lesbian, bisexual or transgender at the same time, in the same space, and not feel excluded from the two different communities—we were a community together.

For the first year the group went incognito, meeting in a back classroom of the building. We weren't really sure if we wanted everybody to know we existed, because we wanted to make sure that it was a safe environment for everyone who was there. We didn't want any kind of protest, because we knew that the group really needed some protection from that. We needed to heal on our own as a group, and then start to widen to everyone else.

At the students' request, the group was not advertised on the website or promotional materials with the other Wesley Foundation small groups. The students quietly invited their friends to join and, through word-of-mouth, the group began to grow. During this time, they decided to name themselves "Friends of Ben" in honor of their original "token gay"; a name they could laugh about, but that also served a unique purpose. When new LGBTQ students came to visit the Wesley Foundation building to attend the group meeting, they could simply say to any student they encountered in the lobby, "I'm a friend of Ben," and would be directed to the back classroom where Ben was. In this way, LGBTQ students did not need to worry as much about outing themselves to their peers.

By the second year, Friends of Ben became the largest group at the Wesley Foundation, often having twenty-five or thirty students in attendance, including LGBTQ students and heterosexual, cisgender allies. Group meetings included prayer, Bible study, and discussion around the intersection of faith with sexuality and gender identity. As LGBTQ students experienced the welcome and affirmation of this group and began to reconcile their Christian faith with their sexual and gender identities, more began to come out and share their identities with their peers, and became less scared of being outed or protested. They began advertising the group on our website and promotional materials along with the other small groups at the Wesley Foundation. They changed the group name from Friends of Ben to "Refuge," deciding that they no longer needed a code name and that this new name more fully represented their identity as a group that was a safe haven for LGBTQ students.

As more group members felt safe and supported, internalized affirming interpretations of scripture, reconciled their faith and identities, and found the strength to come out to friends and family, many of the Refuge students began to move beyond the walls of the back classroom on Monday nights. Students who would have never previously stepped into a campus ministry or church service were now leading prayers in worship, cooking lunch for their peers, singing in the choir, and participating in other small groups at the Wesley Foundation. The refuge they had been seeking was no longer needed in the same way, and they changed the group name to "Open Doors," representing a removal of the barriers erected to protect group members from the scary voices of the church and outside world.

In subsequent years, group attendance steadily declined, and after four years, meetings stopped altogether. While decline in attendance and the death of a group is often seen as a failure, I counted this as a major success. The students no longer needed a secret group meeting behind a closed door with a code name, their safe refuge. They were ready to move into brave spaces[4] with a more reconciled faith, integrated identity, and resurrected sense of their own belovedness.

Challenges of LGBTQ College Students

College can be a time of intense intrapersonal discovery, as many students are, for the first time, in a context where they can discern and explore their identities with new freedom, a safe distance from their families and communities of origin. While some may have discovered early in life that they do not fit into heteronormative and cis-normative understandings of sexual orientation or gender identity, many persons discern these identities during their college years.

It is common for students to "come out" during this time by sharing their identities with peers, friends, and family members. The coming out process can often produce stress in students, especially in those who fear rejection or other punitive reactions, such as the revocation of financial support from non-affirming parents. Studies show a positive correlation between family rejection of lesbian, gay, bisexual, transgender (LGBT) young adults with an increase in substance abuse, suicidal ideation and behaviors, low self-esteem, and physical and mental health issues including depression.[5]

Other challenges for LGBT and queer/questioning (Q) college students include higher rates of harassment on campus, particularly for transgender and gender nonconforming students.

---

[4] The term and framework of *brave space* was developed by Brian Arao and Kristi Clemens. See Brian Arao and Kristi Clemens, "From Safe Spaces to Brave Spaces: A New Way to Frame Dialogue Around Diversity and Social Justice" in *The Art of Effective Facilitation*, ed. Lisa M. Landreman (Sterling, VA: Stylus Publishing, 2013).

[5] Caitlin Ryan et al., "Family Acceptance in Adolescence and the Health of LGBT Young Adults." *Journal of Child and Adolescent Psychiatric Nursing* 23, no. 4 (November 2010): 206–8.

Students with intersecting marginal identities (i.e., minority racial and gender or sexual identities) are more likely experience multiple forms of harassment on campus. LGBTQ students are more likely to have a negative perception of campus climates, particularly students with intersecting marginal identities and/ or who are transgender or gender nonconforming. Studies showed that LGBTQ college students were more likely to feel physically unsafe on campus, avoided "coming out" for fear of negative consequences, and more often seriously considered leaving their institutions.[6] While many campuses now employ nondiscrimination policies, some universities still do not; some even employ prohibitions against "homosexual acts," or include other policies that are not affirming of LGBTQ students. These factors can all negatively impact the experiences of LGBTQ students on college campuses.

The Role of Collegiate Ministries

In the face of these challenges, collegiate ministries can provide a community for students to live out their Christian faith and discern their unique identities. They offer a space for students to discern vocation, explore a call to ministry, and discover the ways God has created and gifted them to live and serve in the world. Collegiate ministries can make space for holy conversation around sexual orientation, gender identity, scripture, and faith. They can help students to have a safe community with which to heal from the wounds of rejection and reconcile their identities with their faith. Most important, collegiate ministries can help all students know that they are unconditionally loved by God.

However, collegiate ministries can also be places of judgment and rejection and can reinforce internalized shame,

---

[6] Sue Rankin et al., "2010 State of Higher Education for LGBT People" (Charlotte, NC: Campus Pride, 2010).

fear, and the belief that LGBTQ identities are irreconcilable with Christian faith. This is a notion to which young people are increasingly disillusioned. More than 66 percent of religiously unaffiliated young adults consider Christians to be antigay. According to researchers, unaffiliated young adults largely view Christians as hypocritical and judgmental, and "think Christians no longer represent what Jesus had in mind."[7]

Compassion as Christian Teaching

It is in fact Christian teachings that encourage many faithful Christians to welcome, embrace, and support LGBTQ persons. For United Methodists, the primary source of Christian teachings is scripture, which is faithfully interpreted through the lenses of tradition, reason, and experience to develop a deeper understanding.[8] Scripture has often been a bludgeon used to harm LGBTQ persons, but it can also be a salve which offers healing and affirmation.

The United Methodist position is that Christian teaching does not affirm same-sex relationships. While there are many faithful scholars who agree with this stance, there are also many faithful scholars that, interpreting scripture through the Wesleyan Quadrilateral,[9] believe homosexuality and other queer identities are compatible with Christian teaching. Within this group there is diversity and a variety of perspectives.

Some scholars say that those who reject LGBTQ persons often focus on a few misappropriated Bible verses and passages that have little or nothing to do with homosexuality or gender identity as they are widely understood today. They say the

---

[7] David Kinnaman and Gabe Lyons, *UnChristian: What a New Generation Really Thinks about Christianity . . . and Why It Matters* (Grand Rapids, MI: Baker, 2007). 15.
[8] See Tim Moore's chapter in this book: "Sunesis: Understanding via Interplay."
[9] Ibid.

biblical references to same-sex behavior do not speak to orientations or identities, since the writers' common conception was that all persons were heterosexual and cisgender. Culturally, same-sex behavior was equated with rape, lust, promiscuity, prostitution, idolatry, domination, violence, exploitation, and other sinful practices. The biblical writers had no conception of loving, committed, monogamous same-sex relationships, nor did they conceive of persons whose gender identity and/or expression is different than their sex assigned at birth.[10]

Other scholars say that homosexuality and queer identities as they are understood today may have actually existed in similar form during the time the biblical authors lived. If this is true, it does indeed seem like there were negative references to same-sex intimacy. Though these passages have been interpreted by some to condemn homosexuality, this group of scholars would assert that these scriptural interpretations do not reflect God's timeless will for humanity.[11] While the Bible has been quoted to promote slavery and the second-class citizenship of women, many Christians have discerned that these scriptural interpretations do not reflect God's timeless will, and The United Methodist Church has taken a strong stance against slavery and affirmed the equal status of women. Perhaps then, the condemnatory interpretations of the same-sex intimacy passages also do not represent God's timeless will.

Other scholars believe that "queerness" is not only present in scripture, but that positive examples can be found throughout the Bible—from the elevation of men with traditionally feminine qualities like Jacob and Joseph, to the

---

[10] Based on a lecture by Dr. Jaime Clark-Soles, New Testament professor at Southern Methodist University Perkins School of Theology.

[11] Adam Hamilton, "On Homosexuality, Many Christians Get the Bible Wrong," *Washington Post*, February 13, 2013, http://www.faithstreet.com/onfaith/2013/02/13/on-homosexuality-many-christians-get-the-bible-wrong/15775.

covenant relationships between David and Jonathan or Ruth and Naomi, to Jesus's affirmation of eunuchs.[12] Some of the very same scriptural passages used to condemn LGBTQ persons can also be interpreted in ways that are affirming. For example, while the story of Sodom and Gomorrah has famously been interpreted as a story of God's wrath against gay persons, the prophet Ezekiel writes, "This was the guilt of your sister Sodom: she and her daughters had pride, excess of food, and prosperous ease, but did not aid the poor and needy." [13] Jesus later implies that the sin of the people[14] of Sodom was inhospitality in Luke 10:10-12.[15] While the story of Sodom may not speak directly to LGBTQ identities or relationships, it has much to share about welcoming the stranger, the outcast, and those from other lands. It calls us to be open, hospitable, and generous to those who are different, such as LGBTQ persons. In the same way, Romans 1:26-27 has frequently been quoted in an effort to condemn homosexuality, as Paul lists the consequences of a fallen state of humanity.[16] According

---

[12] Scholars hold diverse opinions about what a eunuch was—whether this implied castration, celibacy, or even same-sex attraction. It is clear, however, that eunuchs were outside the realm of conventional gender identity and/or sexuality, and yet they were not condemned by Jesus. In contrast, Jesus seems to imply in Matthew that being a eunuch is a special calling, saying, "Not everyone can accept this teaching, but only those to whom it is given. For there are eunuchs who have been so from birth, and there are eunuchs who have been made eunuchs by others, and there are eunuchs who have made themselves eunuchs for the sake of the kingdom of heaven. Let anyone accept this who can" (Matt 19:11-12).
[13] Ezekiel 16:49.
[14] Hebrew Bible scholar John Holbert writes, "In its original Hebrew, two different nouns are used to refer to the people of the city, and neither is gender-specific. Hence the scene is perhaps not one of homosexual rape, but rather of depraved violence by the entire town—men, women, and children—against strangers who have come for refuge." From John Holbert, "What Does the Bible Say about Homosexuality?" in *Finishing the Journey: Questions and Answers from United Methodists of Conviction*, ed. John Thornburg and Alicia Dean (Dallas: Northaven United Methodist Church, 2000), 15.
[15] Luke 10:10-12.
[16] Ibid., 16. According to Holbert, "These famous lines list examples of Paul's understanding of the consequences of the fallen state of humanity. He wrote here, as some of his contemporaries wrote, of out-of-control passions that had become ends

to social ethicist and pastor Dave Barnhart, to get stuck on this list is to misunderstand the purpose of Paul's message. He writes,

> The whole point of Paul's tirade is what comes next. He goes on to say that it is not the ignorant people of Gentile nations, but "you who pass judgment on others" who "have no excuse" (2:1). Ultimately, Paul says, it is not being Gentile or Jew that saves us from God's anger, but God's own grace. Why?
>
> "Because God shows no partiality" (Rom. 2:11).
>
> The very passage from Romans that modern Christians use to condemn homosexuality as sin is the one that summarizes Paul's lifetime of mission and ministry, doing his best to reconcile Jews and Gentiles in the early church.[17]

These are just a few of many scriptures that can be interpreted in ways that encourage the reconciliation of diverse groups and the embrace of those who are labeled as others, strangers, or outcasts.

These diverse perspectives point to the ambiguity of scripture in speaking to LGBTQ identities. While the dominant perspective in The United Methodist Church is that homosexuality is

---

in themselves. The men and women whom Paul described in these lines were, in fact, heterosexuals performing homosexual acts. As was the case with his contemporaries, Paul knew nothing of homosexual orientation; he assumed all people were by nature heterosexual, and if they were engaging in homosexual acts, they could be nothing but terrible examples of human sinfulness. Paul's imperfect knowledge of this issue was fully reflective of the imperfect knowledge of his culture. We ought not ascribe to Paul the last word on the question of same-sex relationships any more than we should assume that his comments concerning the length of men's and women's hair (1 Cor 11:2-6) are definitive for all time."

[17] Dave Barnhart, *God Shows No Partiality: The Forgotten Slogan of the Early Church* (n.p.: printed by author, 2012), 61-62.

incompatible with Christian teaching,[18] many faithful United Methodists believe Christian teachings rooted in scripture, tradition, reason, and experience can fully support the inclusion and affirmation of LGBTQ individuals. LGBTQ persons are no less beloved and worthy of a relationship with God than heterosexual and cisgender persons, but that relationship can be wounded by the condemnation of the church. The healing of these wounds can be facilitated through the bold proclamation of good news that God's love is for all people without condition.

Proclaiming the truth about God's unconditional love for all people does not mean the end of moral virtue. Evil and sin are ever-present realities to which the church must speak out. The institutional and corporate sins of racism, sexism, classism, ageism, nationalism, heterosexism, and others are rampant and pervasive. In the context of Christian sexual ethics, it is important to remember that sin, including sexual sin, is widespread among heterosexual and cisgender individuals and communities as well as LGBTQ individuals and communities. In the face of institutional and individual sin, the church must always be a force for good, moving people and systems away from sin and guiding us toward the kin-dom[19] of God. To do this, we need a Christian sexual ethics which promotes accountability for all people.

Ethics of Accountability

Progressive Christians often shy away from developing sexual ethics for the LGBTQ community, because their sexual expression has been so frequently demonized. For decades, LGBTQ persons have been lambasted by the church, and told

---

[18] As demonstrated by current church doctrine and polity in the *Book of Discipline*, and the inability to make changes to this language by majority vote at previous General Conferences.
[19] "Kin-dom" is an anti-imperialist conception of the kingdom of God in which all people are reconciled to God and one another.

either explicitly or implicitly that that their expression of sexuality is immoral and irreconcilable with the Bible and the Christian faith. In an effort to remedy this wound, the pendulum of progressive Christianity has swung the opposite direction, largely neglecting to offer any semblance of sexual ethics for fear that this might be perceived as judgmental.

A few years ago, before same-sex marriage had been legalized, I remember sitting with Jake,[20] a gay college student, who had been engaging in risky sexual behavior with men he met online. He shared with me that these casual sexual encounters made him feel empty inside. Prior to coming out as gay, Jake had abstained from sex, wore a "purity ring," and planned to save sex for marriage. After realizing his sexuality, he believed that he would no longer be able to have the marriage he had been hoping for, with a wedding blessed by the church he grew up in. Jake took the purity ring off, again realizing he would never be able to have the marriage he desired. As his hopes for marriage ceased, so did his long-held sexual ethics.

As Jake's minister, I grieved with him that he did not feel he could have the marriage he had hoped for. I wanted Jake to know that he was of sacred worth, even though the church would not bless his relationship. I wanted Jake to cease engaging in casual sex with strangers because Jake said these encounters made him feel empty.[21] As a child of God, Jake is deserving of the type of committed, loving, blessed relationship he has always wanted. As we sat together, I invited him to explore the idea that he might still be able to have that relationship after all, even if not affirmed by the church.

---

[20] Name and significant details have been changed to protect anonymity.

[21] Engaging in sexual behavior that makes one feel empty is a form of sexual vice, later defined by Elaine Heath as "behavior that in some way does violence to self," including emotional violence.

Jake's initial inability to imagine having a committed, loving, blessed marriage is a direct result of the shame induced by the church's judgment of same-sex relationships. LGBTQ persons have been told that their relationships are sinful. These teachings often cause deep wounds that can lead to profoundly negative effects on the psychological, emotional, and spiritual well-being of LGBTQ individuals, and cast a shadow of shame on their relationships. It requires an exorbitant amount of resilience for LGBTQ children of the church to live healthy lives, and even to live, when the church imposes such judgment on them. Furthermore, it is incredibly difficult for LGBTQ persons to develop healthy sexual ethics under a cloud of shame-inducing theology. To promote healing and wholeness for LGBTQ persons, the church must embrace their identities, work to cast out shame-inducing theology, and promote a holistic sexual ethics that honors the image of God in all people.

It is important to promote sexual ethics for all persons, especially for college students as they navigate young adulthood in societies pervaded with messages promoting sexual vice and violence. The rape, lust, promiscuity, prostitution, idolatry, domination, violence, and exploitation denounced in scripture are always sinful, regardless of the genders of persons involved. Theologian Elaine Heath asserts that when it comes to sexuality, we are asking the wrong questions. About the discussion of sexuality in churches, she writes:

> The problem, we think, is that the wrong set of questions shapes the discussion. Are you homo (bad) or hetero (good)? Having sex with anyone besides your own spouse (bad)? Married (good) or single (highly suspect)? These questions are too simplistic and too dualistic. They assume too much and ask too little. It is past time to ask new, better questions about sexual virtue and sexual vice. The springboard for the new questions is not genitalia

but *imago dei*, the inherent sanctity and dignity of human life.

The homo that has our attention is *homo sapiens*. Do we understand ourselves and others as human beings made in the image of God?"[22]

According to Heath, sexual vice is behavior that inflicts sexual violence on self or others, which can be physical, verbal, mental, and/or emotional. She writes,

Sexual vice is sinful first and foremost because it violates, exploits, objectifies, manipulates, takes advantage of, and uses human beings. It treats humans made in the image of God, as commodities. Sometimes sexual vice is carried out to give pleasure to the perpetrator of the sin. Often it is an act in which domination is the goal, rather than sex per se. Sexualizing others, internet bullying around sexuality, sexual abuse of all kinds, sexual domestic violence . . . these are just a few of the possible sexual sins. So much of the fruit of sexual vice is sexual self-loathing, self-harm, and self-deception about one's sexuality."[23]

For far too long the conversation around sexuality in the church has been simplistic, framed in a way that leads us to ask the wrong questions. This type of discussion can also produce deep shame for LGBTQ persons.

Heath calls the church to promote sexual virtue, which she describes as a "deep integrity, respectfulness, and authenticity in how one lives one's sexuality," which begins with "a fundamental

---

[22] Elaine Heath, "A New Set of Questions about Sex and Sin," January 5, 2014. Accessed May 15, 2015. https://elaineaheath.wordpress.com/2014/01/05/a-new-set-of-questions-about-sex-and-sin/.

[23] Ibid.

respect for one's identity as someone made in the image of God," and extends outward to other persons. It is "inherently reverent of embodiedness," neither beginning nor ending with genitalia, but with "fully accepting, loving, and wisely stewarding our whole, embodied life as human beings. It begins with a deep commitment to the theological concept of *imago dei* and loving one's neighbor as oneself. It grows with a daily commitment to first do no harm and second, do all the good we can to ourselves, our neighbors, and our enemies." If sexual virtue and sexual vice are addressed with a better set of questions, Heath asserts "we will find our way out of the morass of violence against the sexual 'other,'" moving into a more holy understanding of embodiment, and becoming better practitioners of sexual virtue.[24]

The church needs to offer a sexual ethics of accountability for all persons, regardless of orientation or identity, ethics that denounce sexual violence and vice and uplift the virtues of love and commitment to neighbor and self. We need not fear this discussion. If we are asking the right questions and uplifting virtue while denouncing vice and violence, this conversation will not shame the identities of LGBTQ persons. Instead, it will encourage them to embrace themselves as individuals created in the image of God and give them a framework by which to live into a virtuous expression of their sexuality. With this framework, Jake and others like him will no longer feel the need to choose between their identities and sexual expression, but will know that they too can live a life firmly rooted in the Christian faith that embraces both their identities and virtuous sexual expression.

It would be sin for any person to deny their identity as a child of God, created in God's image. Sexuality is a gift from God, and to deny this part of one's identity would be to deny that divine gift.

---

[24] Ibid.

Collegiate ministries can help move students from vice to virtue by helping them to discern their unique identities as children of God, which includes their gender and sexual identities. To do this, we must promote an environment in which it is safe to explore questions of identity, and where the revelations of students about their gender and sexuality are affirmed.

Offering sexual ethics also includes encouraging a holistic understanding of relationships. Sexual expression is just one part of romantic relationships, but an important part nonetheless. For most people,[25] healthy relationships require spiritual, emotional, intellectual, and sexual connection. In a kind of *perichoresis*,[26] these elements are interdependent and are in unity with one another. Without each of these components, romantic relationships can be stunted. It is unethical for churches to tell LGBTQ persons that they cannot express their sexuality, because in doing so, the church is saying that they are not worthy of the holistic, healthy relationships that require sexual connection alongside emotional, intellectual, and spiritual elements. Condemning an LGBTQ person's identity and/or sexual expression is in itself a form of vice, in that it reinforces shame and inflicts spiritual harm. Instead, the church can encourage the expression of virtuous sexuality as a significant component of relationships that honor self and neighbor.

Compassion in Action

In the context of collegiate ministry, compassionate work with LGBTQ college students can take many forms. The

---

[25] It is important to note that physical/sexual intimacy is essential for most romantic relationships, but not for all. For example, people who identify as asexual may not see sexual intercourse as a fundamental part of healthy relationships. Celibacy should always be based on personal identity or calling and not a demand of society or the church.

[26] Refers to the interdependent, interrelatedness of the persons of the Trinity.

first way to offer compassion is to provide a visible welcome. Collegiate ministries can be safe spaces for LGBTQ college students as they discern their sexual and gender identities or heal from the wounds of rejection, but it often requires a visible affirmation before LGBTQ students will consider involvement. Many LGBTQ students have faced rejection from the church either directly or indirectly, so there is often an understandable assumption on their part that there is no collegiate ministry that will embrace them, or that ministries will expect them to change their identities. A visible welcome can come in the form of a mission or inclusivity statement which explicitly names its affirmation of students of all sexual orientations and gender identities, prominently displayed on the ministry website or flyers, or it may come in the form of an inclusive symbol on a ministry building door or window, like a rainbow flag or sticker.

Even when it seems that we are not reaching LGBTQ students, it is also important for campus ministries to recognize that LGBTQ students may already be involved in our ministries, however these students may be closeted or have yet to discern or develop their identities. For these students, it may be helpful to provide opportunities for discussion around sexual orientation and gender identity. Riley,[27] who identifies as a non-binary queer trans person, grew up in The United Methodist Church and was deeply involved in his Wesley Foundation in college, shares this reflection on their experience as someone who, as a college student, had not yet discerned their queer identity:

> While I was in school, the Wesley Foundation was a very important aspect of my life. The community it provided for me was absolutely irreplaceable. It was certainly not even on my radar at the time that I might

---

[27] Name and significant details have been changed to protect anonymity.

be queer or trans. The local Methodist community was not, in any form or fashion, accepting of LGBTQ people. I knew only a small handful of gay people, and certainly the word "trans" had yet to enter my vocabulary or worldview. At the time, the Wesley Foundation reflected the wider community, and in that way we absolutely never talked about sexual orientation or gender identity. For me, not ever having conversations about it at all just served to solidify the fact that any deviation from the norm in this way was wrong; and it was so wrong that we didn't even need to give it the time of day for discussion. It took me going to seminary before I had anybody in my life offer any sort of theological or biblical approach to sexuality or gender that was expansive, inclusive, or even thought-provoking.[28]

Having these conversations around sexuality and gender identity is not only compassionate towards LGBTQ students directly involved in the collegiate ministry, but also can help heterosexual and cisgender students develop and articulate their own compassionate response to those who are LGBTQ, as Riley illustrates:

I also think it is likely that those conversations would have helped prevent me from doing as much harm as I fear I did to the few gay people in my life at the time. When it comes to teaching or affirming prejudice in the name of God, college ministry becomes not only about the people directly involved, but also the people the participants interact with. I think that if I had a leader that was affirming of LGBTQ people, I would have at least been less confident in assuring gay people that there was

---

[28] Excerpt from interview in May 2015.

something sinful about their actions. I of course know now the damage that such teaching does, and I wish I would have had a person of faith in my life who could have revealed to me that there was a different approach to faith, sexuality, and gender identity.[29]

Conversations around sexuality and gender identity can happen in a variety of ways. In my own collegiate ministry experience, we hosted events on campus in which students would watch a documentary[30] focusing on faith, sexuality and gender identity, followed by guided discussion. We also hosted a panel discussion, in which LGBTQ-supportive United Methodist pastors and LGBTQ students shared about the intersection of faith with sexuality and gender identity, followed by interactive discussion. When selecting panel members for the event, we were careful to invite pastors who were already known to be supportive of LGBTQ persons. When planning and implementing programs like these, it is important to remember that discussions around the intersection of faith, scripture, sexuality, and gender identity can be very sensitive. If not done thoughtfully, dialogue can quickly become harmful, especially when the discussion becomes akin to the institutional dialogues that engage *issues* above actual persons who are LGBTQ. We must always put persons first, recognizing that LGBTQ persons are present in most rooms and can be deeply harmed when we are not sensitive in the way we engage discussion about their identities and faith. We should not shy away from these programs out of fear, but should take time to educate ourselves so that we can lead in a way that best honors LGBTQ students.

---

[29] Ibid.

[30] Good documentaries for discussion include the films *Fish out of Water* and *For the Bible Tells Me So*.

Collegiate ministry leaders can do this by pursuing educational opportunities around how to be allies through their language and action. The transition to using affirming language can be a difficult one, even for LGBTQ persons themselves; but taking this step can help leaders facilitate a welcoming atmosphere for LGBTQ students. This includes knowing what terms to use when talking with or referencing the LGBTQ community; for example, saying "gay" instead of "homosexual," or "transgender" instead of "transgendered." This also includes knowing how to create a safe environment for students, for example, by not "outing" them or by calling transgender students by their preferred pronouns. Many universities now offer LGBTQ "Ally" or "Safe Zone" trainings, which are available to university staff, students, and community members, and can offer education for collegiate ministers and students.

Collegiate ministries can also support LGBTQ students with small groups for these students and their allies. These groups can look very different depending on the context. For example, the Friends of Ben/Refuge/Open Doors group met weekly for Bible study, prayer, and discussion. Bible study often engaged LGBTQ-affirming interpretations of scripture like those discussed earlier in this chapter, and students would take turns bringing favorite Bible passages to talk about. Discussion included sharing coming out stories, faith experiences, individual stages of LGBTQ identity development,[31] Christian sexual ethics, and the spectrum of sexual and gender identity. Group meetings began by shaping and recalling the group covenant and ground rules, in order to offer the safest space possible. This is just one of many forms a group like this

---

[31] See: V. Cass, "Homosexual Identity Formation: A Theoretical Model," *Journal of Homosexuality* 4, no. 3 (1979): 219–35.

can take. Group structure and content may vary depending on students' stages of identity development, which may, for example, vary from identity confusion to pride in lesbian or gay students.[1] These groups usually are able to reach more students when offered in connection and with support from any LGBTQ student center or student groups on campus.

Though the concept of "safe space" is appealing, no space can be completely safe, and we can never fully protect students from harm. However, collegiate ministries can work to be spaces that are less likely to cause harm. Collegiate ministries can be spaces of healing and of reconciling faith and identity. They can offer sexual ethics that promote accountability while affirming students' identities and compassionately offer a space for students to experience the love of God and neighbor.

A Transformed Narrative

Today in The United Methodist Church, we are faced with very different—but deeply connected—narratives. One is the institutional narrative that LGBTQ persons are an *issue* to be debated. The other, as demonstrated by "Friends of Ben," is that LGBTQ college students often do not feel safe in the church, even within our United Methodist collegiate ministries. The fact that members of the group felt they had to be closeted in the back classroom and have a code name to ensure they had a place of refuge speaks to the lack of safety they have experienced in the church. While many of our college students are unaware of official denominational policies, our institutional narrative of condemnation, people as *issues,* and the reinforcement of *don't ask, don't tell inclusion* trickles down into the everyday work of ministry and into the lives of

---

[1] Examples of stages from Cass Identity Model. See V. Cass, "Homosexual Identity Formation: A Theoretical Model."

the students we serve with. They are profoundly impacted by church teachings and dialogues that promote shame.

The narrative I am most familiar with is that LGBTQ persons deeply long to be welcomed and celebrated by the church. LGBTQ college students want to serve in worship, cook lunch for their peers, sing in the choir, and be full participants in our collegiate ministries. They want to be extended compassion and have a model for sexual virtue. Due to the damage already done by the church, this will likely happen only after we intentionally create spaces where students can heal and be reminded of their own belovedness.

Moving forward, what will our shared narrative be? Will our narrative be one of brokenness and division or of healing, reconciliation, and liberation? I pray that the narrative can be redeemed and transformed into one in which all people are celebrated in their identities, reconciled to one another, and will deeply know that they are beloved children of God.

VOCATION

*Clearness Committees Revisited:
Gathering Young Adults for
Contemplative Discernment*

*Discovering Calling at the Center
and the Edge*

*Wesley, Integrity, and Vocation: The
Power and Possibility of Collegiate
Intentional Christian Community*

CLEARNESS COMMITTEES REVISITED: GATHERING YOUNG ADULTS FOR CONTEMPLATIVE DISCERNMENT

Dori Grinenko Baker and L. Callid Keefe-Perry

O n a spring afternoon near Tacoma, Washington, a group of twenty-somethings sit in the sun-drenched picnic area of a Lutheran camp. Drawing their lingering lunch conversations to a close, fifteen of them stand, stretch, breathe and look up, taking in tall evergreens and blue sky. They enter a long rectangular room that was used as a middle-school worship space just days before. Large green construction paper leaves line the ceilings and walls: a jungle theme.

These young adults have come from across the United States and Canada for a weekend retreat, an interlude midway through a year of volunteering in a homeless shelter, as an immigration advocate, or in an afterschool program for underserved youth. They settle into seats, kick off their shoes, wrap themselves into chairs, and begin to enter a time set apart for them to imagine that the Spirit is present and will ask something of them.[1]

"What are you majoring in?" "What job do you want?" "What do you want to do with your life?"

Though these questions have a place, the impulse to imagine a future any different than the present is difficult. Young people awakened to the realities of police brutality, pervasive racism, sexual violence, ecological degradation, and other social ills want to imagine how their lives might contribute to a more hopeful and just future. Rather than viewing discernment

---

[1] The vignettes in this paper come from research encounters. The names of participants and details of content have been altered to protect confidentiality.

as a treasure hunt in which one's vocation is a sought-after prize, we reframe discernment as a practice that invites imagination, a bit of risk, and the hope of deepening community.

Finding the next right step—whether that has to do with ending mass incarceration, getting an MBA, or even, for some, deciding whether to get up in the morning—is hard work; young people engaged in this work deserve the best tools available.

This chapter grows out of our work exploring practices that help young adults answer deep questions about meaning and purpose. Callid is a Quaker minister and consultant formed in the traditions of the Religious Society of Friends, particularly those that arise from explicitly Christian theology. He is a member of Fresh Pond Meeting of New England Yearly Meeting. Dori is a United Methodist pastor, scholar, and consultant for a national nonprofit called the Forum for Theological Exploration (FTE). FTE is a leadership incubator for the church and religious academy; it hosts retreats like the one described in the vignette above.

We are both theologians who merge scholarship and practice. Following a long tradition of collegiality between the Wesleyan tradition and the Religious Society of Friends,[2] we embrace our traditions as renewal movements that seeded prophetic witness in the world. We see resonances between the symbols, language, and beauty of Methodism's youth and

---

[2] Many thanks to David White and John Tyson who point us to clear cross-pollination between the Wesleys and the Friends in the early years including their practice around field preaching, lay preaching, plain speech and attire, inner witness, and roles of women. While no direct proof exists that John Wesley read the journal of George Fox (a founder of Quakerism), there is a good discussion of their similarities in the introduction to the bicentennial edition of his journal in *Wesley's Works*. It is clear, however, that John Wesley read and reacted to Robert Barclay's *Apology*. For more on these connections see also, Carol Spencer, "The Relationship between Quakers and Methodists in the Eighteenth Century" in *Holiness: The Soul of Quakerism: An Historical Analysis of the Theology of Holiness in the Quaker Tradition* (Eugene, OR: Wipf & Stock, 2007).

the theological lexicon of the Friends. We believe the sparse elegance of Friends' practice and its emphasis on the validity of human experience might speak to young adults today.[3] Out of these contexts, we invite campus ministers into a robust encounter based on Clearness Committees (CCs) and other traditions stewarded by the Religious Society of Friends.

A Clearness Committee (CC) gathers a small group of people around one "focus person," who seeks help discerning around a choice, situation, or life experience. The group enters a prayerfully deep listening and questioning space and practice the discipline of not offering advice. Sometimes the focus person arrives at a new sense of purpose or clarity or the ability to name a next step; other times the outcome is less concrete but nonetheless a practice of discernment. This practice grows out of Friends' traditional ways of silent worship, which will be described in greater detail below. While significant scholarship describes the CC itself, little work has been done to explore its applicability to young adults, especially in diverse populations. Our larger research project—from which this chapter arises— invites adaptations of the Clearness Committee, particularly the possibility of emerging from the space having discerned a "next most faithful step." The research project involves 250 young adults over the course of three years, 160 of whom we've already led in this practice.

After careful preparation, the group of fifteen is ready to begin a Clearness Committee. During a break, James approaches Callid with a look of concern. "I don't know about this . . . It seems like mumbo-jumbo" he says. "I'm not sure this process is even biblical." A member of a fast-growing conservative church-planting movement, James expresses his

---

[3] We are not arguing for the universal application of contemplative practices, or that they will speak to all young people; this paper concerns *a* practice to be considered.

belief that women should not be ordained or pursue church leadership. This occurs just moments after a woman in the group has lifted up her own sense of call to ordination as focusing question for the Clearness Committee. James is unsure if he should continue in the Clearness Committee given what he believes.

Callid responds: "Do you think you can hang in? This process is not about what you believe. It's about your listening for what God might be asking her through you. Do you think you can keep listening with an open heart? I don't need you to give up on what you believe. I just need to be prayerfully open to the possibility that God can be here with us. Can you swing that?" James reaches for his hat, twists the brim to the left and nods: affirmative and skeptical.

Not only does James participate, he later offers aloud to the whole of the retreat that he found brothers and sisters where he thought there were none. "God sure does surprise us sometimes, right?"

Potential Prophets and the Questions They Ask

James's discomfort arose in a group of eighteen- to thirty-year-olds. This group included an indigenous woman from Canada, a transgender white male from the West Coast, and a Latino hip-hop artist from Philadelphia. In groups like this, we've heard the following questions, often posed with great passion, even angst: How can I help make sure kids on my block live to see their twenty-first birthday? What can I do to end mass incarceration? How do I help start a community garden in the middle of this food desert? These young adults, while coming from vastly diverse backgrounds, share generational and developmental characteristics borne out in the research on today's emerging adults.

Millennials and Emerging Adults

Millennials are the largest living generation, making up one-third of the current US population. Their likes and dislikes will dictate trends across sectors of public life for decades to come. They are also the most racially, ethnically, and religiously diverse generational cohort to exist in the United States and are also the most tolerant of diversity. Significantly, they are increasingly unattached to organized religion. Their sheer numbers drive the national statistics making "no religious affiliation" the largest part of the US population. Emerging adulthood describes a distinct new developmental period of life between late teens and mid-to-late twenties, marked by delay in reaching traditional measures of adult status, particularly marriage and parenthood. This is the time during which most identity exploration and achievement take place.[4]

Like Starbucks and Target, denominations mindful of trends among millennials often try to listen for clues that would help their "products" appeal to these consumers. While this approach makes sense within an economic framework, a theological framework suggests an alternative response. Christian tradition has stewarded a vast array of spiritual practices, transferring them to new generations and allowing them to be transformed in the process.[5] Might these practices be seen as *tools we can give away*, with no strings attached, as part of God's "gift economy," rather than *tools used* to market an already over-marketed-to cohort? Might contemplative practices—those that draw on the numinous, mystical, experiential aspects of divine nature—be perhaps power gifts to offer from the

---

[4] Jeffrey Jensen Arnett, *Emerging Adulthood: the Winding Road from the Late Teens through the Twenties*, (Oxford, U.K.: Oxford University Press, 2004), 4–9.
[5] Mary Elizabeth Moore, *Education for Continuity and Change: A New Model for Christian Religious Education* (Abingdon, 1983).

Christian tradition? In that spirit of giving, we turn to the reasons we think CCs might be a welcome resource for contemporary collegiate ministry. While they might not *immediately* appeal in a flashy way, our research suggests that group-based contemplative discernment can indeed be compelling and useful to young adults.

Three Points of Connection

Our hunch is that contemplative practices in general—and CCs in particular—hold promise for young people living into the "big questions" about meaning and purpose in the United States today because they align with three values observed among millennials. These three values are:

- a desire to make a difference in the world

- a decreasing religiosity coupled with increasing spiritual curiosity

- a hunger for ways to explore their "inward landscape"[6]

This generation wants to make a difference in the world and believes in its ability to do so. As the capacity for abstract thinking develops, one begins to see one's place in the universe. This means that young adults awaken to social ills as the best of higher education and life experience broadens their intellectual and relational repertoire. But in the midst of this dawning awareness can come a sense of feeling overwhelmed. Emerging adults are not likely to look to traditional religious spaces as a place to sort through the stuff of their lives. Indeed, the most notable sociological trend among millennials is a decline in their affiliation with organized religion.[7]

---

[6] Brian Drayton and William P. Taber, *A Language for the Inward Landscape: Spiritual Wisdom from the Quaker Tradition* (Philadelphia: Tract Association of Friends, n.d.).
[7] Michael Lipkka, "Millennials Increasingly Are Driving Growth of 'Nones,'" Pew Research Center. Accessed May 12, 2015. http://www.pewresearch.org/fact-tank/2015/05/12/millennials-increasingly-are-driving-growth-of-nones/.

Accompanying the disaffiliation with institutional religion is an *increased* interest in spirituality. Most people who claim to be "nothing in particular" or "none" were raised to be at least nominally religious. In other words, many of the "nones" are not actively hostile to religion, and might actually be open to "new" forms of it.[8]

Given the way we frame the CC for participants, it breaks down "making a difference in the world" into small, manageable next steps, helping people avoid a sense of immobilization and compassion fatigue. Because millennials are interested in exploring spirituality but are averse to religious institution, they may find this practice to be an accessible tool that does not require the "churchy" language associated with contemporary Christianity, both liberal and conservative. In introducing the practice, we frame the invitation as taking an imaginative leap toward attentiveness to the divine. It is an explicitly theological exercise, however, it is practiced in a way that engenders openness and exploration. Although most of our experience has been with students who self-identify as Christian or of multiple religious identities, it is possible to introduce communal discernment using non-specific Christian language, inviting the spiritual but not religious. In short, a participant could enter into a CC without ever encountering the words Marcus Borg describes as "speaking Christian," those words and phrases that have lost their meaning, or worse, grown negative associations because of their emphasis on proscriptive social norms.[9]

---

[8] See Alexander W. Campbell, Helen S. and Jennifer A. Lindholm. *Cultivating the Spirit: How College Can Enhance Students' Inner Lives* (San Francisco: Jossey-Bass, 2012).

[9] Marcus Borg, *Speaking Christian: Why Christian Words Have Lost Their Meaning and Power—And How They Can Be Restored* (NY: HarperCollins/HarperOne, 2011).

* * *

Index cards pass from hand to hand around the circle. Dori says, "Go take a walk outside. Listen carefully to what's been bubbling up in you this weekend. Is there a question you'd like greater clarity around as you consider your future? Remember, it might be about baby steps, not necessarily a five-year plan."

Twenty minutes later, people have returned. Dori asks for volunteers: "Does anyone feel like they have something they're carrying that they would like to work with in discernment?" After a pause four hands rise. Their questions? Should I stay enrolled next semester, or go home to help my mom through her kidney transplant? Am I supposed to go to seminary after graduation, or continue this project of translating the New Testament into my native language? Should I keep living with my current roommates, or move into the service-learning dorm? What am I supposed to do about mass incarceration after my year of service ends? Each of the four becomes a focus person as small groups assemble in the corners of the room.

* * *

Clearness Committees: Preparation and Practice

The four questions above are a small slice of a vast possible range of questions that might surface among young adults on any given day. We have facilitated CCs with questions ranging from "Am I being called into ordained ministry?" and "Should I break up with my partner?" to smaller decisions like what courses to take next semester. Practicing discernment about even small daily decisions can develop the muscle needed for discerning more significant life choices.[10]

---

[10] Lloyd Lee Wilson's "Discernment: Coming Under the Guidance of the Holy Spirit," *Journal of the North Carolina Yearly Meeting*, no. 6 (2012). (Conservative).

Our CC events have two steps: first preparation then practice. Preparation for soul care is never to be taken lightly. The groups where we have introduced this practice are usually ones where leaders have mindfully created community norms that that engender "brave spaces" prior to our gathering.[11] If that's the case, we remind people of these norms, particularly emphasizing the need to maintain confidentiality about the content of the CC. If norms haven't been established, we do so using "covenants of presence."[12] We then spend an hour defining the terms *vocation* and *discernment,* using resources from our own lives, etymology, scripture, and religious tradition in what we call "Discernment and Vocation 101."[13]

Briefly, we reflect that discernment involves figuring out the next most faithful step—not figuring out the entire length story of a life or knowing its ultimate destination. Lives unfold; interruptions happen. Sometimes our stories are more of an improvisation than they are a Homeric journey.[14] We invite young adults to think about discerning in the daily realities of their lived existence—what *mujerista* theologians call *lo cotidiano.*[15]

Referencing the struggle of immigrant Latin@s[16] is intentional; we recognize that many people in the room navigate lives in which hunger, abuse, and multiple oppressions are daily realities. While we note that doing discernment often means relinquishing some

---

[11] Brian Arao and Kristi Clemens, "From Safe Spaces to Brave Spaces: A New Way to Frame Dialogue around Diversity and Social Justice" in *The Art of Effective Facilitation: Reflections from Social Justice Educators,* ed. L. Landreman (Sterling, VA: Stylus Publishing, 2013), 135–50.

[12] For a list of these covenants, see "Guide to Vocation Care," p 11. http://fteleaders. org/uploads/files/GUIDE%20TO%20VOCATIONCARE%202012%20Low.pdf.

[13] A full description of this training, including scriptural reflection is in our book, *Finding a Way* (St. Louis: Chalice Press, forthcoming 2017).

[14] Mary Catherine Bateson, *Composing a Life* (New York: Grove Press, 2007).

[15] Ada Maria Isasi-Diaz, *Mujerista Theology: A Theology for the Twenty-first Century* (Maryknoll, NY: Orbis Books, 1996), 172.

[16] This is a gender neutral way of saying Latinos/Latinas.

parts of our past, we equally emphasize that discernment can yield joy. Sometimes the thing that needs to be left behind is better discarded! Other times it means that a difficult part of one's past stays present but transformed into new energy for identity and purpose. We sometimes mention the idea of post-traumatic growth.[17] We ground these ideas in some of the biblical texts engaging discernment, connecting it to four New Testament passages that continue to thicken the concept.[18] Each of these passages helps us remember that, throughout time, people have struggled to figure out how to live according to a greater good. Discernment is possible and we can take concrete steps to discern the will of God and seek to be transformed into greater degrees of glory and freedom.[19]

The Preparation

Building upon this biblical understanding of discernment, we turn to three sources in Christian tradition that deal particularly well with the topic: Ignatius of Loyola,[20] United Methodist doctrine, and Friends' theology. In United Methodist tradition, discernment is seen as "a gift of deep intuition and insight."[21] The United Methodist Church's spiritual gifts assessment literature posits that "discerning people can separate truth from fiction and know at a visceral level when people are being honest. Deeply sensitive and "tuned in," those with the gift of discernment are open to feelings, new ideas, and

---

[17] Lawrence G. Calhoun and Richard G. Tedeschi, eds., *The Handbook of Posttraumatic Growth: Research and Practice* (Mahwah, NJ: Lawrence Erlbaum Associates, 2006).

[18] 1 Corinthians 12:7-10, 2 Corinthians 3:17-18, Romans 12:2.

[19] 2 Corinthians 3:17-18.

[20] We draw frequently on David L. Fleming, *What Is Ignatian Spirituality?* (Chicago: Loyola Press, 2008).

[21] http://www.umc.org/what-we-believe/spiritual-gifts-discernment.

intuition as valid and credible information."[22] We suggest that this description, while helpful, makes discernment sound a little too much like a superpower or a once-and-for all and infallible activity. We encourage participants to consider that discernment is a practice available to all, though in varying degree. This resonates with the perspective we offer from the Religious Society of Friends:

> Discernment is . . . the ability to see into people, situations, and possibilities to identify what is being called forth by God and what is of the numerous other sources in ourselves—and what may be both. It is that fallible, intuitive gift we use in attempting to discriminate the course to which we are personally led by God in a given situation, from our other impulses, and from the generalized judgments of conscience . . . The gift is not the result of training, technique, or analysis . . . but as we grow and are faithful in the spiritual life we may well be given more.[23]

We share Parker Palmer's position that "vocation does not come from a voice 'out there,' calling me to becoming something I am not. It comes from a voice 'in here' calling me to be the person I was born to be, to fulfill the original selfhood given me at birth by God."[24] However, we modulate his comment somewhat, suggesting that while we too are entirely uneager to have our goals become supplanted by the "voice" of patriarchy or consumerism, we *do* think that there is a voice "out there" calling. That is, we offer that the voice "in here" and the voice "out there" are facets of one another working within us and all around us to call us forward.

---

[22] Ibid.

[23] Patricia Loring, *Spiritual Discernment* (Wallingford, Pennsylvania: Pendle Hill Publications, 1992), 3.

[24] Parker J. Palmer, *Let Your Life Speak* (San Francisco: Jossey-Bass), 10.

After exploring "discernment" and "vocation," participants have added words, biblical voices, historical descriptions, and points of their own life experience through which to view the CC. At this point we stop and take part in a direct experience of holy listening.[25] Asking them to turn to another person, we invite them to take a few moments, one at a time, to answer the question: "Any guess as to what you are being called into?" Our instructions begin with Douglas Steere's claim that "to 'listen' another's soul into a condition of disclosure and discovery may be almost the greatest service than any human being ever performs for one another."[26]

Part of what we are doing in the CC is opening ourselves to imagining the world as full of possibility, with a place for us to exercise our gifts in the midst of the cacophony of competing needs. While much of contemporary media focuses on the horror and pain, without giving much cause for hope, practices of contemplative discernment make space for pain *and* ask us to imagine how God may be calling out to our communities from within the pain. Far from suggesting that we forget our wounds or dismiss them, we live out a response to them through our next most faithful step.

A red flag goes up here. Amid conversation about vocation, numerous deep issues may arise. Many people are dealing with every day consequences of violence and abuse, symptoms such as anxiety and depression, or other psychological disorders. All of this creates a climate in which the need for counseling services often exceeds the capacity

---

[25] For more instructions on leading holy listening exercise, see *Lives to Offer: Accompanying Young People on the Quest for Vocation* (Cleveland: Pilgrim Press, 2007), 57.
[26] As cited in Patricia Loring, *Listening Spirituality* vol. 2 (n.p.: Openings Press, 2002), 149.

to provide them. Indeed, on college campuses today, redefining sexual consent and rape is a pressing concern that could weigh heavily on a person's lived reality on any given day. We want to be clear that the CC is a place to establish and honor clear boundaries. It is not a therapy session or a place to bring concrete, immediate crises; however, it is a place in which great care must be taken to do no harm around people's deep needs. This may mean interrupting a planned session to make sure someone gets the appropriate referral to a mental health expert. Above all, it means first establishing the covenants noted earlier. In the context of a retreat or other time-bound gathering, these can be explicitly addressed at the beginning of the event and brought back to mind regularly. If CCs are repeated as part of a community's ethos, it is wise to keep the covenants regularly at hand. In either case, the "container" in which the practice is done must be an intentional one grounded in the care for souls, and always mindful of ethical and legal realities around mandatory reporting.[27]

The Practice

After we have laid the groundwork for the CC, we invite people into actually doing one. Drawing on the experience of numerous personal encounters with the practice of Clearness Committees, as well as extant denominational writing on the topic,[28] Callid explains the eight movements

---

[27] Campus ministers, chaplains, and other religious officials must be aware of their particular state laws and institutional policies regarding mandatory reporting of sexual abuse and the intent to harm self or others, as well as those around sexual harassment and other difficult situations that could potentially arise. Equally important is training in sharing laws and policies that apply to lay or peer leaders facilitating CCs within institutions.

[28] Patricia Loring's pamphlet and *Listening Spirituality*; Scott Pierce Coleman's "The Clearness Committee Process"; Parker Palmer's "The Clearness Committee: A

of the CC. He offers time suggestions as loose guidelines.[29]

1. Gathering (3 minutes)
2. Sharing (10 minutes)
3. Clarification (5 minutes)
4. Deepening (5 minutes)
5. Querying (25 minutes)
6. Affirmation (5 minutes)
7. Reflection (5 minutes)
8. Thanksgiving (2 minutes)

As we progress, movements 1–4 feel like one piece, movement 5 feels like its own, and 6–8 feel like the closing. Querying—and the holy listening that supports it—is the heart of the practice.

During the Gathering, participants come together, settling into stillness and silently waiting for the possible presence of the Spirit and for ears and hearts to be open. In Sharing, the focus person brings the question to the group, providing context and depth to help the participants understand why it is that this question feels important.[30] In Clarification, the non-focus persons ask questions—if needed—to make sure they comprehend the question and related context(s). No probing questions or reflections are offered, just clarification. In Deepening the group settles back into silence, waiting for guidance and hope with expectation. From the silence, queries begin as people feel led to ask questions.

Communal Approach to Discernment"; and Jan Hoffman's "Clearness Committees and Their Use in Personal Discernment."

[29] After a group has been through the process several times, it can allow for more flexible timing, particularly more time spent in querying. This might mean both a greater total length for the whole of the process and a more organic flow from one movement to the next. When first teaching it, however, we have found that when participants have some sense of the flow and timing of the process it reduces anxiety and allows for more openness.

[30] Participants are given some reflection activities in advance to help them consider what aspect(s) of their lives they may want to take into consideration via discernment. For these reflections see appendix C in *Finding a Way* (St. Louis: Chalice Press, forthcoming 2017).

In Querying, people may ask questions of the focus person as they occur, attempting to discern whether the question "rising up" is merely a trivial point of interest, or whether it perhaps is something more. The goal is to help distinguish between questions arising from curiosity or one's own agenda and those that bubble up from a deeper place or a desire to awaken another to the guidance of their "Inner Teacher." Querying is a time for the whole of the group to be listening for the right questions, a communal gathering around one person, with everyone searching asking to be given the questions which might prompt "disclosure and discovery."

During the preparation time we often share the kinds of questions that *might* emerge, so as to diminish any anxiety around getting them "right." As the focus person receives the questions offered from the group, she decides whether or not to respond verbally. Sometimes simply hearing a question writes it on our heart in a way that has profound implications. If the focus person does respond, group members refrain from engaging in dialogue: until Affirmation, the only spoken comments are questions. Time elapses intentionally between questions and responses, and again between responses and more questions. This process proceeds and repeats, often with the spaces in between growing longer.

In Affirmation, the participants speak statements for the first time, acknowledging the vulnerability and openness of the focus person, affirming the confidentiality of the process, and naming the ways in which they saw the focus person taking healthy risks, asking bold questions, preparing for prophetic action, and so on. It is during this time that the group members share what, if anything, they heard in response to the focus question. For example one might say something like "I heard a strong sense that you feel you are called to apply to grad school this year." This is sensitive work as "I heard . . . " statements can tend to drift into thinly veiled "I think you should . . . " statements; however the group is asked to be mindful of this and proceed in trust.

In Reflection, the focus person has an opportunity to respond to the process as a whole, commenting on any aspect of it and their own sense of clarity arising from it. In Thanksgiving, the whole of the group—either in silence or in vocal prayer—offers gratitude for the ability to be open and present to one another and to God.

The CC is an opportunity to practice skills that can help us to orient our lives in a way that allows for deeper listening as a part of daily living. The whole of the process leans into creating the conditions for "the rational to combine with the intuitive and numinous,"[31] and while we hope that the focus person reaches some measure of clarity, the goal is not exclusively about getting to "the answer." What the CC provides is a powerful opportunity to be together and present to each other and God in a receptive and open space of possibility, imagination, and radical hospitality.

Sources for the CC

We draw from three living traditions in developing the CC. Primarily, we draw from the long history of communal discernment lying at the heart of the Religious Society of Friends, particularly as understood in the explicitly Christian streams of the tradition.[32] Our second source is The Center for Courage and Renewal's recrafting of the Clearness Committee, particularly its gifted adaptation for contexts that are not explicitly religious.

---

[31] Suzanne Farnham, Stephanie Hull, and Taylor R. McLean, *Grounded in God, Listening Hearts for Group Deliberations*, (Harrisburg, PA: 1996), 76.

[32] Callid is a Friend whose theology is most resonant with the Christocentric trajectories in the Religious Society of Friends, especially as articulated by Lloyd Lee Wilson of North Carolina Yearly Meeting (Conservative).

Finally, we draw from a nonprofit leadership organization called the Forum for Theological Education, which has blended Parker Palmer's work with that of other innovative leaders.

The Religious Society of Friends

"Clearness Committee" is a term of relatively recent provenance. Its origins are rooted in the Religious Society of Friends, sometime during the 1960s and somewhere near Philadelphia, at the intersection of members of "Young Friends of North America" and "The Movement for a New Society."[33] That being said, the *practice* of communal discernment itself is vital to the exercise of Friends and has been for hundreds of years.[34] That a gathered group of prayerful and listening Friends could hear some measure of God's will is central to the denomination's very existence. Indeed, the name "Friends" comes from John 15:15, "Henceforth I call you not servants; for the servant knoweth not what his lord doeth: but I have called you friends; for all things that I have heard of my Father I have made known unto you."[35] Among early Friends, communal discernment was tantamount to what being a Friend *was*. Community was conceived of as "a resource or blueprint for imagining new, even 'other' futures, in the conviction that these can be realized."[36] The Religious Society of Friends developed the practice of communal discernment in an attempt to learn "what the master is doing" and how to best become part of it.

---

[33] Loring, *Spiritual Discernment*, 21

[34] Jo Farrow. "Discernment in the Quaker Tradition," *The Way: Supplement* 64 (1989), 51–62.

[35] KJV. While mindful of its language being not inclusive, we quote from this translation because of its importance to the tradition of The Religious Society of Friends.

[36] Darrell Jackson, "The Futures of Missiology: Imaginative Practices and the Transformation of Rupture" in *Walk Humbly with the Lord: Church and Mission Engaging Plurality*, ed. Viggo Mortensen and Andreas Osterund Nielsen (Grand Rapids, MI: Eerdmans, 2010), 284.

Religious persecution meant that most Friends lived in close-knit, homogeneous neighborhoods or villages that created "social space in which different forms of existence are nurtured."[37] This meant that worship and discernment were not limited to a certain morning of the week or even to planned events. Due to close proximity and shared practice, Friends were easily able to seek each other out in prayer and counsel to become more clear on God's will at any time. In worship, Friends would gather in silence, none preparing spoken ministry in advance, but any able to offer it should they feel compelled by the movement of the Spirit. Alexander Parkman, a Friend from the first generation of the tradition, offered this instruction about silent worship in 1660:

> The first that enters into the place of your meeting, be not careless, nor wander up and down either in body or mind, but innocently sit down in some place and turn in thy mind to the Light, and wait upon God simply, as if none were present but the Lord, and here thou art strong. When the next that come in, let them in simplicity and heart sit down and turn to the same Light, and wait in the Spirit, and so all the rest coming in fear of the Lord sit down in pure stillness and silence. . . . Those who are brought to a pure, still waiting on God in the Spirit are come nearer to God than words are . . . though not a word be spoken to the hearing of the ear.[38]

Things have changed somewhat, though. Friends today rarely live in such homogeneous communities and often only

---

[37] Gay Pilgrim, "British Quakerism as Heterotopic," in *The Quaker Condition: The Sociology of a Liberal Religion*, ed. Ben Pink Dandelion and Peter J. Collins (Newcastle: Cambridge Scholars, 2008), 53–69.

[38] Alexander Parker, *Letters of Early Friends*, ed. A. R. Barclay (London; Darton and Harvey, 1841), 365–66.

worship together on Sundays. When they do meet they rarely do so with the same length of worship as in centuries past.[39] There is still an emphasis on the "still small voice" mentioned in 1 Kings 19:12 and on the psalmist's advice in 46:10 to "Be still and know that I am God"; however occasions for spontaneous discernment in community are greatly diminished. Consequently, Friends developed the practice of the Clearness Committee to explicitly call for the kind of gathered support that was more frequent in the early years of the tradition. The process is still used today when people are considering marriage, becoming a member of a Meeting, and for other types of significant personal events such as buying a home, entering graduate school, or changing jobs. Our sense is that just as CCs themselves are an adaptation of an earlier practice, they continue to evolve in changing circumstances and contexts.

The CC seems to offer a way back into community support and guidance at critical times in peoples' lives. While functioning as an instrument for discernment, it also helps recover the communal dimension of the spiritual life in relationships, in the vitality and authority that come of profound union in and commitment to God. One mark of the Clearness Committee's vitality is that it has not been codified but continues to be flexible. Its flexibility lets it be adapted to a variety of uses and settings—and lets it continue to evolve.[40]

The Center for Courage and Renewal

The most popularized use of the CC is in the work of Quaker writer and teacher Parker Palmer via the Center for

---

[39] It should be noted that even among Friends only 10 per cent or so still worship in the silent, expectant worship. Most congregations are part of branches of the tradition that have been influenced by Wesleyanism and the Holiness movement and have gatherings that include sermons, hymns, and a prepared order of service.

[40] Loring, *Spiritual Discernment*, 21.

Courage and Renewal, a nonprofit organization launched to train facilitators in "Circles of Trust." Circles of Trust—which have international and secular reach—are communities formed around the beliefs that each of us has an inner teacher and that each of us needs a circle of others to help amplify and invite the inner teacher's wisdom.[41] Palmer's work is an excellent resource for people interested in engaging with CCs beyond the boundaries of the Religious Society of Friends, particularly his oft-cited article "The Clearness Committee: A Communal Approach to Discernment." Indeed, CCs lie at the heart of the work of Circles of Trust, which carefully prepare participants for "holding one another's souls." They are not without limitation, however.

For our work, we consider three limitations that prompted us to further adapt the practice. First, unlike Patricia Loring's vision of the CC as "uncodified and therefore flexible," the work in Circles of Trust proscribes numerous rules for the precise application of the Clearness Committee. The depth of detail and training needed may serve as an obstacle to young adults. This seems to be confirmed by the second item we identify as a limitation: the Center for Courage and Renewal reports that it serves a population that is mostly white, middle-class, and middle-aged. This means that CCs are scarcely known among people in the first third of life.[42] Finally, although certainly working to expand their diversity in age and ethnicity, the Center's work remains expensive, involving highly trained paid facilitators.

While recognizing the need to mindfully prepare participants entering into the vulnerable work of soul care, we think young adults from diverse contexts can benefit from

---

[41] Parker J. Palmer, *A Hidden Wholeness* (San Francisco: Jossey-Bass, 2004 and CCR website.

[42] The Center for Courage and Renewal's "Courage to Lead for Clergy and Congregational Leaders 2005 – 2008" Phase 1 Summary Report. Participant demographics include 95 percent European American and 92 percent age of forty years and above.

structured practices of contemplative communal discernment with minimal regulation. The development of our two-step CC gatherings attempts to strike a balance between methodical preparation and the assumption that all people can enter into "a pure, still waiting on God in the Spirit."

The Forum for Theological Exploration (FTE)

FTE is a leadership incubator for the ecumenical church and religious academy. In 2001, FTE began doing CCs with young adults within a number of its program offerings.[43] Melissa Wiginton, former FTE vice president, began experimenting with the practice among undergraduates and seminary students whom FTE gathered annually as part of its fellowship programs.[44] She found with careful preparation, young adults in small groups could guide themselves through the process, often arriving at a very deep place of listening. "It didn't take an expert, because we provided a careful structure," she said.[45] "I was always amazed at how the Spirit moved, how the participants respected the process and respected each other. I've found it to be a really good exercise in taking your life seriously."[46] Wiginton continues to use CCs as a retreat leader, administrator, and faculty member at Austin Theological Seminary in Austin, Texas. By the time she left FTE in 2010, adaptations of the CC and Circles of Trust had entered the bloodstream of the organization.[47]

---

[43] Melissa Wiginton, interview, July 7, 2015.

[44] At that time, FTE offered competitive fellowships to undergraduate students considering vocations in pastoral ministry, as well as to seminary students. Today, in an effort to widen its reach, it focuses on gathering young adults for discernment retreats and providing grants for mentoring and pastoral internships. Currently it offers financial fellowships only to doctoral students of color who are preparing to be leaders in the religious and theological academy.

[45] Melissa Wiginton, interview, July 7, 2015.

[46] Ibid.

[47] See Dori Baker et al., *The CARE Effect: Living and Leading Change for Good* (St. Louis: Chalice Press, forthcoming).

Two years ago FTE began to engage and adapt the practice of CC more systematically, inviting young adults who attend events to take part in creating space for disclosure and discovery around discerning next most faithful steps. [48] Our CC introduction process was developed to speak to some of the contexts in which FTE operates, based on three hunches about contemplative practices of communal discernment. Intuitively, we believe that these practices can

- appeal to millennials' preference for lived experience as a trustworthy source of wisdom, and that the CC is a simple, repeatable tool that can be offered to young adults for use in the ongoing journey of discernment

- provide opportunity for emerging adults to sort through the vast array of possible ways to make a difference in the world; and

- nourish those who've abandoned traditional religious language but retain an interest in spirituality.

- Our research has been testing these hunches through participant surveys, direct observations, and follow-up interviews.

Callid has finished the "Discernment & Vocation 101" and asks for questions before entering the practice of the communal discernment. Katie stands. "You talked a lot about freedom in your presentation. But most of the time when people I know talk about freedom they're saying things like 'I'm free to

---

[48] Beginning in 2013, Callid was brought on a consultant to help FTE more consistently engage Clearness Committees.

do whatever I want.' And that doesn't seem to be what you're talking about, I don't think. Could you say more?" She laughs. "Maybe something short and tweetable?"

Callid laughs, "It will be a bit long for Twitter . . . I think freedom has three faces. We have to be free from the things that bind us, and until we are free from those things we are not free for the work that God is calling us all into. Until we are free from bondage and free for God's work it is harder to be free in Christ." He pauses. "And sure, I mean this spiritually, but bodily too . . . If you're living in abject poverty and having a hard time feeding yourself and your family it can be harder to listen to God's will . . .You might be too damn hungry. Excuse my language . . . And the same is true for those in bondage to big paychecks or fancy cars . . . We have to get free from the things that hold us back from listening. And, if, as a community of Christians we think we should be encouraging each other into God's will, then we have to do the work of freeing people too. Freeing them into listening for their call." [49]

Initial Findings

In the vignette above, the question about freedom arose directly out of Katie's context amid peer conversations about theology and social justice, midpoint through 2015, a year the *New York Times* says "has seen as much race-related strife and violence as perhaps any since the desegregation battles of the 1960s"[50] Her question invited Callid to move directly into prophetic witness tied to a collective *lo cotidiano*—the stuff around

---

[49] For the video of this moment, go to http://yti.emory.edu/freedom-from-freedom-for-freedom-to/.

[50] Kevin Sack and Megan Thee-Bryan, "Poll Finds Most in U.S. Hold Dim View of Race Relations," July 23, 2015, http://www.nytimes.com/2015/07/24/us/poll-shows-most-americans-think-race-relations-are-bad.html?emc=edit_th_20150724&nl=todays-headlines&nlid=54675593&_r=0.

which we confront choices today and the real dangers facing people of color in the room and their friends, brothers, cousins, and classmates. In this moment of preparation for the CC, a way opened for this young person to ask a question that at once critiqued her own generational norms and allowed others in the room to acknowledge—with audible "Amens" and "Uh-huhs"—the pain of their current historical moment, which is deeply tied to various social locations. Once again they realized that seeking freedom cannot be a solitary act.

Conversations about vocation sometimes immediately zoom out to the big picture, but the CC resists that move. Part of the power of the CC is its capacity to help people take their own lives seriously, in the thick messiness of any given historical moment. Initial results from our research surveys suggest that young people at first resist but later relish this move into messiness. Our research suggests that this is an important aspect of the appeal of contemplative practices of communal discernment.

Forty-two out of a total sixty-three returned surveys from a small college on the West Coast where we introduced the practice.[51] Only eight of those said they did not find the CC effective or were unlikely to recommend it to others.[52] These responses reflected sentiments such as: "It was boring." "I don't like quiet." "The silence was deafening." And, perhaps the most telling, "Awkward . . . It felt like I was asked to jump into someone's soul for a few minutes then leave." Others noted

---

[51] This group ranged in age from eighteen to twenty-seven and self-reported as 54 percent female, 42 percent male, and 2 percent intersex or other. They were 26 percent Caucasian, 21 percent Latin@, 19 percent Multi-Ethnic, 14 percent African American or African, 12 percent Asian or Pacific Islander, 3 percent Native American or First Nations, and 5 percent who identified as Other.

[52] These participants rated the effectiveness of the practice at 4 or lower on a 7 point Likert scale.

that they prefer to process alone or with a few close friends.

Among the thirty-five who rated the practice slightly to greatly effective, we heard the following kinds of comments.

- "Even if you don't know the people doing it well, you all open up."
- "It's like unpeeling an orange and giving a wedge of your life to the ones in the circle.'
- "My experience felt like a meditation by the ocean, quiet, peaceful."
- "heart-lifting"
- "like being in a meditative zone"
- "Like coming to the surface of the ocean . . . like I was drowning before and with each question I came closer and closer until I reached the top and took my first breath of air."

Results, however, were not uniformly positive. Many noted an awkwardness to the process, though most remarked that something happened *after* the awkwardness wore off. For example, it is "at first uncomfortable, then relieving." Numerous respondents described the process as, at first, uncomfortably quiet but growing toward, "enlightening, calming" or bringing "harmony." One person described the process like this:

- quiet, awkward, and enlightening. . . . You start out awkwardly and formally. At first it feels forced and unnatural, but near the end you begin to see how it works. It becomes more natural and you start to enjoy it.

This suggests to us that group-based contemplative discernment has the potential to be compelling to this cohort. The starkest findings, though, lie within the evocative language describing the effect of the gathering.

- "It feels like you're lying on a field at night looking at a clear sky filled with stars while reflecting on your life decisions, then realize there are people around you."

- "It's like I'm in the woods where I'm surrounded by quiet and every once in a while you'll hear a bird chirp. . . . The bird chirping is the questions you encounter during the silence."
- "It's like a birth. Your focus is on the baby."
- "It's like going through a walk in the woods and noticing things on the way in and coming out with a better understanding."
- "It's like watching nature grow, slow and boring but beautiful."
- "Clearing away everyday noise . . . "

Self-reporting results on surveys are also positive, though, as we expected, the greatest benefit was to the focus people. Compared to those who were only part of the discerning group, focus people averaged a very slight increase in how effective they thought the process was. And there is a significant increase among focus people in the degree to which they would recommend the process to a friend.[53]

A general observation across numerous CCs is that the sparse hour in which the practice occurs nonetheless holds an experience in which community catalyzes. Even in retreat settings in which there is a great diversity of perspectives theologically, racially, and politically,[54] participants report feeling connected and "seen" in

---

[53] Survey results show that people who had participated as a Focus Person report that they assess (on average) the practice as effective for helping with decision making as 6.15 while non-Focus Person participants only assess it at 5.67. This is a 7 percent increase for Focus People. The difference is even greater when asked if they could imagine recommending the practice to a friend. Focus People assessed their likelihood at an average 6.75 while non-focus people assessed it at 5.81. This is a 15 percent increase for Focus People.

[54] FTE Youth Leadership retreats are funded by the Lilly Endowment and host gatherings of Christians between the ages of eighteen and thirty who have an interest in social justice and a willingness to explore vocations in pastoral ministry. They are mainline, Pentecostal, nondenominational, evangelical, progressive, and all places in between. Half of our participants come to us by way of national volunteer service

that space. One participant, upon reflection, offered the following:

> It was really amazing! I don't rely on the Holy Spirit to guide me as often as I should, so I was surprised that it wasn't uncomfortable for me. I mean, my friends and family help me to make decisions all the time, but rarely do they sift their thoughts through prayer. I think the prayer [is] what gives clarity and reinforcement to whatever calling is being presented.
>
> It's not making a decision based on what I think + what you think
>
> Or even what I believe God wants + what you think
>
> But, what I believe God wants + what you believe God wants

It confirmed for me that Christianity is a religion meant to be worked out in community, even something as personal as prayer/discernment. Compellingly, this sense of connectedness isn't limited to those serving as the focus person. One participant offered that:

> As a committee member, it was honoring to participate in another's discernment. It's not often that one has the opportunity to purposefully listen and respond to the Spirit in such a tangible, immediate way. It made me feel like an important part of community, like an instrument in God's work on another person's life. It was relieving to not have to share answers or advice, yet know my participation was meaningful.

---

agencies—such as Jesuit Volunteer Corps and Mission Year, and, thus, are mostly recent college graduates. The other half of the participants are currently in college or working. They come to us through pastors and campus ministers who've noticed their gifts and nominate them. These events bring people together for a weekend to be inspired by innovative young pastoral leaders, see each other, and be seen.

We find here an exciting possibility for both long-term community-building and for the spiritual formation that can happen best in groups. This parallels the argument of Quaker scholar John Youngblut, who suggests that the practice of listening spirituality and corporate mysticism helps to develop the capacity for feeling and seeing connected to each other and creation. Entering into the discipline of holy listening helps us to experience the "unity that somehow contains the multiplicity of things, a divine milieu, which is at once the center or core and the environment."[55] In a cultural moment when divisions and differences are very marked, gathering people for a structured process of communal discernment may serve to reground and reconnect us to one another and to the still small voice of God.

Why Are Clearness Committees Compelling?

A seven-year study of college students reported in the book, *Cultivating the Spirit,* names specific experiences that support spiritual growth, including those that expose students to new and diverse people, cultures, and ideas. Experiences such as study abroad, interdisciplinary classes, and service learning fall into this category. What is often missing, according to the authors, is the opportunity for students to do the accompanying "inner work" that helps them integrate dawning awareness about the world around them with their sense of who they are and who they might be becoming.[56] Their study found that *"contemplative practices are among the most powerful tools at*

---

[55] John R. Yungblut, *Discovering God Within* (Philadelphia: Westminster, 1979), 58.
[56] Alexander W. Astin, Helen S. Astin, Jennifer A. Lindholm, *Cultivating the Spirit: How College Can Enhance Students' Inner Lives* (San Francisco: Jossey-Bass, 2011), 137–51.

our disposal for enhancing students' spiritual development."[57] By contemplative practice, they are referring to a collection of diverse methods that share as a goal "the discovery of a deeper realm of experience or awareness beyond the ordinary discursive (thinking) mind." They also point to a growing body of evidence that such practices increase markers of development including interpersonal skills, emotional balance and academic skills.

While a majority of faculty in the study rate the spiritual dimension of their lives as important, they express understandable reluctance to introduce spiritual practices into higher education.[58] Our findings suggest that this void can be addressed by placing CCs in the hands of campus ministers, who then train peer ministers in this simple, repeatable process.

A tension arises as we put our findings in conversation with the experience of diverse millennials and wonderings about prophetic voice. That tension is this: some people have too many choices and some people don't have enough. One version of the millennial narrative is that some people have so many choices that they can't make decisions. Another is that economic realities limit choice. An example of the first narrative goes like this:

> Feeling good about yourself is the most important thing in life. Self-love is not so much a goal as a birthright, affirmed by the cloying lyrics of a hit 1986 Whitney Houston song ("learning to love yourself is the greatest love of all"). Old-fashioned values like hard work and skill have been cast aside in favor of giving

---

[57] Emphasis in original.
[58] Ibid.

everyone a gold star—because they're good enough, smart enough, and doggone it, people like them![59]

Alternatively, Varda Konstam's *Emerging and Young Adulthood,* cites a statement from a twenty-six-year-old research participant:

> My generation is self-centered for a reason. We never felt that the institutions were there for us. Long-term jobs and pensions are not there. Social security is going to disappear. You know what? I have to take care of myself. I felt screwed in my 20s; the baby boomers are to blame; their gain is my loss.[60]

We believe that contemplative practices of communal discernment offer something of value to people who identify with either extreme or someplace in between. To the first, in which young adults are framed as "self-involved, undisciplined, and seeking and expecting immediate gratification as well as unconditional recognition,"[61] the CC is an accessible, low-bar entryway back into the importance of community and a realization that things are not always as certain as they might seem. To the second, in which young adults are responding to "dysfunctional and/or vanishing systems . . . [and] the onerous task of not only having to fend for themselves, but also having to clean up the 'mess' left behind,"[62] CCs affirm the perceived reality of uncertainty.

To both poles of experience, the CC asks participants to narrow the scope of focus to the next faithful step, to what is in front of them and not years off in the future. This temporary

---

[59] Amanda Henry, "Big Babies," *Washington Post*, May 21, 2006, http://www.washingtonpost.com/wp-dyn/content/article/2006/05/18/AR2006051801091.html.

[60] Varda Konstam, *Emerging and Young Adulthood: Multiple Perspectives, Diverse Narratives* (New York: Springer, 2014), 129.

[61] Ibid.

[62] Ibid.

narrowing of focus can come as a great gift. Participants whose contexts seem to provide them with limited choices experience a compounding, negative psychological effect from constantly adjusting to external forces without feeling like they have many options.[63] Inversely, other research suggests that when affluence and privilege yield an abundance of options, the result is "substantial distress . . . when combined with regret, concern about status, adaptation, social comparison, and perhaps most important, the desire to have the best of everything—to maximize."[64] This dual tension is why the CC may be apt for young adults from diverse backgrounds. It is an attempt to create a space that is both hallowed and *narrowed*, turning focus neither to an infinite consideration of options, nor to any assumptions of how it *must* be, but striving to engender the sense that what is important is what *could* be: a next single step. Our own research suggests that this is possible.

Several weeks later, we received this from the Facebook feed of one of the campus ministers.:

---

[63] Kathleen Vohs et al. "Decision Fatigue Exhausts Self-Regulatory Resources—But So Does Accommodating to Unchosen Alternatives," http://www.chicagobooth.edu /research/workshops/marketing/archive/WorkshopPapers/vohs.pdf.

[64] Barry Schwartz, *The Paradox of Choice: Why More Is Less* (New York: HarperCollins, 2004), 221.

Going Forth

The Facebook screenshot speaks volumes. What if a tool exists that one could turn to, again and again along path to adulthood? What if this tool could be helpful to young people of privilege trying to figure out how to dismantle it? What if the tool was also available to a person who navigates a path through college without benefit of parents or grandparents who paved the way? What if you could use it for yourself or offer it to a friend?

Finding a way to live out a life of meaning and purpose is an important developmental move for emerging adults. Given the hesitancy among millennials to take part in organized religion, the task of placing meaningful practices before them challenges pastoral leaders. Revitalized practices of the Clearness Committee in the hands of campus ministers and peer leaders holds great promise. We believe that CCs are a useful tool for those emerging adults who desire to make a difference in the world, who are curious about spiritual practices, and who are destined to create their own religious meanings.

We continue to offer this spiritual practice in spaces that feel less like "church" and more like oases of quiet, stillness, and meditation. We watch young people walk out into their next most faithful step. In these moments, we hold hope that God is speaking through a new generation of prophetic voices.

Note to Reader: Please feel free to contact Dori (www .fteleaders.org or DoriBaker.com) or Callid (CallidKeefePerry. com) with questions or comments.

Discovering Calling at the Center and the Edge

David E. MacDonald

Life at the Center and the Edge

The island of Lindisfarne, also known as Holy Island, is located just off the eastern coast of England in the North Sea. During low-tide periods, the island is accessible via a paved causeway, which is lined with "crow's nests" along the way, as aids for the motorist who might get stranded as the tide rolls back in. The ancient way to access the island, however, is the flat, muddy "pilgrim's causeway," which is unpaved and marked by poles sticking out of the exposed seabed. At one point, Holy Island was the home of Lindisfarne Priory, the home base for a group of Celtic monks, which had been founded by St. Aidan in the seventh century. I first encountered the beauty of Lindisfarne as a tourist in 2002, while living in England as part of the British-American Ministry Programme of the Methodist Church. My initial visit was too short for my taste, and I returned several times to explore this small but powerful site where some of the spiritual giants of Celtic Christianity once lived and worked. Holy Island became, for me, a place of pilgrimage, and my return trips there were a form of *peregrinatio*—a search for the place of my own resurrection.[1]

---

[1] I thank my colleague and friend Karla M. Kincannon for introducing me to the concept of *peregrinatio*. See Karla M. Kincannon, *Creativity and Divine Surprise* (Nashville: Abingdon, 2005), 19–20. Kincannon in turn took the concept from Esther De Waal, noted authority on Celtic spirituality. See Esther De Waal, *The Celtic Way of Prayer* (New York: Doubleday, 1997), 2–3.

On one particular trip to Holy Island, I found myself stopping the car about halfway across the causeway. I suddenly felt the urge to follow in the footsteps of the pilgrims who, centuries ago, sought out the wisdom of the monks who lived here. I turned the car around, parked on the mainland side of the causeway, and hiked the remainder of the way to the island, following the old path set out by my ancestors in the faith. When I arrived at the island, I found my perspective had changed from previous visits. Where once I had been concerned with finding a parking space and getting to my destination on the island as quickly as possible, I now found myself exploring parts of the island that I had never seen before. I lingered especially in the ruins of the priory. Noting the high walls that had been built up around the land once occupied by the monks, I recalled learning about how vulnerable the North Sea monasteries had been to Viking invaders. As I reflected on the radical new message of God's love that the monks had brought to England, I found myself musing on a question: Had the walls been built to protect the monks from the outside world, or could they possibly have been built to protect the outside world from the monks? The answer to this question is undoubtedly the former, but the latter makes sense when seen through the eyes of spiritual imagination. Through such eyes, the monks brought a world-changing message of salvation and peace—both external and internal—that was counter to the culture of the time.

The monks of Lindisfarne lived in relative solitude, secluded from the mainland for long periods of time during high tide. They developed a community of faith that became a spiritual center for them and eventually for the entire Northumbrian region. It was from this center that they ventured into the lands separating the Scots from the Britons, often risking their own lives for the sake of the message of grace and salvation that they carried with them. For the people of those ancient lands, Lindisfarne represented a wild place, an unwelcoming environment, yet a land of strategic importance. It was a place where they could find God and refuge in times of war and invasion. Lindisfarne was a last line of defense against the sea and the pagan Vikings. Though the monastery was ultimately destroyed by the Vikings, the people of Northumberland have come to regard it as an important part of their cultural heritage—the last vestige of the Celtic Christianity, which was destroyed first by outside raiders and then later by compromise and canon law. The beauty of the Lindisfarne Gospels remains as a testimony of how the landscape of Northumberland and the North Sea shaped and inspired the monks of Holy Island.

In his book *The Solace of Fierce Landscapes,* Belden Lane explored the ways that wild places like Lindisfarne forge the spiritual identities of those who choose to live there.[2] In particular, he wrote of the connection between spirituality and the landscapes or environments in which people live, noting that "talk about God cannot be separated from discussions of place."[3] Place and landscape can become internalized within one's spirit to a point where one begins to utilize metaphors that relate to that landscape to describe one's spiritual journey. For example, Lane utilized the landscape image of a desert to describe the experience of witnessing his mother's painful death from bone cancer.[4] In the same way, writers such as Flannery O'Connor, William Faulkner, Kathleen Norris, John O'Donohue, and the poet Janisse Ray have all drawn deeply from the wells of their geographic and cultural locations. In

---

[2] Belden C. Lane, *The Solace of Fierce Landscapes: Exploring Desert and Mountain Spirituality,* (New York: Oxford University Press, 2007).
[3] Ibid., 9.
[4] Ibid., 29–30.

my own life experience, I have found the rivers, ravines, and valleys of my native northeastern Ohio to be rich sources for spiritual reflection, and sitting along the shores of Lake Erie can instantly transport me to the sometimes painful but enlightening experiences of my teenage years, when I first felt the call to ministry at Lakeside Chautauqua. In the same way, the ferocity of storms on the North Sea and the rolling fields of Northumberland have shaped my inner landscape, as has my more recent sojourn into the swamplands and flat, gentle prairies of the western part of Ohio. Some parts of our inner landscapes may be comforting and familiar, but other parts may seem fierce and not at all conducive to comfort. These two extremes of our experiences of landscapes—comforting and uncomfortable—form the basis of a theology of the center and the edge, upon which all that follows will be based.

Ernest Boyer in *A Way in the World* (later republished as *Finding God at Home*), wrote that there are two fundamental aspects of the spiritual life: the edge and the center. The edge represents those places that are uncomfortable, scary, and challenging. The center represents those places that are comfortable, calming, and reassuring.[5] Boyer compares these two aspects to the parts of a wheel. The rim of the wheel, where the rubber literally meets the road, represents life on the edge. This is the part of the wheel that sees the most action, and consequently where most of the change and wear and tear occur. The center of the wheel sees little of the excitement action experienced at the edge. Not much changes at the center, and as a result, life at the center is often predictable and a bit repetitive.[6] The life of the center allows one to be present in the moment and in the day-to-day tasks, which may seem mundane but, in their simple beauty, honor God.[7]

---

[5] Ernest Boyer Jr., *A Way in the World* (San Francisco: HarperCollins, 1984).

[6] Ibid., 27.

[7] Ibid., 54.

Drawing on the work of both Lane and Boyer, I suggest that every person lives a life that has both a center and an edge, and that the interplay between these can lead to spiritual growth and maturity, thus resulting in a person's coming to a sense of vocation or purpose in life. Because the landscapes that shape us in our early lives have such a profound and lasting impact, each person has a spiritual center, which represents where he or she feels most comfortable and comforted. Not all centers can be represented by the image of hearth and home, as was the case for Boyer. Indeed, many people's experience of home is much less than comforting and comfortable. In some cases, one's center may be a sense of family created on the street, among the dispossessed and disenfranchised. This does not diminish the fact that such experiences represent the center for some people. Students coming to a college or university environment might have difficulty adjusting, not because that environment is seen as threatening, but because it is so unlike what they have experienced in their center. I liken the concept of a spiritual center to that of a center of gravity, which may be unique to each individual, and which may shift over time.

Likewise, each person has an edge, represented by the fierce landscapes that awe and inspire but also terrify in their rawness and beauty. As we explore the world, we begin to encounter edge places—places where we find ourselves in unfamiliar spiritual territory. These edges cause us to question our deeply held convictions and may even cause doubts about our faith in God. Such encounters often lead us very quickly to seek out the center—a return to that which we find familiar. As we move from the center to the edge, and then back again, growth gradually occurs, until what was once an edge place may now be a part of a newly found spiritual center, as when the desert became a place of spiritual pilgrimage for early Christians seeking to encounter God outside the safety of the city walls.

The movement from center to edge also provides a framework for the experience of emerging adulthood, much like the spokes of a bicycle wheel provide the necessary tension to keep the wheel in shape.

The alternating placement of the spokes on the wheel, along with the proper tension on the spokes, keeps the wheel round (and thus useful as a wheel). If the spokes on the wheel are either too tight or too loose, the wheel will quickly lose its shape. The journey from the center to the edge can provide useful tension—breaking down old prejudices and stereotypes, and keeping the necessary tension for a person to be able to grow and create a new sense of center.

Within the context of college life, the center/edge metaphor takes on a new significance. Going off to college—moving away from home, and in some cases, being separated from family and friends for the first time—can in and of itself be considered an edge. College life is filled with an abundance of edge experiences— first-time intimate relationships, new ideas, encounters with people of different faiths and cultures all whom have different spiritual centers. When two or more people come together in one place, especially in an environment as dynamic and challenging as a college or university campus, centers and edges inevitably begin to collide. What may be the edge for one person may be another person's center, and vice-versa (see fig. 1).

Figure 1. Centers and Edges Collide

The collision of centers and edges creates something new—a community, made up of diverse individuals, who are now confronted with their own biases and assumptions. Gradually, these biases and assumptions are challenged, rearranged and re-prioritized. What was once of great importance may now play only a minor role in one's life, while what was once foreign and unknown is now familiar and comfortable. This results in the creation of a community that is as unique as the individuals who make up its parts, a dynamic system of centers and edges that interact and have an impact on individuals and the group as a whole.

As a community begins to form within a collegiate setting, many centers and edges come together, with the end result being a web of relationships between those centers and edges, each impacting and changing one another (see fig. 2).

Figure 2. A Community of Centers and Edges

As multiple spiritual centers and edges come into contact with one another, the need for a communal sense of balance begins to emerge, and spiritual direction offers a way to help in the formulation of that balance. This was the impetus for spiritual direction among early monastic communities.[8] The challenge of helping individuals live within a dynamic community is also just as important for collegiate ministers today. Much of what we do in our work is focused on helping students adjust to all the newness represented by college life.

---

[8] Douglas S. Hardy, "Spiritual Direction within a Wesleyan Ecclesiology: the Pursuit of Holiness from the Periphery," *Wesleyan Theological Journal* 41, no. 1 (Spring 2006): 153.

New friends, new classes, new professors, and new freedoms all present opportunities for students to encounter stress or challenges to their faith and beliefs. Chaplains and campus ministers are in the business of helping such students make the adjustment to such changes while also growing into healthy, mature people of faith and citizens of the world.

Center and Edge as Metaphors for Vocational Discernment in Emerging Adulthood

Emerging adulthood is a waypoint on the journey of spiritual development for an individual. Jeffrey Jensen Arnett argued in proposing emerging adulthood as a distinct developmental phase that adolescence can no longer be considered the time when most identity exploration occurs. Instead, he posits that emerging adulthood (the period between ages eighteen and twenty-five) has become the time of greatest identity and spiritual exploration. Rare is the person who can emerge from adolescence completely prepared for the rigors and tests of adulthood. Today, many young people delay decisions such as marriage, childbearing, and career until the college years or early working years are completed. This is emerging adulthood.[9]

Henri Nouwen, in his classic, groundbreaking essay on spiritual direction, wrote that, "The spiritual life is a life in which we struggle to move from absurd living to obedient living."[10] By this, Nouwen meant that, by and large, most human beings eventually cut themselves off from hearing the voice of God (absurdity) and that spiritual direction helps us to again hear God's voice in the world around us, and to follow what God is telling us (obedience). The journey from the center to the

---

[9] Jeffrey Jensen Arnett, "Emerging Adulthood: A Theory of Development from the Late Teens to the Early Twenties," *American Psychologist* 55, no. 5 (May 2000), 473.

[10] Henri Nouwen, "Spiritual Direction," *Worship* 55, no. 5 (September 1981): 399.

edge is a means toward living in obedience to God's call on our lives. It is in the journey from the center to the edge, in which we encounter that which is strange and completely other, that we are able to appreciate what the center truly holds, which is our deepest selves, our core being, the *imago dei.* The *imago dei* can become distorted or hidden from our consciousness by our own actions and sin, and the pressures and noise of the world can drown out the voice of God, calling us to rediscover or discover for the first time God's will for us. It is in the discovery of this will, and our alignment with it, that we discover our calling or vocation.

Speak, Lord: Vocation and Calling

Vocation comes from the Latin word *vocare,* meaning to call or to name something or someone. *Vocare* implies that there is a divine being doing the calling, though in the broadest sense, a call could come from one's community, or even from within oneself. From a Christian perspective, the call comes from God, and vocation is a response to that call; but God also has a reputation for calling the least likely or the overlooked. In 1 Samuel 3:1-10, God repeatedly called Samuel's name. Samuel was just a boy, but that was not what makes him unlikely. Most people would have expected God to call one of the sons of the priest Eli, but the Bible tells us that they were corrupt. So as a leader and judge of Israel, this boy, Samuel, was an unusual choice. One night, as Samuel lay sleeping in the temple. It was early evening for, as the Bible says, "the lamp of God had not yet gone out" (v. 3). Suddenly, Samuel heard a voice calling his name: "Samuel!" So Samuel got up and went to Eli, because he thought Eli was the one calling for him. Eli told Samuel to go back to bed, because he hadn't called him. This scene is repeated two more times, until finally Eli realized that the voice Samuel was hearing was the voice of God. Eli sent Samuel back to bed, this time with specific instructions: "Go, lie down; and if he calls you, you shall say, "Speak, LORD, for your servant is listening" (v. 9). Again, God called Samuel, only this time, instead of returning to his master Eli, the boy said, "Speak, Lord, for your servant is listening" (v. 10). In a similar vein, Isaiah heard the voice of God while sitting in the temple. God called out, "Whom shall I send, and who will go for us?" In this case, the prophet said, "Here am I; send me!" (Isa 6:8). The call of God does not always come quite so audibly, nor even to those who are sitting or sleeping in the temple.

Years later, God directed Samuel to anoint a new king over Israel. This king would replace Saul, whom the people had chosen themselves. In response Samuel went to the home of Jesse. But it was not the eldest, strongest, or most likely son who was chosen. Rather, it was the boy David, the youngest, weakest, and least likely of all (1 Sam 16:1-13).

Jesus continued the trend of calling unlikely people, often from the margins, as he gathered around him tax collectors, prostitutes, and other known sinners. The call of Matthew (also known as Levi) is an excellent example of Jesus overturning expectations of who could or should be one of his disciples, as he beckoned to the tax collector and said, "Follow me" (Matt 9:9). The first person called to witness to others about Jesus was also an improbable choice, as the Samaritan woman left the well and ran to her village after her encounter with him, proclaiming: "Come and see a man who told me everything I have ever done! He cannot be the Messiah, can he?" (John 4:29). Time and time again, Jesus called the least likely people of all to follow him, be his disciples, and share with others the good news.

As God often calls people *from* the margins to follow him, God also calls us *to* the margins. The call of God leads us to the edge places of life, and in those edge places we are challenged to our core. The edge may even make us doubt ourselves and our faith, but such doubts can become, as they were to Tillich, "a necessary element" of faith.[11] As one feels called over and over to the edge, what was once marginal and peripheral is now central to one's experience of the world, creating, as R.S. Sugirtharajah wrote, a "center for critical reflection and clarification rather than as a site opposed to the center or as a state of peripherality."[12]

This re-orienting of the edge as a new and creative center is hinted at in the words of Isaiah: "A voice cries out: / 'In the wilderness prepare the way of the LORD, / make straight in the desert a highway for our God.'" (Isa 40:3) In this reading—taken from the New Revised Standard Version and supported by other translations as well—the call is clearly to go from the city (center) to the wilderness (edge), and there prepare a way for God. The four Gospels reinterpreted this passage in relation to John the Baptizer, saying, "The voice of one crying out in the wilderness: / 'Prepare the way of the Lord, / make his paths straight.'" (Matt 3:3; cf Mark 1:3, Luke 3:4, John 1:23) In the case of the Isaiah passage, the call is from the center to go to the edge, and the prophet is calling for the way of the Lord to be made in the wilderness (edge). In the later use of the passage in the Gospels, the call seems to come from the edge, inviting those who are at the center to prepare the way for God from where they are located, thus keeping the action at the center. For the purposes of this reflection, I will clearly favor the version from Isaiah, which calls for more movement on the part of those at the center, thus calling them to leave behind the comforts of home and hearth for the harsh and

---

[11] Paul Tillich, *Dynamics of Faith* (New York: Harper & Brothers, 1957), 18–19.
[12] R. S. Sugirtharajah, *Voices From the Margin: Interpreting the Bible in the Third World* (Maryknoll, NY: Orbis/SPCK, 1995), 2.

rugged existence of the wilderness. It is in the wilderness where we are able to "prepare the way of the Lord" in our hearts and minds, and where we encounter the living God in splendor and majesty. Upon returning to the center, we are able to reflect upon what we have encountered at the edge, thus deepening and strengthening our faith.

As emerging adults enter into a wilderness phase of their lives, they inevitably find themselves drawn in various ways to the edges of existence. For college students, the experience of learning new concepts and theories and being challenged to question long-held beliefs can be a kind of wilderness-edge experience. College also tends to provide a safe space in which such edge encounters can occur, thus affording students the opportunity to experience the edge places of their lives in a safe and relatively caring environment. The care that must take place must fall to a trusted spiritual guide and friend, traditionally referred to as a spiritual director.

The Spiritual Director as Guide on the Journey

Nouwen's definition of spiritual direction seems simple and forthright: "Spiritual direction is direction given to people in their relationship with God."[13] Rarely is spiritual direction such a seemingly simple task; although I suspect that Father Henri never meant to imply as much. Spiritual direction requires a covenantal relationship between two people who agree to hold one another in prayer and to be in conversation about spiritual practice and struggles with faith, and to share the joys and sorrows of life together. Usually such a relationship consists of a spiritual director, who acts as a guide, and the directee, who agrees to be guided. In some instances, which are

---

[13] Nouwen, "Spiritual Direction," 399.

usually referred to by names such as *spiritual companionship,* both partners in the relationship may act as both director and directee, taking turns and swapping roles as needed and appropriate. This is often the case with persons who practice spiritual direction as a profession, who seek out another professional spiritual director to help them process the information and feelings they take in from their own directees.[14] Nouwen made it clear in his definition of spiritual direction that it is a *discipline of the heart,* which involves "not only listening *to* but listening *with.*"[15] The spiritual director is called upon to listen deeply to not only the words being spoken by the directee but also to the tone, body language, and the pauses or moments of silence, all of which can speak to the directee's spiritual state, and can act as resources for guiding the directee closer to God. As Thomas Merton famously said, "Spiritual direction is, in reality, nothing more than a way of leading us to see and obey the real Director—the Holy Spirit hidden in the depths of our soul."[16]

Spiritual direction has its roots in Catholic monasticism and particularly within the Jesuit movement. The tradition of the Ignatian exercises enriched and deepened the lives of Catholics for centuries before it was "discovered" by Protestants in the latter half of the twentieth century.[17] Since that time, training programs and professional organizations for spiritual directors, retreat leaders, and teachers of spiritual disciplines have blossomed around the world. Practitioners such as Rose Mary Dougherty have adapted spiritual direction for use in

---

[14] Paul W. Jones, *The Art of Spiritual Direction* (Nashville: Upper Room Books, 2002), 15–18.

[15] Nouwen, "Spiritual Direction," 402.

[16] Thomas Merton, *Spiritual Direction and Meditation* (Collegeville, MN: Liturgical Press, 1960), 39.

[17] James M. Houston, "Seeking Historical Perspectives for Spiritual Direction and Soul Care Today," *Journal of Spiritual Formation and Soul Care* 1, no. 1 (Spring 2008): 91.

group settings,[18] and researchers like Len Sperry have sought ways to incorporate spiritual direction into psychotherapy and other therapeutic practices.[19]

As the above examples show, spiritual direction is a widely varied and multifaceted ministry of the church, and there are as many methods and perspectives on it as there are traditions, denominations, and individual practitioners of direction. For the purpose of focusing on vocational discernment as spiritual direction, I would like to hone in on the example of one part of the tradition—and that with which I am most intimately familiar—the Wesleyan/Methodist tradition.

Spiritual Direction and the Wesleyan Tradition

Few Methodists or Wesleyans would identify the movement founded by John Wesley as a movement that is primarily about spiritual direction. Given the evangelical zeal and ardent social consciousness of our founding father, one could easily be convinced that Methodism is all about saving souls and creating justice in the world. This view ignores a third aspect of Wesleyan teaching and practice—that of the bands, class meetings, and societies. In the institutionalization of Methodism into various sects and denominations in the late eighteenth and early nineteenth centuries, the standard practice of every Methodist being involved in a weekly small group, or *band,* generally has been lost to the tradition. Bands were replaced by Sunday school classes and fellowship groups within local churches. Class leaders have largely been abandoned (at least with North American Methodism), and societies long ago converted into local congregations.

---

[18] Rose Mary Dougherty, *Group Spiritual Direction: Community for Discernment* (New York: Paulist Press, 1995).

[19] Len Sperry, "Integrating Spiritual Direction Functions in the Practice of Psychotherapy." *Journal of Psychology and Theology* 31, no. 1 (Spring 2003): 3–13.

In an article in *The Wesleyan Theological Journal* in 2006, Douglas Hardy pointed out that literature on the subject of Wesleyan perspectives on spiritual direction is scarce and that much of what has been produced of late has focused primarily on renewing the communal aspects of Wesleyan spiritual direction (i.e., bands), rather than on how Wesleyan and Methodist practices fit within the wider tradition of spiritual direction.[20] Hardy noted that the distinctive emphases of Wesleyan spiritual direction are:

1. "the search for spiritual authenticity or holiness necessitated looking beyond . . . the existing life of the . . . church";
2. similarities to desert monasticism, especially regarding organization in to small groups;
3. accessibility of spiritual guidance to all levels of society.[21]

What Wesley—and the people who have since been called Methodists—accomplished is creating a system (or method, if you will) of organizing people who are collectively and individually seeking the grace of God and asking how to apply the knowledge of God's grace to their lives. This could also serve as a good definition of spiritual direction.

One concept with which Wesley struggled during his lifetime, and which remains a source struggle for his spiritual descendants today, was that of sanctification or perfection. Sanctification is a process by which one continues to grow in grace following the acceptance of God's grace that comes at the moment of justification. The concept that we are "moving on to perfection" is enshrined in Methodist theology and expected

---

[20] Douglas S. Hardy, "Spiritual Direction within a Wesleyan Ecclesiology: The Pursuit of Holiness from the Periphery," *Wesleyan Theological Journal* 41, no. 1 (Spring 2006): 148–49.
[21] Ibid., 155–56.

of those who would call themselves Methodist—particularly our ordained ministers.[22] Sanctification does not imply that a person has achieved perfection in all things, nor does it imply either works righteousness or even a sense of eternal security of salvation. Once one is justified, one continues to be molded and shaped by God's grace; although through the exercise of free will, one may *backslide* in one's faith. That God's grace continues to operate in, around, and through one who has experienced justification says more about God than it does about the individual, and it implies that God's grace is greater and vaster than anything human beings can imagine.

Throughout one's life from justification until death, various stages of development occur that show evidence of growth in grace toward sanctification. These stages begin with justification, but it is "convincing grace" that leads one to the first step of "repentance before justification," or the acknowledgment of one's sin that leads to a sense that one needs to be justified by God's grace, and therefore allows one to accept that grace and by extension justification.[23] The fruit of the Spirit provide evidence of one's justification and pilgrimage toward sanctification, and one is assured of justification by the testimony of the Holy Spirit, which leads to a certainty that one is a child of God.[24] Sin and doubt may be continually present, even after justification, and therefore necessitate a "repentance after justification." This second repentance leads to new fruit (evidences of the gifts of the Spirit), which are characterized in Wesleyan

---

[22] The United Methodist Church, *The Book of Discipline of The United Methodist Church* (Nashville: The United Methodist Publishing House, 2012), para. 336. "Question 2: Are you going on to perfection? Question 3: Do you expect to be made perfect in love in this life? Question 4: Are you earnestly striving after it?" These are three of the nineteen questions that are asked of ordained elders and deacons who are being admitted into full connection within The United Methodist Church.

[23] Harald Lindström, *Wesley and Sanctification* (Nashville: Abingdon, 1946), 113.

[24] Ibid.,114–15.

parlance as "works of piety" and "works of mercy."[25] The end result of this process is "complete" or "entire" sanctification, in which "all sin is washed away" and which "constitutes a higher stage in the new life."[26] Thus is seems clear that John Wesley's view of a life lived in Christ is one where the Christian moves through stages of growth, leading toward a maturity of faith that he called "perfection." As stated above, this perfection or maturity is measured by the fruit of one's actions. For Wesley, this meant that one had become perfect in love—toward both God and one's neighbor—which could be evidenced by the works of piety and mercy.[27]

Spiritual direction within the Wesleyan tradition, therefore, must by necessity of its identification with the doctrine of sanctification be focused on helping individuals, within the context of a community of accountability, to move toward perfection in love. I would submit that this process of sanctification is the sum total of a Wesleyan understanding of Christian vocation. To that end, I conclude this essay on vocation where it began— by reflecting on finding vocation in the centers and edges of life.

Vocational Discernment at the Center and the Edge

If the commonly accepted definition of vocation is Buechner's meeting of one's deep gladness and the deep hunger of the world[28], then the process of vocational discernment is essentially one of moving from the center (deep gladness) to the edge (deep hunger). Part of the goal of institutions of higher

---

[25] Ibid., 116–17.

[26] Ibid., 118.

[27] Albert C. Outler, *Theology in the Wesleyan Spirit* (Nashville: Discipleship Resources, 1975), 65.

[28] Frederick Buechner, *Wishful Thinking: A Theological ABC* (New York: Harper & Row, 1973), 95.

learning is to help students identify their deep gladness and the center out of which they operate. In the ministry of chaplaincy and campus ministry, we ask questions like: What do you feel called to do? What makes you most happy? Where do you find joy in your life and your studies? In helping students to identify their deep gladness, we intend to help them discover the *why* of vocation. It is the deep joy and gladness that will sustain them through difficult days ahead, when nothing else seems to be going right and they want to give up on their chosen paths.

The best pedagogy and campus ministry will also ask students to confront the harsh realities of life, particularly the conditions faced by the poorest people of the world. Through cultural immersion experiences and mission trips, we seek to help students encounter and then process the feelings that well up when confronted with injustice and oppression. One student with whom I worked as he progressed through the youth ministry major at our institution, went with other students on a Habitat for Humanity work trip each spring break. These experiences with poverty and inadequate housing in the American South led him to refocus his attention from working as a youth pastor in a local church to working full-time for Habitat International. Other students who have gone on university-sponsored mission trips to the Dominican Republic and Haiti have returned with a new sense of vocation. No longer satisfied to be pharmacists, nurses, or engineers simply for the sake of making a living or generically "helping others," these students felt called to using their learning to help those who most desperately need medicine, a caring touch, and passable roads and safe buildings in which to live. By going to the edge, where the world's deep hunger can be found, we are able to help students answer the *what* of vocation.

Both the *why* and the *what* of vocational discernment may leave some students challenged or discouraged. They might think, "But what if I don't want to work as a missionary, or with a nonprofit organization? What if I want to be a retail pharmacist, with a comfortable life and the ability to provide for my family?" Such questions may lead to guilt, as students struggle to discern how they can make a difference in the world while still being able to pay their bills and meet the obligations of a life in the modern world. In such cases, it is incumbent upon those of us who act as guides and mentors to help students discover that their calling may be to something outside of their 9 to 5 job. As in the case of one alumnus of our institution, they may choose to work as an engineer, creating a successful business, while also founding and supporting an orphanage in another country that has been ravaged by poverty and disease, leaving thousands of children without parents to care for them. A student who wishes to be active in the church but also wants to be a college professor might follow the example of one former dean of pharmacy, who also serves as the pastor of a local church. A dual vocation consisting of one type of paid work and a different type of voluntary or less well-paid work is a perfectly feasible approach to life, and one that was practiced by the apostle Paul himself.[29] The educational and programmatic functions of institutions of higher education are not enough, in and of themselves, to provide all students with the answers they need to ask the *why* and *what* of vocational discernment. In many cases, it falls to campus ministers and college or university chaplains to help students sort out these questions. Collegiate ministers often do not have abundant financial and capital resources with which to help students, but

---

[29] Other good examples of this kind of bi-vocational way of living can be found in Bryan J. Dik and Ryan D. Duffy, *Make Your Job a Calling: How the Psychology of Vocation Can Change Your Life at Work*, repr. ed. (West Conshohocken, PA: Templeton Press, 2013). See especially chap. 8.

they do tap into the deep wells of the theological and practical traditions of Christianity to help them guide students in their vocational discernment.

The Role of Collegiate Ministers as Spiritual Directors on the Journey

In my own practice of ministry as a university chaplain, I often encounter students whom I call *doorsteppers*. These students seem to show up on the doorstep of the chapel office out of the blue, often with no prearranged appointments, and more often than not without any formal connection to the religious life program of the campus. They may have been referred to me by a faculty member or a member of the counseling center staff, or they might have heard from a friend of a friend that I was a good person to talk to about life and faith. They are usually shy when they enter the office—one young woman even walked past the office door at least five or six times before she finally got up the courage to come in and ask to see me. Doorsteppers usually have some connection to the Christian faith, even if it is a tenuous one like having once attended vacation Bible school as a child. They also usually come seeking some advice, which they are terribly saddened to later find out is not something that I regularly do for students. Instead, I prefer to engage them in some form of spiritual direction, to help them discover their own answers to their questions. Often, these questions will be about relationship issues or personal crises of some sort, but just as often, they are vocational in nature, even if the student cannot yet identify them as such.

The conversations I have with doorsteppers usually begin with a question from me—"So, why are we here today?" This allows the student the opportunity to frame the conversation. Frequently, the presenting issue that brought the student to my office is one of a vocational nature, such as the case of the young man who came seeking my advice on whether or not he should continue as a physics major. He had recently started attending church and Bible study again, and was feeling conflicted between what he was hearing and reading from his renewed faith and what he was learning in the classroom. He struggled to identify the specific issues that were bothering him, but what he ultimately concluded was that he was having difficulty accepting that he could be a Bible-believing Christian (his words), and also a physicist. "I just can't imagine learning and then teaching all the things I'm required to know about physics while still being true to my faith," he said, and then continued, "And I don't want to have to turn off my brain when I go to church." By engaging this student in a process of spiritual direction, I was able to help him come to terms with what it means for him to be a Christian and a scientist at the same time. He was eventually able to recognize that he did not have to turn off his brain in church, nor did he have to turn off his faith when he was calculating the distance between galaxies. He was able to answer the *what* question of vocation very easily—he wanted to be a scientist who studied the stars and how they interact with each other. Much more difficult to answer was the *why* of his vocation, which he continued to struggle with even after we stopped meeting when he graduated. What he was able to do was to create for himself a kind of placeholder answer—something that would suffice while he continued to discern his sense of vocation—that allowed him to see the beauty of God's creativity within the galaxies and stars he studied. In the end, like Walt Whitman, he was awed by creation, as he "Look'd up in perfect silence at the stars."[30]

---

[30] Wal Whitman, "When I Heard the Learn'd Astronomer," in *Leaves of Grass* (Philadelphia: David McKay, 1900). Online at: http://www.bartleby.com/142/180.html.

For some students, making the journey from the center to the edge can be a frightening experience for which they have been ill prepared. These students may be intelligent, caring, and compassionate individuals, but they have never been afforded the opportunity to be challenged in their beliefs and perceptions about the world. When they arrive on campus for the first time, they may be shocked to encounter people from different cultures, political leanings, and worldviews. Vocational discernment for these students involves helping them make sense of what they are experiencing at the edge. As Dwight Judy wrote in *Discerning Life Transitions,* "Sometimes . . . external crises can bring us face to face with hopes for our life purpose, which we have been neglecting."[31] Collegiate ministers facilitate healthy and productive vocational discernment by helping students clearly identify their center first. In my own practice of spiritual direction, I ask students to identify where or when they feel most comfortable and to create a strong mental image of that place or time. Then, as they have this strong image fresh in their mind's eye, I invite them to encounter the edge that is the current source of anxiety. This might mean talking about a bad experience they have had in a class, or an issue they are having with a roommate or a classmate. It might also involve physically going with them to a place where they feel uncomfortable, such as the local soup kitchen or homeless shelter. Once they confront their edge experience, I ask them to again imagine their center. In this way, they learn to carry their center with them to the edge, confronting that which is scary to them while still maintaining a sense of balance within. Like a spiritual exposure therapy, this process helps directees find their comfortable center within themselves, drawing on

---

[31] Dwight H. Judy, *Discerning Life Transitions: Listening Together in Spiritual Direction* (Harrisburg, PA: Morehouse, 2010), 7.

previously unknown or inchoate inner strengths, which then allows them to go to the edge of their comfort zones, where they can learn and grow.

Vocational discernment, through the constant ebb and flow of movement from the center to the edge, is a process that develops over time. From a Wesleyan theological standpoint, it is also the process of sanctification or perfection, wherein one is shaped and reformed into the *imago dei* by intentional and repeated encounters with the divine through the means of grace. As one moves through the various means of grace, one comes to find within oneself a sense of what it means to be creative, loving, compassionate, merciful, and righteous—which are all attributes of God's self. In a very real sense, then, vocational discernment is the process of becoming fully oneself. That experience is unique to each individual, but it is ultimately lived out to its fullest potential through living in community.

Collegiate ministers who foster a sense of community where students are able to discover their spiritual centers and then explore the edges of their comfort zones, do so as spiritual directors who are journeying with the people of God to the places where they find themselves resurrected into new life in Christ. Practically speaking, we are helping our students acquire the tools they will need to survive and thrive in life, and then helping them discover how to use those tools, not only for their own gain, but for the good of all creation. This is what we were created to be—a beloved community, each recognizing our own centers and edge places, and moving forward together toward perfection in love.

Wesley, Integrity, and Vocation: The Power and Possibility of Collegiate Intentional Christian Communities

A. Rimes McElveen Jr.

I have the good fortune of directing a collegiate ministry, Mere Christianity Forum (MCF), and its intentional Christian community, Vista House, both of which primarily serve the Furman University community in Greenville, South Carolina. MCF's mission is to promote the thoughtful exploration of Christian faith at Furman, and beyond, through our unique blend of faith, reason, and tomfoolery. Each summer MCF hosts a residential ministry, the Servant Scholars Program, at Vista House. It is a ten-week intensive internship and spiritual formation experience for undergraduates and newly graduated young adults. Each summer the servant scholars are matched according to their vocational interests with one of our more than two-dozen partner social service agencies across Greenville County. These outstanding agencies work year-round addressing issues of poverty and injustice among the most vulnerable members of the Greenville community. The agencies provide an enriching internship with leadership and growth opportunities as well as supervision and mentoring for each servant scholar. Over 50 percent of their time is spent in direct engagement with the clients of the agencies. "Poverty" becomes a relational human reality, not just an academic concept or existential social ill. In return, the agency receives ten weeks of forty-hour per week staff support from an extremely capable student.

As part of their covenantal life of intentional Christian community, the servant scholars engage in the shared discipline of morning prayer led by members of the community. Further, each week they read a portion of a book, write a two-page reflection, and engage in a lengthy dinner dialogue with one another and one of nine "conversation conveners" whom we invite to the Vista House dinner table. Three local clergy, three university faculty members, and three nonprofit directors serve as our "conversation conveners." Their dinner dialogue with the students falls into one of three thematic areas corresponding with the reading the students have done for a particular week. The themes include: Christian community/Christian spiritual disciplines; Christian social justice/social action; and Christian vocation/calling. The entire program is funded by local charities and churches that see the value of cultivating deep Christian character in emerging leaders through embodied service among the "least of these" in Greenville County.

This summer we expanded the program to incorporate participants from Claflin University, a United Methodist HBCU[32] in Orangeburg, South Carolina, just a few hours away from Furman. This new partnership was formed through friendship and collegial partnership with Dr. Johnny Hill, chairman of the Religion and Philosophy Department at Claflin. The Mere Christianity Forum recently hosted Dr. Hill for a lecture series based on his compelling book, *Prophetic Rage: A Post-Colonial Theology of Liberation.* His lectures, impact on campus, and pastoral presence at the Vista House during this year of national racial upheaval stirred my imagination for initiating a new relationship with Claflin to include students from both universities in

---

[32] HBCU is the acronym for Historic Black Colleges and Universities.

the crucible of spiritual and vocational formation that is the Servant Scholars experience.

Thanks to Dr. Hill's partnership with MCF, three African American students from Claflin, four Caucasian students from Furman, and a Korean national from Furman joined in the experiment. We also had a recent divinity school graduate pursuing ordination in the Episcopal Church living in the community as the program director for the summer. The community included a beautiful mix of geographic region and nationality, socioeconomic location, male and female, gay and straight, Baptist, Anglican, African Methodist Episcopal, Presbyterian, nondenominational, United Methodist, and Episcopal young adults. Together, along with MCF's assistant director (although she and I do not reside in the house), we embarked on this journey of vulnerability and Christian intentionality in hopes of learning from one another, growing in faithfulness, and laying hold of God's grace along the way. I told the servant scholars from the start that their life together was nothing short of a bold attempt to live Martin Luther King Jr.'s dream that one day "little black boys and black girls will be able to join hands with little white boys and white girls as brothers and sisters in Christ."[33] Indeed, they wouldn't just be holding hands at a playground but in prayer, around the dinner table, at the Communion Table, and living under the same roof as family.

Not ten days into the experience we found ourselves overwhelmed by the horrific race-based violence, in Charleston, South Carolina, just three hours to our south. The heinous murder of nine church members at the historic Emanuel African Methodist Episcopal Church during a Bible study left us with no more room for congeniality or the possibility of

---

[33] http://www.americanrhetoric.com/speeches/mlkihaveadream.htm

cautiously wading into racial and other differences represented in the community "in due time." Our community had family members living in Charleston afraid for their lives and others with family members living within just a few miles of where the perpetrator was apprehended. Our community had members of the same denomination of the church in which the attack took place. Our community had members of the race of those viciously murdered in their church and members of the race of the perpetrator. There was no way to avoid, ignore, or try to "just move on," without facing the tragedy together by God's grace. There were hours spent in prayer, tears, honest conversations, words of confession, moments of deep blindness, hurt, forgiveness, and real God-given grace-filled moments of reconciliation over the course of the summer. Our community survived and at moments even thrived together. The kingdom of God came near. The capacity of intentional Christian community to create safe space for brokenness, healing, and ministry of reconciliation, was not found lacking, but rather a trustworthy context for deep honesty, discernment, and transformation.

A few years ago, a former resident insightfully described the Vista House community in this way:

> I learned that living in community and truly opening up to others means exposing the most fragile aspects of your being. That exposure can be terrifying and at times, heartbreaking, but I do believe that the breakdown ultimately leaves you stronger, that we tear down the weak walls around our beliefs and build up more steady structures in their place. It is a painful process, and you lose things along the way, but what you gain is more valuable in the end."[34]

---

[34] A former Vista House undergraduate resident who shared this quotation with Mere

In my estimation, the power and possibility present in this unique process of working out one's salvation in fear and trembling; sorting out one's identity in Christ; and discerning one's convictional commitments in the context of intentional Christian community cannot be overstated.

Unquestionably, the relationships begun in the Vista House servant scholars' community this summer—authentic transformative friendships spanning deep differences, cultivated in the fertile experience of intentional Christian community—are a foretaste of the communion made possible by the reconciling work of God in Christ. Though there were many relational *dangers, toils, and snares,* the community was protected from implosion and internal calamity by God's grace uniquely mediated by the collective people and practices of this experiment in intentional Christian community. Life in collegiate intentional Christian community is an experience one might consider both crucible and chalice. The essence and excess of students' lives are placed carefully in the crucible of conversation, prayer, possession-sharing, meals, shared hospitality work and worship, study, reflection, and vocational discernment. Their lives are pressed upon within and without by the pestle known as the Holy Spirit, often uncomfortably and occasionally to the point of being broken open, in the hand of the Great Physician. Then together through experiences of grace, healing, and transformation—spoken and unspoken alike—residents become the Blood of Christ, poured out for the world.[35] Their truly Eucharistic community grounded in participation in the life, death, and resurrection of Jesus is God's *kingdom on earth as it is in heaven.*

Christianity Forum in honor of the ten-year anniversary of Vista House in 2013.
[35] "The Great Thanksgiving, *The United Methodist Hymnal,* (Nashville: The United Methodist Publishing House, 1989), 9–11.

Margaret Meade, a renowned cultural anthropologist, is credited for saying, "Never doubt that a small group of committed people can change the world. Indeed, it is the only thing that ever has."[36] As long as these servant scholars remember and share the story of their life together this past summer in South Carolina living in this community, and the goodness, truth, and beauty God wrought among them, the world will be changed for the better.

It is important to remember that involvement in the enterprise of collegiate ministry is meant to be engaged in the quest to change the world for the better; to influence and empower emerging adults to explore life's most persistent questions of meaning, identity, vocational calling, and human flourishing. But good collegiate ministry understands that *cultivating fertile contexts,* wherein robust theological exploration of vocational questions like these, is *as essential as sharing sound doctrine.* A commitment to both process *and* content is vital in contemporary collegiate ministry given the demanding and dynamic challenges facing emerging adults in arguably the most complex global society in history. Along with the anecdotal evidence described above, I suggest that residential intentional Christian communities, particularly among undergraduates and other university-aged persons, is a preeminently vital context for vocational exploration and disciple-making in collegiate ministry.

I am not alone in issuing a call for Christians broadly and United Methodists in particular to prayerfully discern new or renewed expressions of convening disciples and "forming disciples" in the context of intentional Christian communities. The New Monasticism as a movement across denominational and nondenominational ecclesial bodies is gaining momentum

---

[36] https://en.wikiquote.org/wiki/Margaret_Mead.

in depth and breadth and is influencing United Methodist life along the way.[37] Elaine Heath and Scott Kisker have issued the bold call for The United Methodist Church in particular to establish intentional Christian communities in and through existing congregations; to plant new "free standing" monastic communities as full expressions of church; and for seminaries to incorporate intentional Christian communities into their structures of theological education and disciple formation.[38] Though I am only recently aware of their work, in many ways I now extend their call by adding the challenge for United Methodist collegiate ministries, as well as non-United Methodist collegiate ministries, to incorporate intentional Christian communities into their experiential offerings. Likewise, I am calling for United Methodist churches, universities, and judicatories committed to vital collegiate ministries to encourage their existing college ministries to facilitate vibrant intentional Christian communities; to establish new collegiate ministries incorporating intentional Christian communities; and to revitalize their existing intentional Christian communities as rich opportunities for cultivating deep discipleship and vocational discernment.

Murmurs or Movement?

Given the increased hunger for authentic relationships in an age of Facebook-style "friendship," it is no surprise to learn that among the Christian religious tides rising in the United

---

[37] www.communityofcommunities.org continues to grow each year with New Monastic communities. To learn more about the principles and practices of New Monastic communities see Jonathan Wilson-Hartgrove in *Schools For Conversion: 12 Marks of a New Monasticism* (Eugene, OR: The Rutba House,) 2005. And, Ian Mobsby and Mark Berry, *A New Monastic Handbook: From Vision to Practice* (n.p., 2014).

[38] Elaine Heath and Scott T. Kisker, *Longing for Spring: A New Vision for Wesleyan Community*. (Eugene, OR: Cascade Books, 2010), 60.

States, on and off campus, there is a burgeoning interest in living in residential intentional Christian communities (ICCs). There are scores to be found with a simple web search or a slightly more focused inquiry to, among other organizations, the Fellowship for Intentional Communities (www.ic.org) and their extensive list of intentional communities, a subset that includes intentional Christian communities (or Christian intentional communities—CICs). In the November–December, 2012 issue of *Religion Watch*, Mark Killian, a Taft Research Fellow in the University of Cincinnati's Sociology Department at the time, reported "a 70 percent increase in the number of CICs established between 2005 and 2009, compared to those started between 2000 and 2004." Likewise, Killian's research reports a "291 percent increase in the number of CICs in-formation between 2005 and 2009, compared to CICs in-formation between 2000 and 2004."

These statistics indicate a remarkable uptick in the number of people not just *considering* life in an intentional Christian community but those *actually* taking up this ancient Christian way of life. But do these statistics provide a clue or predictor of behavior among undergraduates? If so, which came first? Are more undergraduates living in intentional Christian communities during their college years, and then after graduating, looking to join an existing ICC or establish new ICCs? Or have undergraduates witnessed the trend of more and more Christians embracing nontraditional forms of church such as ICCs and are thus inspired to do likewise on campus? Either way, both interest and opportunity are on the rise on and off campus and people are hungry for thick relationships and communities within which to do faith and life.

But isn't Christianity in decline on campus and in American society? How could we expect "seekers" or even committed Christians to live in such demanding way of life if religiosity is waning on campus? What Killian's findings offer is a sharp example of a countervailing tendency to secularization theorists who assert that with modernity came a hyper-secularization throughout culture, particularly in higher education institutions. Among those who challenge the accuracy of the secularization theory is sociologist Peter Berger, who had this to say in a 1997 interview with the *Christian Century*:

> I think what I and most other sociologists of religion wrote in the 1960s about secularization was a mistake. Our underlying argument was that secularization and modernity go hand in hand. With more modernization comes more secularization. It wasn't a crazy theory. There was some evidence for it. But I think it's basically wrong. Most of the world today is certainly not secular. It's very religious.[39]

Shifting our attention from a broader religious trend in American culture back to a consideration of religious trends in the university milieu, Cherry, DeBerg, and Porterfield, offer a revealing ethnographic account of the state of religion on four university campuses around the United States. In their 2001 work, *Religion on Campus: What Religion Really Means to Today's Undergraduates*, they have this to offer as one dimension of a counter position to secularization theorists' attempts to explain changes on university campuses regarding religiosity: "[T]hese changes seem more clearly to add up to the declericalizing, de-denominationalizing, and, in some cases, de-Christianizing of campuses than to their secularization or their marginalization of religion." They go on to say,

The changes also may very well reflect the protean

---

[39] For the full interview, see http://www.religion-online.org/showarticle.asp?title=240.

flexibility that has characterized American religion as a whole throughout the nation's history. The religion of the American people has demonstrated a large capacity to assume new forms as conditions change and thereby preserve itself as a vital force in American life . . . Given the overall tendency of American religion to assume new shapes as social and cultural conditions change, it is reasonable to assume some new appearances as well, appearances that may have gone unrecognized in the secularization theories.[40]

The popularity of the recent writings of Shane Claiborne, Donald Miller, and Jonathan Wilson-Hartgrove promoting ICC, along with other contemporary proponents of ICC (Sanders, Samson, and Janzen), offer clues to a new or renewed interest in collegiate intentional Christian community as a way of life among undergraduates and in the broader church. I, like Heath and Kisker and a host of others, believe United Methodism has a unique capacity and even calling to faithfully further this movement on campus as well as in the broader church.

History and Particularity of the United Methodist Capacity to Cultivate CICCs

The protean flexibility that has characterized American religion throughout the nation's history has never been more clearly evidenced than in the very birth of the Methodist Church in America as it broke away from its Church of England parentage. John Wesley himself justified the ordination of Methodist bishops like Thomas Coke and Francis Asbury to keep pace with the need for preachers, teachers, and celebrants of Holy Communion out of an urgent missional need because

---

[40] Conrad Cherry, Betty A. DeBerg, and Amanda Porterfield, *Religion on Campus* (Chapel Hill: University of North Carolina Press, 2001), 4–5.

of the rapid growth of the Methodist movement in America. Though he never intended to establish a church other than the Church of England, only to reform it, one might argue that the higher calling to faithfully further the good news of the gospel, to spread of scriptural holiness across the land, and to cultivate faith working through love, outstripped any allegiance to a particular ecclesial body.[41]

This type of innovation and missional flexibility to respond to the movement of the Holy Spirit and the hunger for authentic discipleship is uniquely embedded in the DNA of the Methodist movement. The United Methodist Church today is a global church, millions strong with unique historical, theological, fiscal, physical, connectional, and experiential gifts to contribute to the movement of God in Christ on collegiate campuses around the world. And Methodist, as a whole, bears the particular marks of faithful discipleship and vocational discernment born of vital collegiate ministry in its original mission and vision.

Charles Wesley, as a student at Oxford, created a group who called themselves "The Holy Club." Later John Wesley joined the group, and soon after, the zeal of the group and the discipline with which the group operated matured under John's leadership. The group insisted on wedding personal piety and holiness with social engagement. Despite, or perhaps because of their commitment, the Holy Club members were dubbed "Methodists" by jeering peers at Oxford, looking to poke fun at the group due to their fastidious approach and methodical tendencies. The Holy Club members limited their number to twenty-five members, fasted on Wednesdays and Fridays; gave

---

[41] *History of the American Methodist Church: The Christmas Conference,* http://wesley.nnu.edu/holiness-classics-library/history-of-the-methodist-episcopal-church/volume-2-book-iii-chapter-3/

alms diligently; attended weekly worship to take the Eucharist; studied and discussed the Greek New Testament and other vital Christian theological texts; met daily for prayer; and systemically opened their lives for one another's accountability and examination.[42] As the leader, John stressed the need for combining a deep inward faith with practical service to those in need, so eventually the group began ministering with widows, the sick, and those in prison in the area of Oxford.

Other significant members of the Holy Club, in addition to Charles and John Wesley, went on to play pivotal roles in the growth and influence of Christianity in England, America, and beyond, adding further evidence to the God-given power of that collegiate ministry.

John Gambold later became a Moravian bishop.

John Clayton became a distinguished Anglican churchman.

James Hervey became a noted religious writer.

Benjamin Ignham became a Yorkshire evangelist.

Thomas Brougham became secretary of the Society for Promoting Christian Knowledge.

George Whitefield, who joined the club just before the Wesleys departed for Georgia in 1735, became a prominent preacher and leader associated both with the Great Awakening in America and the Evangelical Revival in England.

Reflecting back from 1781 John Wesley remarked that he saw in the Holy Club the first rise of Methodism. The second rise was in Georgia in 1736, when he met with selected members of his congregation on Sunday afternoons. From these earlier experiences of intense discernment and discipleship grew the idea for "Methodist societies" that became the backbone of the Methodist organization.[43]

---

[42] A list of the original twenty-two questions each Holy Club member asked of themselves daily can be found here: http://hopefaithprayer.com/john-wesley-holy-club-questions/.

[43] Richard Heitzenrater, *Wesley and the People Called Methodist*, 2nd ed. (Nashville:

There is little doubt that global Methodism is the broadest and most vital branch of the church to spring forth from that collegiate ministry organization, initiated by Charles and intensified by John. It also seems apparent that those formative years were simultaneously the refiner's fire for the discernment of the Wesleys' theological, ecclesial, and social vision and vocation, as well as proving grounds for what would become the "United Societies" and the entire Methodist movement worldwide.

It was ten years after his prominent role in the Holy Club's development that John Wesley was approached in London by a group of earnest seekers to receive direction and counsel— essentially to be a disciple—by someone they witnessed who possessed great wisdom, piety, and Christian integrity:

In the latter part of the year 1739, eight or ten persons, who appeared to be deeply convinced of sin and earnestly groaning for redemption, came to Mr. Wesley in London. They desired, as did two or three more the next day, that he would spend some time with them in prayer and advise them how to flee from the wrath to come, which they saw continually hanging over their heads. That he might have more time for this great work he appointed a day when they might all come together, which they did every week thereafter, namely, on Thursday evenings. To these and as many more as desired to join with them (for their number increased daily), Wesley gave needed advice and always concluded their meeting with prayer. This was the rise of the United Society, first in London and then in America. This society was none other than "a company of men having the *form* and seeking the *power* of godliness, united in order to pray together, to receive the word of exhortation, and to watch over one another in love, that they may help each other to work out their salvation."[44]

Abingdon, 2013), 37–80.
[44] See *The United Methodist Church Book of Discipline*, 75–76.

In those pivotal moments the seeds of experiential wisdom, sown in the Oxford Holy Club, sprang up to become the movement that would soon follow. Today the Wesleyan/Methodist tradition remains a global movement of people striving to work out their own salvation through the gifts and calling of personal piety, communal Christianity, and scriptural and social holiness made manifest in the Wesleyan maxim, "faith working through love."[45]

Today, there are more than 500 United Methodist campus ministries around the United States, an estimated 600 more internationally. There are approximately 120 United Methodist schools, colleges, universities, and theological schools, along with hundreds of local United Methodist Churches with collegiate ministries of all shapes and sizes. These are just the United Methodist variety within the broader Methodist family. There are hundreds more that are part of the broader Wesleyan theological family. All of which share the same "Holy Club" DNA. A grace-infused Christian heritage rooted in a unique collegiate ministry where John and Charles Wesley began to work out their own callings and refine their theological convictions for the sake of gospel witness and social engagement.

What a compelling vision for collegiate ministry, in particular, and church ministry broadly understood: a relatively small set of Christian friends pouring over scripture and other vital Christian theological resources together; praying regularly with and for one another; engaging in weekly worship with Eucharist; laying open their lives before one another for accountability and encouragement; sharing resources sacrificially; and ministering with the poor, the

---

[45] Heitzenrater, *Wesley and the People Called Methodist*, 115.

sick, the imprisoned, and brokenhearted in their community. These students did things that the church of their time had never done before. They took the church to the people, rather than demand that people come to the church to meet the face of Christ. But what possibility and relevance does such a vision for ministry have in relationship to the contemporary American collegiate experience or the burgeoning interest among undergraduates and young adults to live in intentional Christian community and the complex relationship between church and higher education?

Build It and They Will Come Live There

I have spent the last several years in search of answers to that complex question. Since beginning my work in collegiate ministry eight years ago, I turned to contemporary Christian authors and activists like Shane Claiborne, Donald Miller, and Jonathan Wilson-Hartgrove, championing publically in word and deed the call to live in intentional Christian communities. There seems to be a clear increase in momentum in establishing such communities among young adults, particularly among undergraduates. Over the course of the last four years, I've spent extensive time compiling a list of college and university-related intentional Christian communities, over half of which were started fewer than twenty-five years ago. I have identified more than one hundred collegiate-related intentional Christian communities (CICCs) across the United States and am aware of scores that are more loosely formed and often "student initiated/run," as opposed to those more formally facilitated by church, para-church, and university related entities. It is an incredibly diverse set of communities theologically, geographically, and socially, operating in a diverse set of higher education institutions.

I have grouped the list of CICCs across the United States into four categories according to their institutional genesis and their ongoing operational underpinnings. The four categories are:

1. Student-run. Some of this type function with modest oversight and support from alumni, but most are comprised of students, who pass the baton to the next group of residents of a particular house, apartment, or even dorm. These communities simply emerge for a handful of years and then often expire. However, a compelling example of one that has endured over the years is the University Christian Union operating at the University of Washington in Seattle, where it has been more or less in operation since the 1930s. Today roughly twenty-five men and twenty women constitute this unique CICC. It can be found online at: http://www.ucu.com.

2. University-run. With these a university provides an experiential opportunity for its undergraduates. These CICCs seem to last as long as there is student or administrative interest/funding as well as university staff and facilities necessary for the task. An interesting example is the Emmaus Scholars Program at Hope College in Holland, Michigan. It can be found online at: http://www.hope.edu/emmaus.

3. Church/Denomination-run. These are formed by a particular Christian church or judicatory, which is responsible for the CICC. These are often housed in the denominational campus ministry's facility/house. There are United Methodist, Episcopal, Baptist, Catholic, Lutheran, Presbyterian, Mennonite, and other CICS around the country. A unique example where underutilized parsonages have been repurposed to create five CICCs is the Wesley Foundation at FIU-MDC in Miami, Florida and can be found here: http://www.fiumdcwesley.org/#!wesley-house/clh2

4. Para-church organization-run. These involve a religiously independent para-church entity, typically a nonprofit campus

ministry such as Inter-Varsity, Young Life, Campus Crusade, or a Christian Study Center, which is responsible for operating the community as an extension of its ministry programming. One of the best examples is Chesterton House at Cornell in Ithaca, New York, which can be found here: http://www.chestertonhouse.org.

Vista House

I have spent much of the past eight years shepherding a community run by a para-church organization, Vista House (www.vistahouse.org), in my role as executive director of Mere Christianity Forum. In that time more than one hundred undergraduates and a handful of young graduates have lived together in intentional Christian community at Vista House during the academic year CICC experience and/or during the summer Servant Scholars Program (www.servantscholars.org) described above.

Since its beginning in 2003, the Vista House CICC and its residents have sought to embody an alternative way of Christian collegiate life, undergirded by a shared covenantal commitment to following Jesus through hospitality, community, and the arts. Each community cocreates their communal covenant during an opening retreat and revisits the covenant regularly throughout their time living together in community. The habit of revisiting the content of the covenant regularly cannot be underestimated. (Imagine a married couple looking into one another's eyes over dinner at least once a month while remembering and reciting some part or all of the content of their wedding ceremony, specifically their marriage vows, and you begin to get an idea of how influential is the community's diligence in revisiting their covenant regularly.) When consistently revisited, their covenant becomes the spiritual plumb line by which their intentionality and faithfulness are measured and maintained, as well as the pathway by which the Holy Spirit helps them grow in grace as individuals and as a community. One of the most powerful practices of remembering the covenant is the monthly (or more frequent) discipline of residents confessing their failure to uphold elements of the covenant and/or naming aspects of the covenant they sense the Holy Spirit's conviction to more faithfully engage. The flip side of that discipline that makes it complete is the additional naming of specific affirmations of other community members who they have witnessed fulfilling aspects of their shared covenant.[46]

Vista House residents model many of the historic habits and practices of men and women who have lived together in intentional Christian communities, monastic and lay, for centuries. They engage in daily prayers; enjoy weekly shared "closed table" meals; read and reflect independently and as a group on particular Biblical texts and other Christian theological resources; strive for simplicity and sharing; practice Christian hospitality through serving guests who come for retreat in the Vista House guest room; and serve free meals at weekly "open table" fellowship meals that host between twenty and forty peer guests as well as biweekly dinner dialogues for fifteen peers and a guest of honor, who then shares his or her vocation/calling story and leads the group in a theological discussion of issues pertinent to undergraduate life. Likewise, the residents host numerous other informal and formal gatherings for fellowship and Christian conviviality, including book discussions, Bible studies, and creative arts events. In so doing they are modeling for a watching world how college-age Christians can take their faith seriously without taking themselves too seriously.

---

[46] James 5:16, John 21:20-23, Hebrews 10:24-25.

Vista House residents, like other students living in CICCs around the country, also take part in another time-honored practice common to Christian and non-Christian college students alike—sinfulness. They fail to uphold their covenant; they hurt one another; they become tired, short tempered, and engage in passive aggressive triangulation in relationships; and they leave their filthy dishes in the sink, on the counter, and in their rooms like every other roommate that's ever graced the hallowed halls of higher education institutions around the world. However, in those moments of failure, sin, and brokenness, if they choose to reach for the rich resources to which their shared covenant points, they discover their collective capacity to experience the high and holy moments of God's grace in Jesus that is sufficient for their journey. During the initial orientation for each community the entire experience of Vista House is set in the context of covenantal Eucharistic community wherein the biblical drama of creation, fall, confession, repentance, forgiveness, and reconciliation will be relived throughout their time together.

The hurts and selfishness can thereby be transformed into sacred moments of confession and responsibility taking, forgiveness, and reconciliation. By God's grace, the collective experience as a Christian community of imperfect people is made perfect, which is to say whole and holy by the author and perfecter of their faith. Jesus' promises to be found when two or three are gathered in his name, seeking God's presence and to be with his disciples "even unto the end of the age" are fulfilled in CICC. As these inspiring students' faith is practiced, Jesus' words become reality year after year as Vista House residents live with one another and experience the goodness, truth, and beauty of CICC. God's grace is never found lacking at the moments of pain and brokenness if we are faithful to the discipline of exercising a covenantal way of life, vulnerably giving ourselves to one another, and to the God who calls us to this unique and venerable vocation.

The Role of CICCs in United Methodist Collegiate Ministry

What exactly is the unique vocation of collegiate intentional Christian communities and what role might such communities play in a United Methodist vision of collegiate ministry? Discerning the Christian vocation of an organization or an individual requires deep reflection, holy inspiration, and a capacity for making connections between the movements of the Holy Spirit and the unique gifts of the person and/or organization. It also requires discerning the call to act in the temporal context at the intersection of God's will and God's people in a given time and place.

At the present moment, higher education institutions, both public and private, are facing mounting pressure in the face of increased skepticism by funders, parents, and students alike, regarding the value of a liberal arts-based education in today's market. Pat McCrory, governor of North Carolina, shortly after being elected in 2013, said he asked his staff to "write legislation that he can send to lawmakers to change state funding formulas for public institutions of higher education that would link the funds to the number of graduates who get jobs after they graduate." More specifically, he said funding should not be "based on how many butts in seats, but how many of those butts can get jobs."[47] It is a bit of a crass sentiment held by an increasing number of lawmakers and other powerful people in their hyper-reductionist

---

[47] Valerie Strauss, "N.C. Governor Attacks Higher Ed, Proposes Funding Colleges by Graduates' Jobs." See: http://www.washingtonpost.com/blogs/answer-sheet/wp/2013/02/07/n-c-governor-attacks-higher-ed-proposes-funding-colleges-by-graduates-jobs/.

assessment of the value of higher education.

Colleges, universities, and higher education as a whole are being challenged to find ways to meet the increasingly diverse needs of its student-constituent-customers and to assure its students and their parents the price tag and experience is worth the skyrocketing costs when calculating their return on investment in terms of job readiness and acquisition—all while servicing the dramatic costs of maintaining and updating their facilities. There is a increasing pressure on students to make sure every part of their college experience is in service to the single goal of acquiring a job when they graduate, largely due to the mountain of debt most undergraduates and graduate students incur to complete their degrees. United Methodist higher education institutions and students are not immune from these challenges.

There is a parallel theme at work among United Methodist campus ministries and United Methodist Annual Conferences. Increasingly, Wesley Foundations/Fellowships and other United Methodist collegiate ministries are experiencing decreasing funding from Annual Conferences and are finding themselves spending dramatically increased time fund-raising in order to facilitate the ministry they are called to on campus. In order to fulfill their own personal and organizational vocation on campuses across the country, they are learning to adapt or become extinct. While funding has never been adequate, many ministries are also finding themselves with aging facilities, which must be renovated, sold, or repurposed. What better ministry than CICC might such facilities be repurposed for in service to collegiate ministry? The FIU-MDC Wesley in Miami alone has already repurposed nearly half a dozen parsonages as CICCs. The growth, maturation, adaptation, and innovation necessary for facilitating dynamic collegiate ministries requires immense fortitude, staff longevity, board and donor generosity, and a hefty dose of the original Wesleyan DNA born of the Holy Club. Staff, students, judicatory leaders, and other supporters alike must be true champions for collegiate ministry and power and possibility of CICCs as a part of such ministries.

I am convinced that the ministry of CICC should be explored as a key ingredient to virtually any vibrant Methodist expression of collegiate ministry. The theological heritage is readily accessible within the Methodist tradition, and many Wesley Foundations already have CICCs as part of their ministry. Here is a list of key examples from which we might learn vital lessons:

The Wesley Foundation at the University of Kentucky
Kansas State Wesley Foundation
FIU-MDC Wesley, Miami, Florida
Florida State Wesley Foundation
University of Florida Wesley
The University of Virginia Wesley
Wesley House of the University of Cincinnati
Wesley Foundation of Western Michigan

Tennessee State Wesley Foundation

Each of these United Methodist CICCs have much to teach regarding the rich potential to fulfill the call to make disciples of Jesus Christ and transform the world. We would do well to mine their experiential wisdom for clues about the vocation of CICC in a collegiate context and how to plant new or enhancing existing United Methodist CICCs.

Other Examples

Are there other examples from which to learn? Absolutely. I have discovered a wealth of other collegiate intentional communities that are theme-based including interfaith, environmental/sustainability, curricular, athletic, vocation, arts, and other unique communities. They share living space, resources, common philosophical or social values, and a particular set of practices or even vows. Many such communities fall into a category of "living-learning communities," "service-learning communities," or "engaged learning communities" associated with universities that have embraced "themed housing" offerings for their students as a way of appealing to the niche of micro associations of student interests and preferences. Many of these communities are a part of university efforts to facilitate student experiences of specialize housing opportunities where living with other students who have the same majors or minors or service learning interests are highly valued.

One of the most interesting studies of such a community is described in Tim Clydesdale's *The Purposeful Graduate: Why Colleges Must Talk to Students about Vocation*. In the chapter entitled "Matters of Design," Clydesdale describes in detail the impact of one such CIC on sophomores and juniors at "Richboro University," a university (given a fictional name for anonymity's sake), which was responsible for a vocational exploration themed CIC on campus. The university conducted extensive evaluation of the impact of the program on its students and the university community more broadly. They found that participants had a "two-year gain in maturity" when tested by an outside psychology firm. The CIC was described as having been a great success and was given unofficial credit for upping applications, matriculation rates, and retention rates after becoming a staple on university tours by prospective students and having slots for 20 percent of its sophomore students. Likewise, the university study found that students who participated showed more signs of a capacity to deal with difficulty and disappointment and overall described themselves as more fulfilled in life. It was also noted by Clydesdale that the university made the resident community a staple when courting donors and they had little difficulty raising three million dollars to endow the program in perpetuity.[48]

The Importance of Cultivating Integrity in an Age of Principled Pluralism

What is at the heart of the CICC experience and what is the essence of such communities' formational gifts to their residents? Simply stated, I believe it is their unique capacity to cultivate deep Christian integrity individually and communally. In an age when college students care less and less about people's titles or offices and more about their experiential credentials, integrity is in high demand.

College students, like youth, can smell incongruence and pharisaism from a mile away. In a postmodern, post-Christian, global, pluralistic society, integrity is the only true social currency left to trade on in the public square. Gone are the days of students automatically ascribing deep respect to public figures, clergy, even faculty. They want to size them up and discern for themselves whether or not the person before them in a person of deep integrity, even if they may disagree with the person in a variety of subject matter or philosophy. My students are often unimpressed by how many books the guest speakers we host have written, how many degrees they have earned, or their job title. Instead, they want to hear our guests' stories around a dinner table, listen intently to the person, and discern whether or not they are witnessing for themselves the embodiment of Quintilian's maxim of "the good person speaking well" right in front of them.

Parker Palmer describes integrity and wholeness in almost

---

[48] Tim Clydesdale, *The Purposeful Graduate: Why Colleges Must Talk to Students about Vocation* (Chicago: University of Chicago Press, 2015), 75–79.

parallel terms in his book *A Hidden Wholeness*: "Wholeness does not mean perfection: it means embracing brokenness as an integral part of life." He diagnoses the divided life as our denial of brokenness as virtually a personal pathology that leads to personal and public ruin due to the compartmentalizing of one's beliefs, convictions, habits, and persona separated from one another. Instead he commends integrity rather than a mere attempt at "adherence to a moral code." He writes that integrity is the state or quality of being entire, complete, and unbroken . . . like unto "a jack pine or the human self—in its 'unimpaired, unadulterated, or genuine state, corresponding to its original condition.'" Palmer goes on to say that humans cannot embrace wholeness alone, because "we need trustworthy relationships, and tenacious communities of support, if we are to sustain the journey toward an undivided life."[49] No integrity without community. Palmer's wisdom is a truth that is integral to any viable conception of the Christian life and certainly any Wesleyan notion of collegiate ministry.

College life is, if nothing else, a fertile ground for seeding and cultivating deep vocational exploration and discernment for those who dare, and often times even for those who do not willingly dare! There is an opportunity to reflect significantly on one's deep longings and their intersection with the world's great needs, to paraphrase Frederick Buechner's well-known description of vocation. And in my experience, there is no more potent a context within which to faithfully cultivate vocational discernment and Christian integrity than collegiate intentional Christian community.

Conclusion

I believe CICCs have both the capacity and one might argue, the vocation, to cultivate deep vocational discernment among

---

[49] Parker J. Palmer, *A Hidden Wholeness: The Journey toward an Undivided Life*. (San Francisco: Jossey-Bass. 2004).

emerging adults around the world. Likewise, I am convinced that United Methodist Collegiate ministries are uniquely gifted and called to this ministry. I am not here merely commending the consideration of CICCs by Methodist-related universities, churches, and collegiate ministries. Rather, I am issuing a clear call to rise up in faithfulness and heed Elaine Heath and Scott Kisker's timely challenge to "imagine how Methodism can and should wholeheartedly advance the new monasticism (on and near campuses) as a vital form of holistic evangelism in the twenty-first century."[50]

Collegiate ministry is in the Wesleyan DNA. It is credited by John Wesley as being responsible for the "first rise" of Methodism in the Holy Club he and Charles anchored at Oxford. And there is no more compelling context or process I know of with the same caliber of potential for deep cultivation of Christian discipleship, vocation, and integrity among emerging adults than life in intentional Christian community. According to Bonhoeffer, author of *Life Together*, the stories and wisdom born of the seminary-based intentional Christian community in Germany during World War II had this to say in a letter to his brother on January 14th, 1935:

> The restoration of the church will surely come only from a new type of monasticism which has nothing in common with the old but a complete lack of compromise in a life lived in accordance with the Sermon on the Mount in the discipleship of Christ. I think it is time to gather people together to do this.[51]

No doubt this is deep wisdom that remains relevant today in our quest for faithfulness in contemporary collegiate ministry.

---

[50] Elaine Heath and Scott T. Kisker. *Longing for Spring: A New Vision for Wesleyan Community* (Eugene, OR: Cascade Books 2010), 48.

[51] Extract of a letter written by Dietrich Bonhoeffer to his brother Karl-Friedrich on January, 14, 1935. (Source: John Skinner, Northumbria Community).

CPSIA information can be obtained at www.ICGtesting.com
Printed in the USA
LVOW08s0157240516

489600LV00002B/4/P